"This is a bold, brave and brilliant book, one that is truly boundary-breaking. Amos Yong offers a critique of pentecostal and evangelical theology that is sharp and penetrating, but nevertheless life-giving and transformative. He offers encouragement to Asian and Asian American evangelicals and pentecostals to find their own voice in exploring their Christian faith, but the book is also a call to other Asian and Asian American Christians. In some ways that are even more important, however, this is a call to all Christians to trust their experience, context and culture and to construct theologies that are both rooted in their lives and that can be shared across them."

Stephen Bevans, S.V.D., Catholic Theological Union

"Amos Yong delivers to Protestantism a beautiful matrix of biblical and cultural analysis that provides a model for the types of discussions we must have if evangelicalism is to have a future in the West. Yong helps us see that recapturing evangelicalism's past is not the way forward, given the fact that ethnic minorities and immigrants, and Asian Americans in particular, are among the most vibrant and growing sectors of evangelicalism today. Yong will not only increase the reader's cultural intelligence, but the book provides the right questions and categories that all strands of American Protestantism must engage in the twenty-first century. This book is essential reading for those who care about the future of Christianity in the West."

Anthony B. Bradley, The King's College, New York

The Future of
EVANGELICAL THEOLOGY

SOUNDINGS
FROM THE
ASIAN AMERICAN
DIASPORA

AMOS YONG

IVP Academic

An imprint of InterVarsity Press
Downers Grove, Illinois

InterVarsity Press
P.O. Box 1400, Downers Grove, IL 60515-1426
World Wide Web: www.ivpress.com
Email: email@ivpress.com

InterVarsity Press® is the book-publishing division of InterVarsity Christian Fellowship/USA®, a movement of students and faculty active on campus at hundreds of universities, colleges and schools of nursing in the United States of America, and a member movement of the International Fellowship of Evangelical Students. For information about local and regional activities, visit www.intervarsity.org.

Scripture quotations, unless otherwise noted, are from the New Revised Standard Version of the Bible, copyright 1989 by the Division of Christian Education of the National Council of the Churches of Christ in the USA. Used by permission. All rights reserved.

See pages 15-16 for additional permissions.

Cover design: Cindy Kiple
Interior design: Beth McGill
Images: Easter weekend: Easter Weekend by Willie Rodger. Private Collection. The Bridgeman Art Library.
        Chinese art illustration: © koey/iStockphoto

ISBN 978-0-8308-4060-1 (print)
ISBN 978-0-8308-9675-2 (digital)

Printed in the United States of America ∞

Library of Congress Cataloging-in-Publication Data
A catalog record for this book is available from the Library of Congress.

P 25 24 23 22 21 20 19 18 17 16 15 14 13 12 11 10 9 8 7 6 5 4 3 2 1

Y 36 35 34 33 32 31 30 29 28 27 26 25 24 23 22 21 20 19 18 17 16 15 14

To Paul Lim

In anticipation of a new Asian American evangelicalism

and of the revitalization of evangelical theology

CONTENTS

PREFACE

This book emerged out of conversations between Gary Deddo and me when Gary was still one of the senior editors at IVP. I am appreciative of Gary's inviting me to think about publishing with IVP and I am happy that my first book with IVP is on a topic—Asian American Evangelicalism—that they have been invested in at some level over the decades. David Congdon has been helpful in assisting me in navigating the IVP world since Gary's departure, and Claire VanderVelde Brubaker and Karli Saner have been professional throughout the editing and production process.

The following provided feedback at the proposal stage of conceptualizing the volume: Jonathan Tan, Timothy Tseng, Billy Vo, Young Lee Hertig and Grace Ji-Sun Kim. My doctoral students from across Asia who have also served as graduate assistants over the past few years have aided immeasurably: Timothy Lim Teck Ngern provided very important perspective on the organization and flow of the book at the beginning stages; Vince Le proofread the manuscript; and Enoch Charles developed the index.

I am grateful also to the following for reading through the full draft of the manuscript and sending me immensely helpful comments: Jonathan Tan, Grace Hsiao Hanford, David Fitch, Christopher (Crip) Stephenson, Derek Cooper, Daniel Hawk and Tony Richie. Billy Vo, Bo Lim and Brian Bantum, my friends at Seattle Pacific University who also contribute variously to their School of Theology's Asian American Ministry program, each read parts of the manuscript and provided critical perspective for the final draft. All of these friends have helped me say better to my Asian American evangelical readers what I as a one-and-a-half generation Asian American have only limited perspective on even as they have assisted me in more appropriately addressing white evangelical readers from my Asian American location. Needless to say, all errors of fact or interpretation remain my own responsibility.

As will be clear from the pages below, I present only one Asian American pentecostal perspective intended toward revitalizing evangelical theology in the twenty-first century. Many other perspectives from many other evangelical families or traditions as well as many other ethnic or minority group vantage points are needed. One other urgent set of lenses for this conversation is also represented in my household through my Mexican American wife. Alma has been my constant and unfailing companion through more than a quarter-century of marriage. Her love, loyalty and strength make it possible for me to do everything I do as a theologian. It is unfathomable to me that any other theologian in the world has been blessed as much as I have, so I can only thank God for such an undeserved gift. And thank you also, Alma, for being the wonderful and amazing woman you are.

I should also say that, as the acknowledgments page (to follow) exhibits, this volume represents a substantial reworking of a number of articles and essays previously published in various venues. Only the final chapter seven is completely new and written expressly for the book. This means that I have not been able to provide the kind of overarching and foundational theological consideration of how Asian American evangelical perspectives can inform the broader evangelical and global theological enterprise, which is what is ultimately envisioned. Rather these represent piecemeal approaches to this grander task, albeit ones that now reorganize and rearticulate such previous efforts into a whole that can be said to be coherent only in that it represents where this material has led me at present. If I were to write this book afresh, beginning from the ground up, it would be wholly different. However, constraints of time, place and finitude dictate that the best I can do as this juncture is to reweave my prior thinking into what is hopefully a more-or-less original whole that can catalyze others to fulfill the larger task gestured to in this book. I thus hope my readers will trek with me despite some of the repetition unavoidable even when previously published material is reworked. Where I have fallen short, as I am painfully aware of in penning this preface, may my critics be inspired not to just point out my deficiencies but also to do better in executing a global Christian and evangelical theology in light of local and contextual realities.

This preface is being revisited on the eve of the book's going to press, in an empty office at Fuller Seminary, where I have relocated in the summer of 2014. Much of the book, including the prologue, was written while I was at Regent University, first as professor and then as dean of the School of Divinity. I am grateful to former dean Michael Palmer at Regent for giving me the time and space to write, and to the wonderful staff in the School of Divinity and the library who have supported my work over the last nine years. I am also grateful for the warm welcome at Fuller Seminary, and am looking forward to working with its Asian American Initiative going forward.

This book is dedicated to my Asian American theologian, brother (in Christ), friend and confidant Paul Chang-Ha Lim. His parents are Korean, mine Chinese; we are both immigrants to the United States—he at fifteen and I at ten. Paul was trained as a historical theologian (of early modern England), I as a systematician (of pentecostal persuasion), both with deep evangelical roots and commitments. Both of us are turning slowly to engaging explicitly the specifically Asian and Asian American horizons that have otherwise percolated beneath our thinking. His no-nonsense honesty, scholarly erudition, and ongoing and unabashed Christian commitments give me hope for the future of evangelical theology. I am privileged and blessed beyond measure to have had sojourners along this evangelical theological path like Paul.

ACKNOWLEDGMENTS

I am grateful to the following for approval to revise and use previously published material:

- Asian Pentecostal Theological Seminary Press for permission related to my "The Future of Asian Pentecostal Theology: An Asian American Assessment," *Asian Journal of Pentecostal Studies* 10, no. 1 (2007): 22-41—which provided part of the structure and content for chapter four;

- The Association for Theological Education in South East Asia (ATESEA) for permission related to my "The Future of Evangelical Theology: Asian and Asian American Interrogations," *The Asia Journal of Theology* 21, no. 2 (October 2007): 371-97—which has been dispersed in chapters one, two and four;

- Edinburgh 2010 and Regnum International for permission related to my "From Every Tribe, Language, People, and Nation: Diaspora, Hybridity, and the Coming Reign of God," pp. 261-69, in Chandler Im and Amos Yong, eds., *Global Diasporas and Mission* (Oxford: Regnum Books International, 2014)—now worked into the epilogue;

- IVP Academic for permission related to my "Asian American Evangelical Theology," pp. 195-209, in Jeffrey Greenman and Gene L. Green, eds., *Global Theology in Evangelical Perspective: Exploring the Contextual Nature of Theology and Mission* (Downers Grove, IL: InterVarsity Press, 2012)—which has been redistributed into chapters two and three;

- The Institute for the Study of Asian American Christianity (ISAAC) and Society of Asian North American Christian Studies for permission related to my "Asian American Historicity: The Problem and Promise of Evangelical Theology," *SANACS Journal* 4 (2012–2013): 29-48—now the basis for chapter three;

- Palgrave Macmillan for permission related to my "The Im/migrant Spirit: De/constructing a Pentecostal Theology of Migration," forthcoming, in Peter C. Phan and Elaine Padilla, eds., *Migration, World Christianity, Theology* (New York: Palgrave Macmillan, 2014)—now the foundation for chapter five;

- P & R Publishing for permission related to my "Race, Racialization, and Asian-American Leaders in Post-Racist Evangelicalism," pp. 45-58, in Anthony B. Bradley, ed., *Aliens in the Promised Land: Why Minority Leadership Is Overlooked in White Christian Churches and Institutions* (Phillipsburg, NJ: P&R, 2013)—part of which has been revised and appears in the prologue;

- Sopher Press for permission related to my "Informality, Illegality, and Improvisation: Theological Reflections on Money, Migration, and Ministry in Chinatown, NYC, and Beyond," pp. 248-68, in Eleazar S. Fernandez, ed., *New Overtures: Asian North American Theology in the 21st Century—Essays in Honor of Fumitaka Matsuoka* (Upland, CA: Sopher, 2012), originally published in the *Journal of Race, Ethnicity, and Religion* 3, no. 2 (2012)— upon which chapter six has been expanded;

- University of California Press for permission related to my "Asian American Religion: A Review Essay," *Nova Religio: The Journal of Alternative and Emergent Religions* 9, no. 3 (2006): 92-107—parts of which found its way across chapter two;

- World Evangelical Alliance for permission related to my "Whither Asian American Evangelical Theology? What Asian? Which American? Whose *Evangelion*?" *Evangelical Review of Theology* 32, no. 1 (2008): 22-37; and "Restoring, Reforming, Renewing: Accompaniments to *The Cambridge Companion to Evangelical Theology*," *Evangelical Review of Theology* 33, no. 2 (2009): 179-83—the former now contributes to chapters one through four while the latter has been absorbed into a section of chapter one.

PROLOGUE

Autobiographical Reflections and Anticipations of an Asian American Pent-evangelical Sojourner

I begin this book with a testimony, a primary expression of the pentecostal spirituality of my upbringing, about growing up yellow in nonyellow parts of the world.[1] Yet precisely as testimony, I cannot and do not speak for other yellow people, much less all other Asian Americans.[2] There are too many differences from South Asia (India) to East Asia (Korean and Japan), not to mention from North Asia (Mongolia and China) to Southeast and Southern Asia (Malaysia, Singapore and Indonesia) and to the Pacific Rim (the Philippines).[3] I therefore

---

[1]For more on the role of testimony in pentecostal spirituality and theology, see Mark J. Cartledge, *Testimony in the Spirit: Rescripting Ordinary Pentecostal Theology* (Burlington, VT: Ashgate, 2010), pp. 17-18, and especially Tony Richie, *Speaking by the Spirit: A Pentecostal Model for Interreligious Dialogue* (Wilmore, KY: Emeth, 2011), chap. 4.

[2]As we shall see later, the Asian American nomenclature was first promulgated for political reasons coming out of the civil rights movement in the 1960s. This volume assumes and builds on the existing literature. It also hopes to be suggestive not only for Asian perspectives from the United States but also from Canada, although it does not make much of an effort to address the extensive Asian Canadian literature. For discussion of how Asian American ought to be understood as Asian North American so as not to overlook Canadian voices and experiences, see the introduction to Eleanor Ty and Donald C. Goellnicht, eds., *Asian North American Identities Beyond the Hyphen* (Bloomington: Indiana University Press, 2004).

[3]The United States Census Bureau defines *Asian* as: "A person having origins in any of the original peoples of the Far East, Southeast Asia, or the Indian subcontinent including, for example, Cambodia, China, India, Japan, Korea, Malaysia, Pakistan, the Philippine Islands, Thailand, and Vietnam. It includes people who indicate their race as 'Asian Indian,' 'Chinese,' 'Filipino,' 'Korean,' 'Japanese,' 'Vietnamese,' and 'Other Asian' or provide other detailed Asian responses" (see "Race," United States Census Bureau, accessed June 21, 2013, http://quickfacts.census.gov/qfd/meta/long_RHI505210.htm—thanks to Grace Hsiao Hanford for reference to this site). Asian Americans, then, are immigrants to the U.S. from these countries or their descendants.

give what I call a "slanted" or biased perspective,[4] obviously playing off my phe-
notypical features as a Malaysian-born Chinese immigrant, naturalized since my
teenage years, in the U.S. Yet the following is not merely to be read autobiographically. As a pentecostal and evangelical theologian,[5] I believe that our testimonies are also modes of witness that potentially declare the wondrous works
of God for God's glory (Acts 2:11). Hence, the following weaves personal and
theological considerations together.

I was born in Muslim-controlled Malaysia in the same year (1965) that the
United States passed the Immigration Act, opening the door for massive migration from Asian countries and elsewhere. Yet even before leaving for the
United States, I was racialized in a complex multicultural society.[6] As a person
of Chinese descent, I was a minority in a Muslim-dominated nation that had
only just achieved independence from the British a few years before (in 1957).
Malaysia was thus an emerging postcolonial state, struggling to finds its own
way in the modernizing world. I had to learn Malay, the national language, and
English (British English, to be precise) during my first few years of elementary
public school education, but that also meant that I had no opportunity to
learn how to speak Chinese, except with my grandparents whenever they
visited us or we them. The Malaysian Chinese thus experienced racialization,
if not racism, first- and secondhand: from their Muslim "lords" and through
the legacy of the colonial enterprise.

My parents were first-generation converts to Christianity through the ministry of pentecostal Assemblies of God (AG) missionaries from the United

---

[4]I am also playing off Sharon Betcher's "theology on the slant"—in her *Spirit and the Politics of
Disablement* (Minneapolis: Fortress Press, 2007)—developed in order to show how disability perspectives and a theology of the Holy Spirit can be brought together to reconsider classical theological topics that have worked to marginalize and even oppress people with disabilities. I myself
have developed a pneumatological theology of disability in other books—notably, *The Bible, Disability, and the Church: A New Vision of the People of God* (Grand Rapids: Eerdmans, 2011)—but
am in this book addressing Asian and Asian American ecclesial life and theological work.

[5]In this book, I capitalize "Evangelicalism"/"Evangelicals" and "Pentecostalism"/"Pentecostals"
when used as nouns but not when used as adjectives.

[6]Racialization is distinct from racism; all of us are racialized in terms of having adapted to a world
in which the color of our skin, the looks of our faces or the sounds of our speech make a difference
in how we approach and are received by others. Racism, however, involves prejudicial or discrimi-
natory attitudes or behaviors, intended or not, directed to others for no other reason than that they
are ethnically and racially different from ourselves. So while we are all racialized, some of us are, in
addition and consciously are not, also racist. I hope to clarify the differences further as we proceed
in this book.

States. My father trained for the ministry and had a congregation before I came around, so I grew up as a pentecostal "preacher's kid." Because it was against the law to proselytize and evangelize Muslims, our pentecostal churches were predominantly Chinese (who make up about twenty-five percent of the Malaysian population), with a very small number of South Indian congregants (about seven percent of the overall Malaysian population). I will forever be grateful for the US missionaries under whose labors my parents and I became Christians and grew in our faith. However, they also bequeathed to us a racialized view of the world, about which I will say more in a moment.

In 1975, my parents received an invitation from an AG missionary to Malaysia whose burden for Chinese-speaking peoples led her to plant AG churches for immigrants from Hong Kong and southern China in her home state of California. To oversee these churches, she sponsored the immigration of a number of Malaysian pastors to California. My parents were among those who came. I now became a "missionary kid" to the United States, and part of the earliest wave of what missiologists call "reverse mission" from the Global South to the Western world.[7] Yet while coming to the United States opened up new opportunities for their children, my parents' "American experience" was anything but a success story. My father had left a thriving church in Kuala Lumpur to take the pastorate of a small church in the Californian city of Stockton. Both of my parents struggled, in their middle-age years, to adjust to their new world during what was the last quarter of the twentieth century, their distinctive foreign accent exacerbating their sense of being in a strange and alien land. Their church never grew to much more than a hundred adherents, and even that high point did not last long. Mom and Dad almost never felt as if they had misheard God's call but always struggled to understand their roles amidst what was apparently an unsuccessful (when measured

---

[7]The richness of the "reverse mission" from Fuzhou, China and West Africa are brilliantly documented, respectively, by Kenneth J. Guest, *God in Chinatown: Religion and Survival in New York's Evolving Immigrant Community* (New York: New York University Press, 2003); and a trio of recent volumes: Afe Adogame and James V. Spickard, eds., *Religion Crossing Boundaries: Transnational Religious and Social Dynamics in Africa and the New African Diaspora* (Leiden: Brill, 2010); Frieder Ludwig and J. Kwabena Asamoah-Gyadu, eds., *African Christian Presence in the West: New Immigrant Congregations and Transnational Networks in North America and Europe* (Trenton, NJ: Africa World Press, 2011); and Mark Gornik, *Word Made Global: Stories of African Christianity in New York City* (Grand Rapids: Eerdmans, 2011). We return to discuss Guest's book in chapter 6.

according to the usual quantitative standards) ministry. Yet they have persisted in faithfulness, and still to the present time labor in service to those who
do frequent their nondenominational (independent) and pan-Asian International Christian Fellowship (formed in 1987).

I first experienced the overt realities of US racism during my junior high
school years in the San Joaquin Valley of California. I stood out not only because I had slanted eyes and a foreign accent, but also as a missionary family
supported by the AG district's "home missions" (low) budget—my parents
called it "living by faith"—I wore hand-me-downs that the sponsoring (white)
churches collected and gave to us each Christmas. On a few instances, I almost
got into fights because I resented being called a "chink." I am not sure where
this feistiness came from but in hindsight, these were more instinctive reactions than anything as I struggled not only to find acceptance but also to
survive in an unfamiliar world. I worked hard during these years, not only
dealing with adolescence but also ridding myself of my Malaysian-Chinese
accent. I still get comments to this day: "Oh, I thought you were born here,
you don't sound like a foreigner." Now (as of the time of writing), I am en-
rolled in a college Chinese (Mandarin) course and am doing my best to speak
Chinese "right"! Is it too late to undo what was done?

When I was in junior high school, my wrestling-with-identity issues prompted
a series of discussions with my parents, especially my father. I wanted to know
what my culture was. Was I Malaysian, Chinese, American or some kind of
hybrid?[8] My father said I did not have to worry about cultural aspects of my
identity since we were Christians; so, we were culturally Christian, I concluded.
I accepted this answer at that time, but I have since learned that it was typical of
the kinds of thinking present among AG missionaries, pastors and church
leaders during the middle quarters of the twentieth century. Of course, the AG
also belonged to a wider North American pentecostal and evangelical world,
and such ideas were just as prominent there as well. The point was that Christianity was characterized by such North American cultural habits, and converts
to Christianity were expected to leave their cultural traditions behind in turning
to Christ. What they were not told—because it was not even understood as such

---

[8]I discuss this briefly in my *Beyond the Impasse: Toward a Pneumatological Theology of Religions*
(Grand Rapids: Baker Academic, 2003), pp. 9-10.

by the missionaries—was that turning to Christ involved embracing the culture of the missionaries also.[9] There were subtle and more obvious ways this "truth" was communicated. Nevertheless, my father "got it," and he passed it on to me when I inquired. Such a racialized self-understanding—which presumed the superiority of white and Western culture and downplayed the importance and value of being Malaysian or Chinese—followed me for many more years. I thus accepted that, to use theological notions I later learned, Christian faith transcended culture in a real sense; but I did not see the other important side to this truth: that Christian faith was also always manifest in and through culture as well, supremely in the incarnate Son of God.

It just turned out that during my high school years, from which I graduated as one of six valedictorians (with two other Asians alongside!), I fit the stereotype of Asians as "model minority" immigrants.[10] This, however, is unfair on at least three counts. It is unfair to Asians since there are a diversity of cultures with a range of work and other habits. Why should we measure all ethnic and cultural Asians by norms attained by only a very small slice of them? It is also unfair to other immigrants and peoples of color, especially African Americans, since it suggests that they are of an inferior type or quality when compared to Asian ones. Last but not least, it is unfair to all Americans, period: stereotypes raise hopes, and incorrect stereotypes set everyone up for failed expectations. Judging people by their skin color or their looks is a form of racism; the repetition of stereotypes about "model minorities" perpetuates such racism, however unintentionally, in a supposedly postracist world.[11]

---

[9]This understanding was promulgated not only by missionaries in Asia and the Global South, but even in North America, among Native Americans; see Kirk Dombrowski, *Against Culture: Development, Politics, and Religion in Indian Alaska* (Lincoln. University of Nebraska Press, 2001).

[10]The by-now classic discussion that shows the deep faults and flaws of the "model minority" stereotype is Frank H. Wu, *Yellow: Race in America Beyond Black and White* (New York: Basic Books, 2002), chap. 2; see also Stacey J. Lee, *Unraveling the "Model Minority" Stereotype: Listening to Asian American Youth* (New York and London: Teachers College Press, 1996), esp. chap. 6, and the compactly insightful discussion of Ronald Takaki, *Strangers from a Different Shore: A History of Asian Americans* (Boston: Little, Brown, & Company, 1989), pp. 474-84, about the economic inequalities, structural problems, "glass ceiling" realities, misleading and harmful stereotypes, and violence masked by the "myth" of the model minority.

[11]Henry Yu, *Thinking Orientals: Migration, Contact, and Exoticism in Modern America* (Oxford: Oxford University Press, 2001), shows how the processes of racialization or racial differentiation have resulted in the marginalization of, as well as discrimination against, "Orientals"—the former term which "Asian American" has replaced since the 1970s—even on the eve of the twenty-first century.

I went to Bethany College in California—a school founded in the Bible-institute tradition of classical Pentecostalism—for my undergraduate studies to prepare for what I felt God calling me to: Christian ministry. From there I went on to get a master's degree in the history of Christianity from Western Evangelical Seminary (now part of George Fox University) in the Wesleyan-Holiness tradition, and then a second master's in intellectual history from Portland State University, a secular institution, both in the Portland, Oregon, area. My studies were thoroughly Western. I do not recall having any teachers or professors of color, and the curriculum was dominated by Anglo-American perspectives. Bethany, as a denominationally affiliated school, inculcated (indoctrinated may be too strong) students with the values and ethos of the AG, and also of the wider North American evangelical movement. Western Seminary introduced me to the broader Western Christian tradition (I actually wrote my master's thesis on the reception of the Chalcedonian doctrine of the two natures of Christ in the West), and Portland State immersed me in the Western canon of "Great Books." I do not recall much discussion about race. It was as if race realities did not exist (although I should acknowledge also that I was probably not yet ready to be impressed by such discussions, oblivious as I was to these critical discursive perspectives). Yet, not talking about race itself has allowed the negative aspects of racialization to persist.[12] In any case, even in such a white world, I still managed to meet and marry a Mexican American fellow student at Bethany, and, with that, my racialized identity complexified. I return to this part of the story in a moment.

I should note that I first encountered the non-Western world during my coursework at Portland State through a professor who had us reading the philosophy of Alfred North Whitehead (1861–1947), whose ideas continue to be well received internationally. It was there that I learned of the growing dialogue between Western and Eastern philosophers, striving toward articulation

---

[12]So while descriptively racialization can be understood simply as the process of categorizing by race or ethnicity, the result, whether intended or not, is also the creation of "a racial hierarchy in the Unites States, with Asian Americans and Latinos positioned in between African Americans and whites," so that like it or not, Asian Americans are contributing to the racist structural inequalities that have plagued American culture for two centuries; see Russell Jeung, Carolyn Chen and Jerry Z. Park, "Introduction: Religious, Racial, and Ethnic Identities of the New Second Generation," in Carolyn Chen and Russell Jeung, eds., *Sustaining Faith Traditions: Race, Ethnicity, and Religion Among the Latino and Asian American Second Generation* (New York and London: New York University Press, 2012), pp. 1-22, quotation from p. 7.

of what is called "world philosophy." I began then to observe that there were similar trends afoot in theological circles, especially mainline Protestant and Roman Catholic, about the importance of engaging with Eastern or Asian perspectives. All this was part of my doctoral course of study at Boston University in the mid-1990s.[13] Although the Western philosophical and theological tradition was still the starting point for much of what we studied at Boston, there were also intentional efforts to register the perspectives of women and people of color, and to engage with ethnic, cultural, philosophical and religious traditions in the Global South.

Not too long after completing my PhD at Boston, I landed a theology position at Bethel University in St. Paul, Minnesota. I worked there and thrived for six years. A department chair who recognized the need to diversify the theology faculty welcomed me, and I found nothing but support from the wider faculty and Bethel administration. This does not mean Bethel was exempt from the racialized realities of North American Evangelicalism. Ethnically, Bethel is affiliated with the Baptist General Conference (BGC), a pietist denomination with deep roots in the Swedish immigration in the mid-nineteenth century to the Upper Midwest region of the United States. My blonde-haired and blue-eyed Scandinavian students put up with me while I had to learn how to talk to them about the importance of "global perspectives." Denominationally, the BGC considers itself broadly evangelical and certainly sees itself as contributing to the discussion of what it means to be evangelical in the twenty-first century. As a Chinese American pentecostal and evangelical theologian, I found myself thrust into a set of discussions, even debates, carried out mostly by white Evangelicals. Culturally, it was at Bethel that for the first time I experienced what my father said, but in a way that he did not mean. Conversion to Christianity did bring with it a conversion to Christian culture at some level; the only thing is that in the Upper Midwest such "Christian culture" takes on a very white form of life.

Our family moved in 2005 when I joined the faculty at Regent University in Virginia. After having lived on the West coast of the country and in the

---

[13]My *doktorvater*, Robert Cummings Neville, has worked hard as a systematic philosopher and theologian over the decades to engage Eastern traditions and integrate them into the overall philosophical enterprise, beginning with his third and fourth books, *Soldier, Sage, Saint* (New York: Fordham University Press, 1978), and *The Tao and the Daimon: Segments of a Religious Inquiry* (Albany: State University of New York Press, 1982).

Northeast and Upper Midwest, we finally experienced in a more palpable way the stain of the long history of slavery when we arrived in this northernmost of the Southern states. Service workers remain largely African Americans in this part of the country, and there would probably be more people of color in these professions if it were not that the demographics here in the Commonwealth of Virginia are largely black-and-white. Yet my colleagues here at Regent are committed to an inclusive vision of the coming reign of God. Charismatic evangelical minister, entrepreneur and one-time presidential aspirant M. G. "Pat" Robertson founded Regent in the late 1970s, and he has always had a heart for the Chinese people. Our diverse faculty, at least in the School of Divinity, where I am located, strives to engage students with a global vision, which includes heeding the voices and perspectives of women and people of color.

While I feel quite accepted here at Regent, I have heard that even in the recent past, my ethnic minority (especially African American) colleagues still occasionally face racist attitudes, from other colleagues no less. I wonder sometimes whether being Asian in what for some is still a starkly black-and-white North America, not to mention the American South, protects me to some degree. I also wonder whether people will like me less if I began to write and speak more intentionally about racism and racialization. Perhaps I am "safe" because I have earned my academic stripes, so to speak, by talking about matters that do not set in relief the underlying realities of race in what we would like to think is a postracist world. Yet to put things this way also turns a blind eye and deaf ear to the distinctive forms of racism, oppression and marginalization that are experienced by nonblack and nonwhite people, including yellow people like me.[14]

By now, of course, I have become quite comfortable in the racialized world that I inhabit. After all, I have a named chair to my position and have some degree of influence as dean of the divinity school here at my institution. My parents are proud of my achievements. Although my youngest brother, Mark, born with Down syndrome, remains at home,[15] my second brother, Eben, has

---

[14]As noted by Sang Hyun Lee, *From a Liminal Place: An Asian American Theology* (Minneapolis: Fortress, 2010). In fact, to be "neither black nor white" is also an experience of marginality for many Asian Americans; see the introductory chapter of Angelo N. Ancheta, *Race, Right, and the Asian American Experience* (New Brunswick, NJ: Rutgers University Press, 1998).

[15]I tell the story of growing up and living with Mark and his disability in the introductory vignettes

long had a successful professional position in the information technology in-dustry. We are living out the American dream, and through us, so are our parents. We have come a long ways from our humble beginnings as immi-grants, and there is much to thank God for.

My wife has also come from a similarly modest background. She was born to Mexican American farmworkers who traversed the migrant trail from Texas up north to Wisconsin and then westward to the eastern part of Washington state, where the family finally settled. Still, growing up she had to leave school late in the spring before the year ended since migrant farm-work season opened up in Montana and North Dakota before summer break arrived. Both of us recall the embarrassment of having to get in the "free lunch" line at school be-cause our parents qualified for this (although now, looking back, we are grateful to have gotten fed daily). As the first college attendee and graduate in her family, and still the only one with a graduate degree, my wife has also grown up with firsthand experience of the racialized US. Now she is a successful high school Spanish and social studies teacher in a very diverse public school system that is especially sensitive to the plight of English-as-a-second-language students.

To be sure, our three children have interesting questions about whether they should embrace more the Chinese or the Mexican aspects of their identity, and they usually figure out that there are advantages to be able to claim either depending on the situation.[16] They certainly inhabit and benefit from the cultural styles of the middle-class United States in ways that their parents never did growing up. Are not my family and I examples of the dawn of a postracist North American culture and Evangelicalism? That is certainly the mantra of the dominant (white) culture: that regardless of one's skin color, all one has to do is to work hard to attain the American dream. On the flip side is the often-unthought but certainly unsaid as-sumption that those who are less or not successful are to be blamed for not working hard enough. Are both sides of this notion true in the end, or do they mask more fundamental and racial realities within which all of us—

---

of each chapter in *Theology and Down Syndrome: Reimagining Disability in Late Modernity* (Waco, TX: Baylor University Press, 2007); see also my *The Bible, Disability, and the Church*, pp. 1-5.

[16]My Chinese Mexican American children live out what Brian Bantum calls "mulattic existence," which simultaneously gives us a window into God's identity in Christ; see Bantum, *Redeeming Mulatto: A Theology of Race and Christian Hybridity* (Waco, TX: Baylor University Press, 2010).

white and black, and even yellow and brown—are entangled?[17]

While elsewhere I have reflected autobiographically in nonethnic and non-racial terms,[18] the preceding sets in relief the ethnic and racial dimensions of my journey. As already indicated, I did not always consciously understand these aspects of my personal, much less theological, identity. In many ways, these have grown on me, perhaps largely in part because I chose to minimize them and was able to successfully—measured by promotions I received—navigate my theological profession without making too much ado about such. Yet, there is no doubt that at least the educational periods of my life as well as my initial entry into the theological academy were prepared if not explicitly carried by affirmative action policies and sentiments favorable to the acceptance, hiring and promotion of people of color. Beyond this sociological datum, from a more theological angle, I have from the very beginning of my scholarly work been engaged with the horizon of Asian religious, cultural and philosophical traditions, and in hindsight I very easily see that these passions were one way in which I explored what it meant to do theology as an Asian American theologian.[19]

It was also during the period when I was relocating to Regent that I began, for the first time, following the growing literature about Asian American migration, Christianity and theology. Over the last almost-ten years, I have not studied this multifaceted and interrelated set of topics in depth, but I have begun to think more intentionally about my work as a pentecostal and evangelical theologian at this intersection. Gradual reading in and around the various literatures meeting at this juncture led to various review and other exploratory essays in different venues. Then, a growing involvement with networks such as the Institute for the Study of Asian American Christianity and conversations with

---

[17]Beyond the racialized dimensions of the "American dream" are (largely) unexplored presuppositions at the intersection of theology and economics; I return to comment on these in the sixth chapter.

[18]See, e.g., Yong, "Between the Local and the Global: Autobiographical Reflections on the Emergence of the Global Theological Mind," in Darren C. Marks, ed., *Shaping a Global Theological Mind* (Aldershot, UK: Ashgate, 2008) pp. 187-94; and "The Spirit, Vocation, and the Life of the Mind: A Pentecostal Testimony," in Steven M. Fettke and Robby Waddell, eds., *Pentecostals in the Academy: Testimonies of Call* (Cleveland, TN: CPT Press, 2012), pp. 203-20.

[19]Technically, of course, I am a Chinese American theologian; however, I write this book in solidarity with others who hail from other parts of the Asian continent and who find themselves taking up the theological task in the North American context—so I also embrace, and will use, the "Asian American" self-designation.

other Asian American theologians as well as evangelical and pentecostal theologians sensitive to the contextual character of all theology spurred my thinking and writing. This volume pulls together a number of previously published essays and articles, revising, expanding on and adding to them.

THESIS AND OVERVIEW OF THE VOLUME

If in much of my prior work I have argued that pentecostal theology specifically has much to contribute to the broader Christian theological discussion, in this volume I argue the thesis that Asian American experiences and perspectives have much to contribute to the broader evangelical theological discussion. More precisely I want to press the question of the *what* and *how* of evangelical theology in the emerging global context that we all now inhabit, and do so from the particular angle of Asian American realities. This is not so much because the latter provides some sort of normative viewpoint for the theological task but that the issues raised are representative of the challenges and opportunities before global Evangelicalism in general and evangelical theologians—of whatever background—more specifically. I therefore approach this undertaking utilizing not the standard postmodern, postcolonial, post-Western or even post-Christendom theoretical models—although the influence of and critical engagement with these will be evidenced in what follows—but as a theologian, deploying primarily theological methods of analysis. In particular, I will be arguing my case as a pentecostal and evangelical theologian by drawing primarily from the biblical motif and metaphor of the Day of Pentecost narrative, highlighting how the outpouring of the Spirit of Christ upon all flesh invites a reconfiguration of the global evangelical theological conversation so as to heed the particularities of various linguistic, cultural and social dynamics.

Hence this book is not limited to sketching a way forward for Asian American theology in general and Asian American evangelical theology in particular (about which differences more will be said later), although it certainly also intends both objectives. Rather, the wager is that the achievement of these goals has larger purchase, with implications also for North American evangelical theology specifically but also the global theological discussion. En route to this destination, then, this volume intends to make a contribution along two discrete but related trajectories. It will provide a distinctive pente-costal perspective on Asian American theology and Asian American evan-gelical theology, even as it echoes Asian American pent-evangelical soundings on the global theological register.

To be clear, then, I am writing this book for two primary audiences: other Asian American theological colleagues, especially those in the evangelical world, and the North American evangelical (primarily and predominantly white) theological academy in general. I hope that more of the former see the value of thinking faithfully and creatively out of their Asian American iden-tities, not just for ourselves but for the wider theological discussion. I also pray that the latter will be more intentional about thinking contextually and his-torically in dialogue with Asian American and other perspectives in global context. Of course, if there are also others beyond these two specific groups who find value in what I have to say, that will be an added byproduct for which I can only be thankful.

Chapter one unfolds the contemporary global context of the evangelical theological enterprise. While the contribution of British and US theologians should not be understated with regard to how we have arrived at the present state of contemporary evangelical theology, it is also the case that the shift of the center of gravity of Christianity from the Euro-American West to the Global South invites rethinking about the evangelical theological task. The voices of Asian Evangelicals have gradually emerged over the last generation. This chapter outlines their contributions and overviews the opportunities and challenges related to sounding Asian voices in the evangelical theological conversation.

The second chapter turns specifically to the Asian American context. What are the sociological and demographic changes across the Asian diaspora to North America? By "Asian diaspora to North America," I refer first and foremost not to Asians who are refugees or exiles to the United States, although these are not excluded. Instead, as we shall see, the nomenclature of "Asian American" refers broadly to Asian immigrants to the United States, increasing since 1965. Yet as we shall also see, "Asians" are not a cohesive group, and neither are "Asian Americans." Hence, the "Asian American diaspora" is a shorthand term that masks more than it illuminates. For purposes of jump-starting the discussion, however, we will use this abbreviated reference to refer to immigrants to the

United States (and their descendants) who have come from the Asian continent for whatever reason. More specifically, we are interested in how such immigrants and their children (to a second and later generation, even) relate to Christianity in general and Evangelicalism in particular. How has Asian American Christianity intersected or interfaced with the dominant (white) evangelical culture? What does the existing scholarship by and on Asian Americans reveal? What are the dominant currents and scholarly conversations with which Asian Americans are interfacing? What have been the contributions of Asian American theological voices both in the guild and in relationship to the ongoing life of the church as well? The questions are unpacked in order to provide a broader historical, social, academic and theological context for understanding the task of Asian American Evangelicalism and Asian American evangelical theology. What emerges is a vibrant field of Asian American studies and scholarship on Asian American Christianity from inter- and multidisciplinary perspectives which, as shall be seen in the next chapter, contrasts with the relatively weak Asian American evangelical theological field.

If the first two chapters set the contemporary stage on which Asian American evangelicalism is unfolding, the next chapter gets us to the heart of the present problematic for not only Asian American theology but also for evangelical theology writ large. The question can be posited sharply: why has Asian American evangelical theology been relatively unenergetic, especially when compared to Asian American theology in mainline Protestant and Roman Catholic circles? The third chapter argues that there are many reasons for this and that they relate both to the legacy of the (white) North American evangelical endeavor as a whole and to how this tradition has been received and internalized by Asian American Evangelicals. The result is that while Asian American evangelical theology has been by and large consonant with that of the (white) evangelical establishment, it has not been encouraged to seek after nor has it found much of its own voice. Understanding the cultural, historical and theological forces driving these tendencies allows for the mandate and task of a specifically Asian American evangelical theological contribution to emerge with clarity. The argument unfolded here is at the heart of this book: it claims to address not only challenges confronting Asian American evangelicals but also the blind spots of evangelical theology especially in its American incarnations. If it is successful, then we shall see that the "problem" for Asian American evangelical theology is simultaneously the problem of evangelical theology itself—there is no way to address either without addressing the other. Yet problems are also, when looked at from the glass-half-full perspective, opportunities. Thus evangelical theology in the twenty-first century (which is after all the title and reflects the major thrust of this book) will need to attend to how Asian American Evangelicals confront and respond to this issue, and vice versa.

In order to catalyze the Asian American evangelical theological project, the remainder of this volume will draw from and engage with pentecostal perspectives. This is not only because of the author's pentecostal affiliation and identity but also because the argument can (and will be) made that Pentecostalism can be considered either as a subset of Evangelicalism or vice versa. In chapter four, the fortunes of Asian American pentecostal theology are mapped onto the Asian American evangelical experience in order to identify resources for developing a global pent-evangelical theology that is yet not devoid of the historicity, particularity and contextuality of Asian and Asian American life and experience.

The next chapter (five) burrows deeper into the Asian American experience by examining the realities connected to migration and immigration in a globalizing world. While recognizing that migration is not distinctive to the Asian American experience, nevertheless we observe that Evangelicals have lagged behind in taking up questions related to theology of migration. An evangelical theology of migration is then outlined from a pentecostal perspective by providing an Asian American reading of Luke–Acts, in particular through observing how the apostolic community can be understood as a dynamic community of migration.

However, the issues related to theology of migration are deeper and more complicated than even most treatments of theologies of migration in the wider academy let on, because of the phenomenon of undocumented immigration. In chapter six, then, we focus on a case study of alternative forms of Chinese American immigration. Exploration of the issues related to this understudied "yellow" reality invite theological reflection on social justice, economics and politics. Biblical and pentecostal perspectives on a theology of economics and a theology of migration are developed in dialogue with evangelical and other theological resources.

The final chapter returns us full circle to the task of global evangelical theology, but now informed by our immersion into the Asian American pentecostal and evangelical experience. Paying attention especially to gender, race and political realities as viewed from an Asian American lens, I sketch a programmatic vision here for evangelical theology, inviting Asian American evangelical contributions at one level (which would be parallel to any number of other particularly engaged evangelical theological projects in global context), challenging Western European and North American evangelical expansion at a second level, and then envisioning possibilities for a truly global evangelical theological conversation in conclusion. The argument is that all three levels of theological work need to be engaged simultaneously and dialogically in order for the promise of a global evangelical theology to continue to develop and find traction.

The epilogue returns to expand on some of the autobiographical reflections in the prologue, but now in light of the threads of this book. In particular, I explore the question about theological hybridity, analyzing the Asian and American intersection in a globalizing evangelical conversation. I take up critical questions about theology and hybridity in order to insist that the Asian American evangelical conversation exists only *in media res*, neither merely at the beginning nor close to culmination, interwoven, interlaced and intertwined with the matrix that constitutes evangelical life in the twenty-first century.

Two Caveats

Let me be clear up front, however, about how I understand and what I mean by hybridity, a concept that appears periodically and that will feature prominently in my concluding reflections. I will discuss in the rest of this book how we are all hybridic in some respect, a combination of various biological, cultural and historical realities. That is undeniable as a descriptive statement of historically formed human beings. Yet my argument for a hybridic Christian faith is not intended to justify just any combination that might be appealing or even politically correct. Rather, I understand hybridity primarily theologically: the incarnation provides us with God's embrace of hybridity, most wonderfully and truthfully manifest in Christ, and the many tongues of Pentecost allow us to see how the Holy Spirit can redeem the diversity of languages, cultures and traditions for the glory of God. Christ is hybridic not in the sense that he is composed partly of this and that but that he was, as the historic creeds assert, *fully* divine and *fully* human.[20] Following this christological paradigm, then, those of us shaped by the image of Christ can live fully into— rather than ignoring, denying or erasing—our hybridic dimensions by the redeeming and sanctifying power of his Spirit. My own Asian American soundings thus find inspiration in Paul's description of the one body that yet comprises many members through the charismatic activity of the Holy Spirit. Yet as surely as this rightly and beautifully describes the church as the people of God, the body of Christ and the fellowship of the Spirit in anticipation of the coming reign of God, it also is suggestive for how to understand the truth of the gospel as manifest in individual hybrid (Asian American, etc.) lives. The rest of this book will attempt to make this argument not merely for Asian Americans but for a pent-evangelical theology for the twenty-first century.

One final word about nomenclature before proceeding. This volume intends to make a contribution to evangelical theology from an Asian American and pentecostal perspective. None of these terms is uncontested. *Evangelicalism* has perennially been disputed, and its sociological and theological boundaries will continue to be debated long after this book is out of print. *Pentecostalism* is no less complicated a term depending on who is being asked. Last but not least, we have already noted that what it means to be Asian American is not obvious, even more complex than the so far unsuccessful attempts to understand either *Asian* or *American* on its own. The remainder of this volume, beginning immediately in the next chapter, will provide some guidelines for how I am using these terms even as the cumulative argument will, hopefully, both provide some justification for such choices and demonstrate how these notions contribute toward a richer evangelical theology for the twenty-first century.

---

[20]I find inspiration here from Bantum, *Redeeming Mulatto*, part two.

1

EVANGELICALISM AND GLOBAL THEOLOGY

Emerging Asian and Contextual Voices

This chapter intends to establish the broader global horizons for contemporary evangelical theology, especially when viewed from the Asian and Asian American landscape. To do so, its three sections begin with some of the globalization and world Christianity dynamics that inform the contemporary theological enterprise, move from there to explore more specifically Asian evangelical theological trends and currents, and then shift to the present North American and Asian American evangelical contexts. Our goal is to properly situate the argument of the present volume so as to set in relief the thesis that the vitality of evangelical theology going into the middle of the twenty-first century depends on its contextual inputs—in the case presented in this book, that of Asian American voices and perspectives.

Before proceeding, however, I want to clarify the basic terminology deployed. For purposes of this volume, I basically adhere to the definition of *evangelical* as set forth by David Bebbington.[1] From a historical perspective, Bebbington argues that Evangelicalism has been characterized by four features: a conversionist approach to the Christian life that motivates especially mission and evangelism; an activist spirituality that insists Christian discipleship is expressed in a distinctively and behaviorally observable way of life;

---

[1]David William Bebbington, *Evangelicalism in Modern Britain: A History from the 1730s to the 1980s* (Boston: Unwin Hyman, 1989), esp. chap. 1. Another solid and reliable historical overview, especially of the American evangelical scene that forms the broader context for this volume, is Douglas A. Sweeney, *The American Evangelical Story: A History of the Movement* (Grand Rapids: Baker Academic, 2005).

a deferential and committed biblicism that foregrounds the normative authority of Scripture; and a crucicentric piety that emphasizes the death of
Christ for the salvation of the world. While this definitional quadrilateral is
arguably incomplete, it has found wide acceptance as a generic starting point
for discussion about the nature of evangelical identity.[2] The concern in some
circles that this understanding pertains more to the pietist expressions of the
modern evangelical movement actually becomes one springboard for the
pent-evangelical approach featured in this book.

A second catalyst toward the pent-evangelical framework for this volume
is mediated by the work of Donald Dayton.[3] Dayton's concerns have been to
highlight the role of the nineteenth-century American holiness movements in
the formation of twentieth-century Evangelicalism, in particular emphasizing
how their various social engagements were founding forces for later evangelical developments. As evangelical theology has come to be dominated by
conservative Reformed voices especially in the second half of the twentieth
century, Dayton and his Wesleyan colleagues have been urging against the
reduction of "evangelical" to "Reformed" understandings. While I have elsewhere thrown in my support to the Daytonian thesis,[4] it is interesting to note
in the context of this book that Asian American evangelicals in United States
historically have been drawn much more to Reformed than Wesleyan traditions and streams. While the correlations between Puritan and Confucian
work ethics may go part of the way toward explaining this convergence, there
is no theological rationale for these historical associations, especially not
when there are emerging Asian American appropriations of the Wesleyan tra-

---

[2]This is not to say that the definition of *evangelical* is uncontested; the debates surrounding the term
during the past two generations are succinctly summarized in Jon R. Stone, *On the Boundaries of
American Evangelicalism: The Postwar Evangelical Coalition* (New York: Palgrave Macmillan, 1997).
For broader historical perspective, see the five volumes of A History of Evangelicalism: People,
Movements and Ideas in the English-Speaking World, published by InterVarsity Press from 2003–
2013; an overview of the complexity can be appreciated from the introductory chapter of the inaugural volume in the series: Mark A. Noll, *The Rise of Evangelicalism: The Age of Edwards, White-
field and the Wesleys* (Downers Grove, IL: InterVarsity Press, 2003), pp. 13-26.

[3]Starting with Donald W. Dayton, *Discovering an Evangelical Heritage* (New York: Harper & Row,
1976), and expanded thereafter in many articles and book chapters, among other venues.

[4]See my essay, "Wesley and Fletcher—Dayton and Wood: Appreciating Wesleyan-Holiness Tongues,
Essaying Pentecostal-Charismatic Interpretations," in Christian T. Collins Winn, ed., *From the
Margins: A Celebration of the Theological Work of Donald W. Dayton* (Eugene, OR: Pickwick, 2007),
pp. 179-90.

dition.[5] For our pent-evangelical purposes, then, Dayton's argument is important: it provides historical moorings for the claim that pent-evangelical pietism is as intimately intertwined with and informed by holiness sensibilities as by Reformed commitments.[6]

Building on these Bebbingtonian and Daytonian genealogies, this volume presumes that contemporary pentecostal, charismatic and renewal Christianity[7] can be understood as a subset of Evangelicalism, despite some of the historical and theological difficulties with this mode of categorization.[8] Historically, while the beginnings of modern Pentecostalism are contested among historians, there is no denying the central role of the Azusa Street revival in Los Angeles during the first decade of the twentieth century.[9] The subsequent influence of this revival on later Pentecostalism and charismaticism means that contemporary global renewal movements are also basically pietistic in orientation. To be sure there are challenges to evangelical theology that have accrued from such a pietistic leaven,[10] but there is no way to minimize the fact that pentecostal spirituality both extends and adapts the pietism that the Azusa Street revivalists inherited. However, there is also no doubt that contemporary renewal Christianity, especially across the Global South, includes various streams and currents that are only tangentially related,

---

[5]E.g., Sang-Ehil Han, "A Revisionist Spirit-Christology in Korean Culture" (PhD diss., Emory University, 2004), who writes from a pentecostal perspective.

[6]See also Donald W. Dayton, *Theological Roots of Pentecostalism* (Grand Rapids: Francis Asbury, and Metuchen, NJ: Scarecrow Press, 1987).

[7]In this book, I also do not intend to adjudicate the differences between "pentecostal," "charismatic" and "renewal." Increasingly all three are being used in the scholarly literature. For an overview of the differences, as well as their sufficient similarities so as to be justified in understanding them as relatively synonymous, see my article, "Poured Out on All Flesh: The Spirit, World Pentecostalism, and the Performance of Renewal Theology," *PentecoStudies: An Interdisciplinary Journal for Research on the Pentecostal and Charismatic Movements* 6, no. 1 (2007): 16-46, online at glopent .net/pentecostudies.

[8]Thus is the charismatic renewal in the Church of England included and discussed in the seventh chapter of Bebbington's *Evangelicalism in Modern Britain*.

[9]As urged even by Allan Anderson, *An Introduction to Pentecostalism: Global Charismatic Christianity* (Cambridge: Cambridge University Press, 2004), esp. chap. 2.

[10]E.g., as documented by Ben Witherington III, *The Problem with Evangelical Theology: Testing the Exegetical Foundations of Calvinism, Dispensationalism, and Wesleyanism* (Waco, TX: Baylor University Press, 2005), esp. part III. This volume can be read also as at least a partial response to Witherington's arguments, not necessarily attempting to suggest they are misguided (even if aspects of them can be said to be misconceived or at least overstated) but to show a way forward for evangelical and pietist theology that avoids many of the problems he rightly identifies.

if at all, to the main historical and especially theological lines of the evangelical tradition sketched by Bebbington. Theologically any specific renewal movement will need to be evaluated on a case-by-case basis. Classical pentecostal movements, churches and traditions, however, by and large fit the Bebbingtonian quadrilateral, even if there are strands within such that may deviate from other foundational orthodoxies.[11] More precisely, renewal theological instincts are no less Bible-based, Christ-centered, evangelistically and missionally motivated, and pietistically shaped then their evangelical forebears and cousins.[12] Preliminarily, then, our use of the term "evangelical" and its cognates in this book will generally include the broad range of pentecostal, charismatic and related renewal movements, although in specific instances, specific strands of this latter group will be delineated for various reasons that will be clear in those contexts. I resort to the awkward neologism "pent-evangelical" to remind readers that the evangelical category in this volume includes the pentecostal and charismatic currents. In the end, the argument of this book will be successful if it can be shown that such a pent-evangelical category holds together meaningfully in the context of thinking about global evangelical theology on the one hand as well as about Asian and Asian American contributions to such on the other.[13]

---

[11]I am thinking for instance of Oneness Pentecostalism, which rejects the Nicene trinitarian formulations, although they embrace the biblical affirmations regarding God as Father, Son and Holy Spirit, and the full deity of Christ; for further discussion, see my "Oneness and the Trinity: The Theological and Ecumenical Implications of 'Creation *Ex Nihilo*' for an Intra-Pentecostal Dispute," *Pneuma: The Journal of the Society for Pentecostal Studies* 19, no. 1 (Spring 1997): 81-107.

[12]These depictions of renewal Christianity can be seen in many of my books, two of the most pertinent of which are *The Spirit Poured Out on All Flesh: Pentecostalism and the Possibility of Global Theology* (Grand Rapids: Baker Academic, 2005), and *In the Days of Caesar: Pentecostalism and Political Theology—The Cadbury Lectures 2009*, Sacra Doctrina: Christian Theology for a Postmodern Age series (Grand Rapids: Eerdmans, 2010).

[13]I risk this "pent-evangelical" nomenclature even though there is an emerging pentecostal scholarly and theological academy that, in reacting to the attempts by some Evangelicals to equate "Evangelicalism" with the conservative Reformed tradition, have embraced more Wesleyan—leading to pentecostal and holiness—self-understandings and thus even distanced themselves from the evangelical label. While I have been previously partial also toward carving out a distinctive pentecostal perspective, it is nevertheless clear that the "evangelical" field has been and continues to be contested. This book represents my most direct intervention in this particular debate, and as will be evident, I am hoping that the following Asian American pent-evangelical proposal will be a helpful contribution to the broader and more irenic Evangelicalism that does exist, however loosely, across the North American landscape.

THEOLOGY IN A GLOBALIZING WORLD: EVANGELICAL AND ASIAN INTERSECTIONS

Much is being made currently of the global expansion of Christianity in the twentieth and now twenty-first centuries.[14] In particular, there is the stark realization that the center of gravity for the Christian faith has shifted from the Euro-American West to the Global South.[15] Whereas up until even the middle of the twentieth century, Christian "movers and shakers" came by and large from the Western world, they are now increasingly brown (Latin American), black (African) and shades of yellow (Asian). New discourses and fields of inquiry are emerging, many with the nomenclature of "world Christianity,"[16] although there is still little agreement about what precisely that means or covers. What is increasingly clear is that whatever else may be included under that rubric, contemporary trends indicate that the global explosion of Christianity is driven primarily by evangelical, pentecostal and charismatic renewal churches and movements.[17] Yes, Western Christianity, especially in its American forms, continues to play an important role in the emerging world forum,[18] but there is no denying that Latin American, African and Asian actors and agents will grow in prominence as we move forward.

This is certainly the case in the theological arena. While there is no doubt that evangelical theology, in particular, has had a long and venerable history in the West—with both positive and negative results, as will be clear in the rest of this volume—even Western evangelical theologians are intentionally

---

[14]E.g., Philip Jenkins, *The Next Christendom: The Coming of Global Christianity* (Oxford: Oxford University Press, 2003), and Douglas Jacobsen, *The World's Christians: Who They Are, Where They Are, and How They Got There* (Chichester, UK: Wiley-Blackwell, 2011).

[15]As clearly documented in Todd M. Johnson and Kenneth R. Ross, eds., *Atlas of Global Christianity 1910–2010* (Edinburgh: Edinburgh University Press, 2009).

[16]I discuss some of these developments briefly in an article, "The Emerging Field of World Christianity: A Renewal Reading of the *Cambridge Dictionary of Christianity*," *The Journal of World Christianity* 4, no. 1 (2011): 27-43, online at journalofworldchristianity.org/index.php/jowc/issue/view/13/showToc.

[17]See, e.g., Mark Hutchinson and Ogbu Kalu, eds., *A Global Faith: Essays on Evangelicalism and Globalization* (Macquarie Centre, NSW: Centre for the Study of Australian Christianity, 1998), and Donald M. Lewis, ed., *Christianity Reborn: The Global Expansion of Evangelicalism in the Twentieth Century* (Grand Rapids: Eerdmans, 2004); cf. also Mark Hutchinson and John Wolffe, *A Short History of Global Evangelicalism* (Cambridge: Cambridge University Press, 2012), and Brian Stanley, *The Global Diffusion of Evangelicalism: The Age of Billy Graham and John Stott* (Downers Grove, IL: IVP Academic, 2013).

[18]Mark A. Noll, *The New Shape of World Christianity: How American Experience Reflects Global Faith* (Downers Grove, IL: IVP Academic, 2009).

sensitive to these globalizing dynamics. The turn of the twenty-first century especially has witnessed a spate of new books that both recognize the very Western character of much of what has gone before as evangelical theology and that there is a need to seek out, engage and renew the tradition in dialogue with theologians and perspectives from the Global South.[19] For many reasons, Western Evangelicals will continue to lead the theological charge, but gone are the days when thinkers will be able to ignore either historical, cultural and contextual factors or globalization trends in their envisioning and articulating of the theological task.[20] In fact, even Western Evangelicals are increasingly postcritical and particularistic in working with awareness of how the interpretation of Scripture and the reception of tradition can only be viable if undertaken in a contextually sensitive manner.[21]

Looking backward from this vantage point, however, it is now also increasingly clear that the history of Christianity itself, as well as the evangelical tradition (however that may be understood prior to the twentieth century), has been much more variegated according to its even-then "global" dimensions than the standard textbook accounts of previous generations have let on. Earlier historiographic models tended to consider "Christian history" primarily in terms of the ecclesiastical history of both occidental and Orthodox traditions, which then relegated the growth of Christianity in Africa, Asia and Latin America (after 1492) to the area of "mission studies." While not inaccurate from one angle, this way of organizing the discipline of theology suggested that if we wanted to learn about Christianity, or the church, then the Western story included all that was important to know; concomitantly, exploration of what was happening in the non-Western world taught us not about Christianity or the church as such, but about the latter's evan-

---

[19]Leading the way here was Aída Besançon Spencer and William David Spencer, eds., *The Global God: Multicultural Evangelical Views of God* (Grand Rapids: Baker Books, 1998). See also Craig Ott and Harold A. Netland, eds., *Globalizing Theology: Belief and Practice in an Era of World Christianity* (Grand Rapids: Baker Academic, 2006), and Jeffrey Greenman and Gene L. Green, eds., *Global Theology in Evangelical Perspective: Exploring the Contextual Nature of Theology and Mission* (Downers Grove, IL: IVP Academic, 2012).

[20]Exemplary here is Timothy C. Tennent, *Theology in the Context of World Christianity: How the Global Church Is Influencing the Way We Think About and Discuss Theology* (Grand Rapids: Zondervan, 2007).

[21]As manifest in the collection by mainly British Evangelicals: Tom Greggs, ed., *New Perspectives for Evangelical Theology: Engaging with God, Scripture and the World* (New York: Routledge, 2010).

gelical and evangelistic activities to reach the lost. Needless to say, this older paradigm is being replaced.[22] What is emerging is a more integrated narrative in which Christian history is rearticulated from the perspective of its various agents, regardless of geographic domain.[23] In particular, the notions of a "world Christianity" are being contested also within the discipline of historiography. The point is that there are important ways to understand Christianity as a worldwide phenomenon even prior to the twentieth century, and that these include recognition of the back-and-forth interactions between Western and non-Western Christians across space and time. Further, the bifurcations between history and theology are also being deconstructed, as are those between the ontology of the church (its nature) and its activities (mission), so that it is now possible to tell of the missionary or evangelical initiatives of non-Western churches on their own terms. Last but not least, there is diversity within the Christian tradition not only outside the European and Mediterranean "West" but also within it.

World Christianity: Theology and its translatability. To dive deeper into the nexus of both historical and theological issues opened up by these globalizing forces, let us look at the work of Lamin Sanneh, a Gambian expatriate (to the United States) and (since 1989) Yale Divinity School professor who has written much about world Christianity. Although he began his career as an Islamicist focused on Muslim-Christian relations especially in West Africa, he has since gone on to understand Christian history in terms of how indigenous cultures have received the gospel on their own vernacular terms.[24] This has led, perhaps inexorably, to a reconsideration of Christian historiography as a whole. In one of his more recent books, *Disciples of All Nations: Pillars of World Christianity*,[25] Sanneh argues that the dynamic engine that has driven the missionary expansion of Christianity now becomes the vernacularizing

---

[22]E.g., David Chidester, *Christianity: A Global History* (San Francisco: HarperSanFrancisco, 2001).

[23]Throwing down the gauntlet here is Dale T. Irvin and Scott W. Sunquist, *History of the World Christian Movement*, 2 vols. (Maryknoll, NY: Orbis, 2001 and 2012).

[24]See Lamin O. Sanneh, *Translating the Message: The Missionary Impact on Culture* (Maryknoll, NY: Orbis, 1989); *Encountering the West: Christianity and the Global Cultural Process—The African Dimension* (Maryknoll, NY: Orbis, 1993); and *Whose Religion Is Christianity? The Gospel Beyond the West* (Grand Rapids: Eerdmans, 2003).

[25]Lamin Sanneh, *Disciples of All Nations: Pillars of World Christianity* (New York: Oxford University Press, 2008).

process. Hence rather than being told from a Latin, Western or European (and then North American) set of perspectives, the story of Christianity is deconstructed and told from the "underside" of history, from the viewpoint of the evangelized, as it were. However, the result is no retelling of Christian growth from a "passive" or recipient angle; instead, the Christendom and colonial narratives are revisited from the other side of the margins and boundaries where gospel and culture have interfaced. In Sanneh's account, then, culture has always been caught up in the processes of Christian expansion, but now we realize that the culture under consideration has included that belonging not only to what we call Europe but also to that of Africa, Asia and Latin America, each in all of its complexities and diversities. More to the point, and perhaps more explicitly than has been urged by Sanneh himself, there is no gospel apart from its vernacularized accounts, beginning with the apostolic testimony now preserved in the pages of the New Testament.

The "Contents" page of Sanneh's book fails to tell the reader that the book's subtitle, *Pillars of World Christianity*, actually serves as a metaphor for how Sanneh understands the foundations of Christianity as a worldwide phenomenon. Rather, the subtitles on each of the seven main chapter title pages—which do not appear in the contents page at the beginning—include an adjective describing which "pillar" is being discussed. Sanneh organizes his narrative as follows. The comparative pillar (chapter two) describes Christianity through its encounter with Arab peoples and then through the interactions between Christianity and Islam during the broad scope of the medieval period. Next is the trans-Atlantic pillar (chapter three), which tells the various stories of New World Christianities, especially as viewed through the lens of the slave trade and slave experience. This is followed by the colonial pillar (chapter four), which explores the intertwining of missions and Christian independency in the sub-Saharan context. Enigmatic is the pillar called charismatic renewal (chapter five), since its focus is not on pentecostal or charismatic movements but on the unfolding of various pietist traditions especially in East African contexts. Sanneh then shifts to what he calls the primal pillar (chapter six) of independent forms of Christianity in West Africa. The last two pillars are the critical and the bamboo (chapters 7-8), which discuss the final dissolution of mission as interwoven with the colonial enterprise (as seen through the works of Roland Allen and Vincent Donovan) and the emergence of Christianity from out of the heart of Maoist China.

When put together, Sanneh's portrait of world Christianity is one that emphasizes indigenous agency, vernacularly formulated and articulated practices, and thoroughly diversifying processes from start to finish (or to the present). Even the initial chapter—which is not subtitled using the pillar notion, but which features a number of subsections that identify various pillars—on Christian expansion during what historians have traditionally called the "patristic period" is replete with examples of Christian translation in its movements outward from Jerusalem throughout the Mediterranean world and into England and Ireland. Told from this perspective, Christian uniqueness is constituted precisely by its translatability, mutability and adaptability: "world Christianity" is what it is because of its paradoxical capacity to both be transformed by its encounter with "otherness" on the one hand, while at the same time being able to absorb and even transform "others" also.[26]

Three brief comments suffice. First, missiologically, Sanneh's agenda seems to me to be concisely captured in his summary of Vincent Donovan's assumption: that "God enabled a people, any people, to reach salvation through their culture and tribal, racial customs and traditions."[27] The gist of the idea is that given Christianity's translatability, the distinctiveness of the gospel is its incarnational, contextual and intercultural potency (to use various missiological notions). Most pentecostal missiologists or theologians of mission will probably not have much trouble with the suggestion that local cultures are capable of receiving the gospel in their own languages precisely because (at least in part) the pentecostal worldview and cosmology of angels, demons and spirit-beings dovetails well with indigenous cosmologies. However, Sanneh's discussion of Christian expansion through the encounter, confrontation and interaction with Arab and Islamic cultures suggests that Christian translat-

---

[26]See also many of the chapters in Lamin O. Sanneh and Joel A. Carpenter, eds., *The Changing Face of Christianity: Africa, the West, and the World* (New York: Oxford University Press, 2005), for other details.

[27]Sanneh, *Disciples of All Nations*, p. 237; here engaging especially Vincent Donovan, *Christianity Rediscovered* (Maryknoll, NY: Orbis, 1982).

ability is not limited only to primal traditions.[28] Sanneh does not explicitly say that Christian translation in Arab contexts produced an Arabic form of Christianity, but he does describe in elaborate detail how Christian identities have been forged through brushing up against the Islamic world. A careful reading of Sanneh's work may require evangelical rethinking of the mission to Muslims. But Sanneh's thesis also raises questions that he does not address, namely whether his thesis of translatability is suitable to what we might call secular or modern cultures, especially as seen today in Europe and North America. To be more precise, if Evangelicals can agree with Sanneh about the cultural translatability thesis, does this apply only to indigenous cultures and not to major/world religious cultures (such as Islam) or to modern secularist cultures?

Second, at the level of historiography in general and with regard to the pentecostal case more specifically, Sanneh's approach to world Christianity can be read in some respects as an extension of the theory of pentecostal origins propounded by what has come to be known as the Hollenweger School (including Allan Anderson, Michael Bergunder and others).[29] The latter's emphasis on the indigenous factors behind pentecostal emergence in various locales throughout the Global South can be said to prefigure the story told in *Disciples of All Nations*, except that in Sanneh's case the focus is on Christianity as a whole rather than on one of its (recent) subtraditions. Of course, what is suggested is neither a simplistic identification of Sanneh's methodology with that of Hollenweger and his students, nor that there is a theoretical connection or influence running in either direction. Yet it is fair to surmise that Evangelicals and Pentecostals open to reconceiving pentecostal historiography in accordance with the Hollenwegerian set of approaches (e.g., Anderson's is by no means equivalent to Bergunder's) will not have any trouble following Sanneh's basically post-Christendom and post-colonial account. On the other hand, for those who remain unconvinced

---

[28]Sanneh has also written extensively on the Christian encounter with Islam, including *Piety and Power: Muslims and Christians in West Africa* (Maryknoll, NY: Orbis, 1996).

[29]See Walter J. Hollenweger, *Pentecostalism: Origins and Developments Worldwide* (Peabody, MA: Hendrickson, 1997); cf. Anderson, *Introduction to Pentecostalism*, part I, and Michael Bergunder, "Constructing Indian Pentecostalism: On Issues of Methodology and Representation," in Allan Anderson and Edmond Tang, eds., *Asian and Pentecostal: The Charismatic Face of Christianity in Asia* (London: Regnum International, and Baguio City, Philippines: Asia Pacific Theological Seminary Press, 2005), pp. 177-215.

about the "Hollenwegerian" approach to pentecostal origins, reading Sanneh may lead to one of (at least) two responses: either they will be inclined to revise their estimation of the Hollenwegerian proposals, or they will reject the plausibility and viability of Sanneh's rendition.

Third, and most briefly because of space constraints, Sanneh suggests that the globalization process, if applied to Christianity, will result in its death since globalization can only be understood in terms of homogenization. In this case, the globalization of Christianity would be a twenty-first-century version of the Christendom or colonial projects of the past. Instead, the salvation of Christianity, for Sanneh, consists in its ongoing vernacularization. This is the flip side of recognizing that the genius of the Christian message is its always-already manifestation in local, contextual and historical form. If Sanneh is right, global pent-evangelicalism could hold forth great potential for creative and constructive theological reflection in the twenty-first century since its potency may well reside in the intuition that the gospel always comes in and through the concrete particularities of humankind's many tongues and languages. In this case, whereas the twentieth century saw what we might call the "evangelicalization" and "pentecostalization" of Christianity as a world religion, the twenty-first century possibly will unveil the "evangelicalization" and "pentecostalization" of Christian theology as a form of world religious discourse.[30]

Asian Christianity and its theological trajectories. Whereas Sanneh's springboard has been the West and sub-Saharan African contexts, my own horizon is the Pacific Rim, particularly the forces of globalization propelling Asian immigration to North America. The historiographical and theological issues are no less complicated when attending to the Asian scene. More specifically, Sanneh's thesis about Christianity's translatability finds a great deal of traction in this domain. In fact, those working on the history of Christianity in Asia are now tending to talk about *Christianities* in the plural.[31] The standard histories have long been framed as a series of essays attending to the vastness of the continent, the pluralism of its regions, countries and cultures, the di-

---

[30]I make this argument at greater length in my "Pentecostal and Charismatic Theology," in James Beilby and Chad Meister, eds., *The Routledge Companion to Modern Christian Thought* (New York: Routledge, 2013), pp. 636-46.

[31]See, e.g., Peter C. Phan, ed., *Christianities in Asia* (Malden, MA: Wiley-Blackwell, 2011).

versity of its languages and the multiplicity of its historical strands.[32] Any adequate coverage has to include the central Asian sector (from ancient Persia to its modern states), the South Asian subcontinent (India and its neighbors), the Southeast Asian areas (spread out from Myanmar through Malaysia, Indonesia, Papua New Guinea and the Philippine Islands) and the East Asian countries (China, Mongolia, Korea and Japan). Such historical accounts undeniably struggle not only with this geographic expansiveness but also with the various periodizations that could be applied, depending on which criteria (political, religious, economic, etc.) are prioritized.

Theologically, things are no less complex. In fact, Sanneh's thesis raises questions about whither the theological task when considering the Asian context. Given the vernacularization of Christianity, Asian Christian theology itself is increasingly dominated by local concerns and motivations even as indigenous voices and perspectives are sounding forth with urgent clarity. This is most evident in the fairly recently published three-volume *Asian Christian Theologies*.[33] The central motif around which materials were collected and considered for inclusion in these volumes is that of "local theology." By this, the editors mean theology incarnated or contextualized specifically in the various regions and countries of Asia. Hence, the emphasis throughout is on Asian Christian theologies forged in dialogue with the historical, social, cultural, political, philosophical and religious movements and traditions of Asia.

This organizing principle certainly illuminates the specific character of each region's or country's theologies, but also helps account for the many different Asian Christian theologies as each has responded to the distinctive challenges of its situation. For example—and the following is by no means intended as an exhaustive summary—Aotearean theologies are those developed in terms

---

[32]The standard history at this point is Samuel Hugh Moffett, *A History of Christianity in Asia*, 2 vols. (Maryknoll, NY: Orbis, 1998–2005).

[33]John C. England et al., eds., *Asian Christian Theologies: A Research Guide to Authors, Movements, Sources*, 3 vols. (Maryknoll, NY: Orbis, 2002–2004). Volume 1, *Asia Regions, South Asia, Austral Asia*, provides an introduction to the history of theology in Asia as a whole and focuses on Bangladesh, India, Pakistan, Sri Lanka, Nepal, Australia and Aotearoa New Zealand. Volume 2, *Southeast Asia*, covers Burma/Myanmar, Vietnam, Cambodia, Laos, Thailand, Malaysia, Singapore, Indonesia and the Philippines. Volume 3, *Northeast Asia*, concludes with China, Hong Kong, Japan, Korea (South, primarily, but also North), Macau, Taiwan and inner Asia (especially Mongolia). For the most part, the chapters of each volume are organized by country according to the preceding divisions.

of Maori, Samoan and Pacific Islander categories of thought; Indian theologies have had to deal with the long history of religious pluralism in the Indian subcontinent; Burmese theologies have been influenced by the pervasiveness of folk Buddhism; Indonesian theologies have been shaped (almost literally) by the country's island topography and geography, somehow nourishing a certain mystical religiousness and consciousness; Filipino theologies have wrestled with the quest for political independence and with the animistic and Muslim undercurrents; Thai theologies can be better understood when seen as apologetic efforts against the Theravada Buddhist tradition; Vietnamese theologies have responded to the Confucian-Buddhist synthesis and the recent history of Communism; Chinese theologies have been more creation-centered, perhaps under the influence of the Confucian-Daoist worldview; Hong Kong theologies have labored under the long history of British colonization; Japanese theologies have emerged from a long history of Confucian-Buddhist-Shinto convergence and from the traumas inflicted on the national consciousness by the end of the second World War; and so on. While these comments mislead more than they illuminate what is actually occurring on the Asian ground, they provide some sense of the vibrancy and diversity of Christian theological reflection across the Asian Australasian continents.

Interestingly, given the central criterion of "local theology," the pages of *Asian Christian Theologies* are dominated by Roman Catholic and mainline Protestant theologians, movements and sources.[34] It should not be assumed, however, that these volumes are then only a research guide to more progressive or even liberal versions of Asian Christian theological thinking, since the liberal-conservative dichotomy is itself a Western construct that may be forced when applied to the diversity of Asian contexts. But it is surely the case that there are few recognizably "evangelical" voices throughout these volumes. Volume one mentions Chris Sugden, Vinay Samuel and Lesslie Newbigin, but not Ken Gnanakan, Ajith Fernando or Vinoth Ramachandra. (Its coverage of theology in the land "down under"—Australasia—also includes neither the work of Philip Johnson, who, along with others, has attempted to bring evangelical theology into dialogue with New Age spirituality and themes, nor that

---

[34]This is also the case with Sebastian C. H. Kim, *Christian Theology in Asia* (Cambridge: Cambridge University Press, 2008).

of those connected to the journal *Australasian Pentecostal Studies*.) Volume two introduces the work of Denison Jayasooria, Hwa Yung, Yeow Choo-lak and Simon Chan, among others, but fails to note the work associated with Asia Pacific Theological Seminary (formerly Far East Asian School of Theology) in the Philippines. Volume three presents Jia Yuming, Wang Mingdao and Wang Weifan in China, and Takakura Tokutaro in Japan, but ignores the ministry of David Yonggi Cho and Korean pentecostal scholarship. To be fair, some of these developments in Asian evangelical theology are more recent, but these omissions deserve notation.

We will return in a moment to discuss the contributions of some of these theologians. For the moment, however, it is important to note that the scant attention to Asian evangelical theologies in these volumes raises a number of questions. Are nonevangelical theologians ignorant or intentionally dismissive of evangelical theologies, and if so, why? Part of the reason for this may be because evangelical theologians, churches and movements have been less concerned with "local" or "indigenous" theological reflection. More precisely, some Evangelicals may not be as enthusiastic about "local theology" because they are concerned that overemphasis on the context of theology potentially subordinates the biblical horizon to contemporary perceptions. From this perspective, the diversity of Asian theologies either threatens to dissolve into dissonant voices or leads into a parochial or ghettoized set of perspectives that speak only in local tongues. Ironically, concerned Evangelicals conclude, while the market is forging a common economic world, Christianity's vernacularizing tendencies may be producing a fragmented message and perhaps even gospel. As shall be further clarified later in this chapter, this may be one of the major concerns evangelical theologians have with current trends.

Meanwhile, Asian evangelical theologians can and ought to press beyond the liberal-conservative divide.[35] If Roman Catholic theologians do not fit neatly into either category, evangelical theologians should work more intentionally at articulating afresh an Asian evangelical theology that is not held captive by the issues stemming from the early twentieth-century modernist-

---

[35]That this is happening, albeit gradually, can be seen in such volumes as Paul S. Chung, Veli-Matti Kärkkäinen and Kim Kyoung-Jae, eds., *Asian Contextual Theology for the Third Millennium: A Theology of Minjung in Fourth-Eye Formation* (Eugene, OR: Pickwick, 2007).

fundamentalist debates in North America. Further, Asian evangelical theologians also have at their disposal the wealth of theological resources from East and West to find a way between and beyond dichotomistic understandings of individualistic pietism and social liberationism, literalistic biblicism and hermeneutical relativism, and this-worldly versus other-worldly orientations. The fact is, actually, that there are multiple mediating trajectories in Asian evangelical theology, although they are less well known outside evangelical circles.

ASIAN EVANGELICAL THEOLOGY: RAMPING UP

It is true that relative to the length of time that Christianity has been present even across the South, Southeast and East Asian regions, Asian evangelical theology is a relatively new undertaking. This is due in part to the fact that evangelical theology itself is a more recent development, even as it is also true that many evangelical theologians would not recognize the long history of theology in South Asia (in India since, arguably, the second century) and East Asia (since the middle of the first millennium) as being "evangelical" according to the contemporary movement's self-understanding.[36] Not surprisingly, much of the motivation behind this discussion has been missiological, coming on the heels of the 1974 Lausanne Covenant, which mobilized evangelical efforts toward world evangelization.[37] Yet even within this overarching missiological frame of reference, two major tributaries can be discerned.

The first, not surprisingly, concerns articulation of an Asian evangelical theology that is both biblically faithful and culturally relevant in ways that advance the cause of the gospel.[38] Evangelicals are sensitive to the cultural and

---

[36]For historical-theological perspective on Asian theology prior to the Reformation, see Dale T. Irvin and Scott W. Sunquist, *History of the World Christian Movement: Earliest Christianity to 1453* (Maryknoll, NY: Orbis, 2001), esp. chap. 25.

[37]See, e.g., Bong Rin Ro, "Basic Issues in the Asian Church," in Waldron Scott, ed., *Evangelical Strategies for the Eighties* (Colorado Springs: World Evangelical Fellowship, 1980), pp. 47-56; cf. Saphir Athyal, ed., *Church in Asia Today: Opportunities and Challenges* (Singapore: Asia Lausanne Committee for World Evangelization, 1996).

[38]Bong Rin Ro and Ruth Eshenaur, eds., *The Bible and Theology in Asian Contexts: An Evangelical Perspective on Asian Theology* (Taiwan: Asia Theological Association, 1984); Rin Ro and Mark C. Albrecht, eds., *God in Asian Contexts: Communicating the God of the Bible in Asia* (Taiwan: Asia Theological Association, 1988); and Ken Gnanakan, ed., *Biblical Theology in Asia* (Bangalore: Theological Book Trust and Asia Theological Association, 1995).

especially religious pluralism across the Asian landscape. While some Evangelicals are not wishing to tow a hard exclusivist line that insists salvation can come only through personal knowledge and confession of Christ, there is nevertheless no underemphasizing the urgency of mission and evangelization. The point is that even though God can save as God wills through the cross of Christ and the work of the Holy Spirit, this does not lessen the importance of the Great Commission.[39] There is thus an increasing openness to learning about other religions,[40] although again, the incentive is to enable more confident dialogue that leads to witness. Throughout, the goal is to avoid any "syncretism" of the biblical message with local traditions or practices. It is not that Evangelicals are unaware that any meeting of the biblical horizon with the contemporary world will produce a fusion of sorts. But they are concerned that convergences, such as there may be, not confuse the laity in ways that keep them beholden to their former ways of living and thinking rather than be liberated by the salvific power of the gospel.[41]

A second line of Asian evangelical theology may be a bit more unexpected: the focus on poverty.[42] It is certainly the case that there is widespread poverty throughout the Asian continent, and no sensitive evangelical missionary initiative can ignore this fundamental reality. At the same time, the Lausanne

---

[39] See Hwa Yung, "Towards an Evangelical Approach to Religions and Cultures," in David Emmanuel Singh and Bernard C. Farr, eds., *Christianity and Cultures: Shaping Christian Thinking in Context* (Carlisle, UK: Regnum, 2008), pp. 17-29.

[40] See, for instance, the special issue of the *Journal of Asian Evangelical Theology* 15, no. 1 (June 2007), which is devoted to recent trends in dialogue with Confucian, Buddhist and other Asian religious traditions; cf. also the observable shifts in tenor that are clear in moving from Bruce J. Nicholls, ed., *The Unique Christ in Our Pluralist World* (Grand Rapids: Baker Book House, 1994), to Ken Gnanakan, *Proclaiming Christ in a Pluralistic Context* (Bangalore: Theological Book Trust, 2002), and Ivan M. Satyavrata, *God Has Not Left Himself Without Witness* (Eugene, OR: Wipf & Stock, 2011).

[41] Thus, for instance, Evangelicals have worked diligently on establishing alternatives to ancestor worship. More classical forms of ancestor veneration perpetuate some of the older assumptions, so transformation of such practices necessitates new ways of honoring prior generations in accordance with biblical teaching. See, for instance, Bong Rin Ro, ed., *Christian Alternatives to Ancestor Practices* (1985; repr., Seoul: Asia Theological Association and Word of Life Press, 1991).

[42] See Vinay Samuel and Chris Sugden, eds., *Sharing Jesus in the Two Thirds World: Evangelical Christologies from the Contexts of Poverty, Powerlessness and Religious Pluralism* (Grand Rapids: Eerdmans, 1983); Bruce J. Nicholls and Beulah R. Wood, eds., *Sharing the Good News with the Poor: A Reader for Concerned Christians* (Grand Rapids: Baker Book House, 1996); and Chris Sugden, *Seeking the Asian Face of Jesus: A Critical and Comparative Study of the Practice and Theology of Christian Social Witness in Indonesia and India Between 1974 and 1996 with Special Reference to the Work of Wayan Mastra in the Protestant Church of Bali and of Vinay Samuel in the Church of South India* (Oxford: Regnum, 1997).

movement's emphasis on a holistic gospel has not only given Evangelicals permission to think about the material, social and economic dimensions of the gospel but perhaps also has provided impetus for theologizing explicitly about such matters.[43] In typical evangelical fashion, however, the approach always foregrounds the teaching of Scripture before moving on to contemporary social analysis. But there is a growing trend to be open to important insights provided via the latter, even to the point of a sympathetic yet not uncritical consideration of liberation theological perspectives, particularly as that informs holistic mission.[44] The point is that Evangelicals have expanded their missionary efforts to include both relief and development initiatives, understood within what is emphasized as a biblical account of social justice.

A Western missionary contribution. This overview sketch needs to be filled in. Yet even in its basic outlines, it overlaps strikingly with Asian Roman Catholic theologians who are emphasizing a "triple dialogue" with the poor, the many cultures and the many religious traditions of Asia.[45] To further probe these opportunities and challenges, we will briefly explore the work of three Asian evangelical theologians: a Western missionary, an Asian evangelical and an Asian pentecostal. Much more certainly could be said about a much wider range of evangelical thinkers past and present. Because of my own Chinese ancestry, I am more drawn toward East Asian trajectories than to South Asian ones; hence I by and large neglect ferment in the Asian Indian evangelical scene. Regardless, the following discussion focuses more on contemporary developments rather than those of prior generations; further, I am also inclined toward more scholarly articulations rather than popular expressions, and this despite the fact that my own constructive pent-evangelical proposal is sympathetic with, if not also deeply informed by, oral theological expressions characteristic

---

[43]See "Lausanne Occasional Paper 33: Holistic Mission," in David Claydon, ed., *A New Vision, a New Heart, a Renewed Call: Lausanne Occasional Papers from the 2004 Forum of World Evangelization Hosted by the Lausanne Committee for World Evangelization—Pataya, Thailand, September 29—October 5, 2004*, vol. 1 (Pasadena, CA: William Carey Library, 2005), pp. 211-88; also note Goh Keat Peng, ed., *Witnessing to the Whole Gospel: Asia Lausanne Consultation on Holistic Models of Evangelism* (Singapore: Asia Lausanne Committee on World Evangelism, 1996).

[44]See Charles Ringma, "Liberation Theologians Speak to Evangelicals: A Theology and Praxis of Serving the Poor," in Lee Wanak, ed., *The Church and Poverty in Asia* (Manila: OMF Literature and Asian Theological Seminary, 2008), pp. 7-53.

[45]See the summary discussion in Thomas C. Fox, *Pentecost in Asia: A New Way of Being Church* (Maryknoll, NY: Orbis, 2002), chap. 2.

of the pentecostal-charismatic stream of the evangelical tradition.[46] In any case, the goal here is neither to provide a comprehensive catalog of Asian evangelicalism nor to exhaustively expound Asian evangelical theology. Rather, we simply desire to highlight some of the major themes of present Asian evangelical theological trends in order to situate the wider global context of Asian American theological reflection that is the task of this volume.

Developing an Asian Evangelical Theology, by Donald Leroy Stults, a missionary, educator and theologian in the Nazarene Church, was one of the first monographs on the topic.[47] The three parts of this book discuss the work of theology (including its necessity, the urgency of an authentically Asian theology, the work of the theologian, and the need for a theological and evangelical system), overview the cultural and contextual factors (including the relationship between gospel and culture, which includes religions, philosophies and ideologies), and present a programmatic sketch of an Asian evangelical theology. For Stults, as an evangelical theologian, the parameters for inculturation are strictly established by the primacy of Scripture. However, Scripture's authority is not an abstract norm but is rich in the content of evangelical theology. Evangelical doctrines such as total depravity, salvation by

---

[46]Within the context of this discussion, then, mention should be made of the popular yet enigmatic Chinese revivalist Watchman Nee (Ni Tuosheng, 1903–1972), known best as the founder of the "Little Flock" of anticlerical, antidenominational and anti-Western missionary churches and author of many accessible books that have been translated into numerous languages and have become a staple of popular pent-evangelical consumption over the decades. While Nee's legacy has heretofore not made a significant scholarly contribution to Asian evangelical theology, Dongsheng John Wu's recent Graduate Theological Union PhD dissertation, published as *Understanding Watchman Nee: Spirituality, Knowledge, and Formation* (Eugene, OR: Wipf & Stock, 2012), may signal the emergence of such impact in the coming years in that it attempts both to rescue the heritage of Nee from charges leveled over the years, especially by more conservative Protestant critics, while also locating Nee squarely within developments in twentieth-century Chinese Christianity. Beyond this, Wu, an affiliate faculty member of Regent College in Vancouver, British Columbia, explicates Nee's theological ideas in relationship with Western sources, especially the historic Christian mystical tradition. Wu's thesis is effective not just apologetically but also in its constructive, ecumenical and dialogical potential to bring Nee's work into the mainstream of both Chinese philosophical/religious discourses and Christian traditional ones. If successful, the scholarly relevance of Nee's thinking emerges precisely as he is understood as indigenizing and contextualizing Christian faith and practice in Chinese forms. Toward that same end, then, Asian American evangelical theology will make its contribution when it speaks out of its own distinctive and hybridic voice, not when it mimics the Western (white) tradition. For further historical perspective on Nee, see Lian Xi, *Redeemed by Fire: The Rise of Popular Christianity in Modern China* (New Haven, CT: Yale University Press, 2010), chap. 7.

[47]Donald Leroy Stults, *Developing an Asian Evangelical Theology* (Manila: OMF Literature Inc., 1989; repr., Denver: Academic Books, 2001). I will be referring to the reprinted version.

grace alone, the Great Commission and the return of Christ are nonnegotiable, and evangelical theologians cannot go beyond these traditional formulations without betraying the evangelical label. On this basis Stults proceeds to criticize the general trend of Asian theology—seen in the work of Klaus Klostermaier, M. M. Thomas, Kitamori Kazoh, Brahmabandhav Upadhyaya, A. J. Appasamy and C. S. Song, among others—as politically oriented, syncretistic and normed by social analysis rather than by Scripture.[48] Continuing this same line of thought, while the various Asian religious traditions have some degree of truth and while any Asian Christian theology has to use some concepts and terms from these religions, still evangelical theology must insist that all non-Christian religions are human creations and thus nonsalvific.[49]

Unsurprisingly, within this framework Stults's rendition of an authentically Asian evangelical theology retains the same loci as that developed by post-Reformation dogmatic systematicians. It begins with the doctrine of a trinitarian God, proceeds through christology, theological anthropology, soteriology, ecclesiology and pneumatology, and concludes with eschatology. Along the way, whatever may have been distinctively Asian recedes into the background if not fades away completely. Stults is clear that, "TThe [*sic*] biblical message is constant and unchangeable while the method or systematic approach may differ according to the situation and mode of communication."[50] Stults's assumptions that Evangelicals have understood this message correctly, that the "kernel" and the "husks" can be easily distinguished, and that the modes of communication used by evangelical missionaries have not affected the content of the biblical gospel are widespread

---

[48]In a later work, Stults also criticizes, in dialogue with the work of Lesslie Newbigin, especially Western culture and its theological traditions to the degree that they have been touched by the crisis of Western thought; see Stults, *Grasping Truth and Reality: Lesslie Newbigin's Theology of Mission to the Western World* (Cambridge: James Clarke & Co., 2009).

[49]Stults, *Developing an Asian Evangelical Theology*, pp. 128-29. As already noted, traditionally, Evangelicals in Asia have been very cautious about dialogue with those in other faiths replacing Christian proclamation, but this is slowly changing. It is possible that Stults's own views on this topic have been moderated since the publication of his book in 1989.

[50]Stults, *Developing an Asian Evangelical Theology*, p. 193. Actually, many of the earliest attempts to develop an Asian evangelical theology follow this line of thought; e.g., Saphir Athyal, "Toward an Asian Christian Theology," in *Voice of the Church in Asia: Report of Proceedings Asia Theological Association Consultation* (Singapore: Asia Theological Association, 1975), pp. 124-39; Han Chul-Ha, "An Asian Critique of Western Theology," *Evangelical Review of Theology* 7, no. 1 (1983): 34-47; and Rodrigo D. Tano, "Toward an Evangelical Asian Theology," *Evangelical Review of Theology* 7, no. 1 (1983): 155-71.

among Evangelicals, Western and Asian alike. However, they deserve more consideration and argument than many provide. Yet one ought not be overly harsh about a volume that was explicitly intended by the author to urge Asian Evangelicals themselves to take up the theological task. In that regard, this volume served as an important clarion call to mobilize others to fulfill the promise of an Asian evangelical theology.

An Asian evangelical approach. Building on Stults's work, Hwa Yung's *Mangoes or Bananas? The Quest for an Authentic Asian Christian Theology* recognizes that a truly indigenous Asian Christian theology has yet to emerge insofar as Asian evangelical theologians have been held captive by Western presuppositions, concerns and methods.[51] This current bishop of the Methodist Church in Malaysia believes that Enlightenment rationality has bequeathed to the contemporary mind what anthropologist Paul Hiebert calls the "flaw of the excluded middle": the arbitrary reduction of reality to two tiers that erroneously dismisses or purposefully ignores the middle realm of spiritual and demonic beings.[52] This results in less than fully contextualized theologies that have only superficially engaged Asian cultures and thought forms, which include ancestors and complex layers of cosmological spirits. Asian Christian theologies have therefore to date been more akin to bananas (Asian-yellow on the outside, but Western-white on the inside) than mangoes (the quintessential Asian fruit, representing an authentic homegrown product).

More adequate contextual Asian Christian theologies, Hwa Yung suggests, must therefore be theologies of mission or missiological theologies. With this in mind, he develops four criteria by which to assess Asian evangelical theologies: (1) their ability to address the diverse Asian sociopolitical and religious contexts in which the churches find themselves; (2) the empowerment they bring to the evangelistic and pastoral tasks of the churches; (3) the means by which they facilitate the inculturation of the gospel; and (4) their faithfulness to the Christian tradition. Theologies are defective if they fail any one of these criteria—for example, if they are overly accommodative to Asian cultures and religions, or if they

---

[51]Hwa Yung, *Mangoes or Bananas? The Quest for an Authentic Asian Christian Theology* (Oxford: Regnum, 1997).

[52]Hwa Yung, *Mangoes or Bananas?* pp. 72-74. See also Paul G. Hiebert, *Anthropological Reflections on Missiological Issues* (Grand Rapids: Baker Books, 1994), part III.

are unconcerned with either social justice or evangelistic proclamation.

To be sure, Hwa Yung's criteria are much more expansive than Stults's. At the same time, while Hwa Yung exposes the inadequacy of the Western evangelical theological paradigm because of its flawed dualism and successfully argues that Asian evangelical theology has yet to achieve emancipation from the West, he does not in turn suggest what kind of worldview is needed for an authentically Asian Christian theology.[53] If "dualism" is to be discarded, is "monism" now favored? Hwa Yung never explicitly says that an Eastern worldview (which Eastern?) is to be preferred to that of the Enlightenment West. This might be implied by his suggestion that a fully contextualized Asian Christian theology must be presented and comprehensible in Asian categories. But his largely critical treatment (similar to Stults's) of theologians such as M. M. Thomas, C. S. Song and Kosuke Koyama seems to assume (problematically, one might add) that the Asian worldview is that to which contextualization is directed rather than the framework within which theologizing occurs.[54] Dialogue with other religions is affirmed, the insights of cultural anthropology are welcomed, and the "power" cosmology of Asian indigenous traditions is acknowledged. Each instance, however, scratches the surface and invites fuller development. Of course, Hwa Yung advocates a biblical worldview, but this gives us little guidance for how to understand the *Asian* of his project in evangelical theology.

Alternatively, Hwa Yung could have engaged more with Asian Pentecostals, given that Asian Pentecostalism has ignored the dualism bequeathed by the Enlightenment. David Yonggi Cho, former founding pastor of a pentecostal megachurch in Seoul (whom Hwa Yung briefly discusses),[55] has managed to

---

[53]Hwa Yung cites favorably Carver T. Yu, *Being and Relation: A Theological Critique of Western Dualism and Individualism* (Edinburgh: Scottish Academic Press, 1987), in particular Yu's call for a return to the nondualistic worldview of the ancient Hebrews, but what that means and how such interfaces with twenty-first-century Asian thinking is less clear.

[54]Elsewhere I have discussed the difficulty of engagement with worldviews as "objects" that can be "handled" by those on the "outside"; see my "To See or Not to See: A Review Essay of Michael Palmer's *Elements of a Christian Worldview*," *Pneuma: The Journal of the Society for Pentecostal Studies* 21, no. 2 (1999): 305-27.

[55]See Hwa Yung, *Mangoes or Bananas?* pp. 205-13. For my own discussion of Cho and his work, see my article "Salvation, Society, and the Spirit: Pentecostal Contextualization and Political Theology from Cleveland to Birmingham, from Springfield to Seoul," *Pax Pneuma: The Journal of Pentecostals & Charismatics for Peace & Justice* 5, no. 2 (2009): 22-34—reprinted in Mun Hong Choi, ed., *The Spirituality of Fourth Dimension and Social Salvation: Studies on Dr. Yonggi Cho's Theology*, Journal of Youngsan Theology Supplement Series 1 (Gunpo City, South Korea: Hansei University Press,

contextualize the gospel in terms accessible to Korean hearts and minds. Central to Cho's proclamation of the *euangelion* are the "fivefold gospel" and the "threefold blessing"—Jesus as savior, Jesus as baptizer in the fullness of the Holy Spirit for power to witness, Jesus as sanctifier, Jesus as healer, and Jesus as coming king; and the spiritual, material/physical and general well-being blessings—which combine to reveal his basically holistic approach to Christian life. Further, Cho's ministry is unabashedly evangelistic without neglecting social justice issues. Finally, Cho's reliance on the Holy Spirit is not at the expense of utilizing mass media and modern technology.[56] Does Cho successfully negotiate the tension between enculturation and faithfulness to the evangelical Christian tradition? Does Pentecostalism's emphasis on the experiential and bodily aspects of spirituality provide common ground for an evangelical dialogue with Asian religions and spiritualities?

An Asian pentecostal proposal. With these thoughts in mind we now turn to look at the work of recognized evangelical-pentecostal theologian Simon Chan, longtime professor at Trinity Theological College in Singapore. While we shall return in chapter four to discuss Asian pentecostal theology more extensively, I introduce the work of Simon Chan here since he has published extensively on evangelical spirituality and theology rather than only on pentecostal theology.[57] Two of his essays are especially pertinent for our topic.[58] In the first essay, Chan is concerned that Asian theologians have focused too

---

2012), pp. 163-88—and my *In the Days of Caesar*, §6.1.2.

[56]For overviews, see Yoo Boo-woong, *Korean Pentecostalism: Its History and Theology* (New York: Peter Lang, 1988); Myung Sung-Hoon and Hong Young-gi, eds., *Charis and Charisma: David Yonggi Cho and the Growth of Yoido Full Gospel Church* (Waynesboro, GA: Paternoster, 2003); Wonsuk Ma, William W. Menzies and Bae Hyeon-sung, eds., *David Yonggi Cho: A Close Look at His Theology and Ministry* (Baguio City, Philippines: Asia Pacific Theological Seminary Press, 2004); and Kim Ig-Jin, *History and Theology of Korean Pentecostalism: Sunbogeum (Pure Gospel) Pentecostalism* (Zoetermeer, The Netherlands: Uitgeverij Boekencentrum, 2003).

[57]Chan has published five other books, two more generally evangelical—*Spiritual Theology: A Systematic Study of the Christian Life* (Downers Grove, IL: InterVarsity Press, 1998) and *Liturgical Theology: The Church as Worshiping Community* (Downers Grove, IL: IVP Academic, 2006)—and two more specifically pentecostal: *Pentecostal Theology and the Christian Spiritual Tradition* (Sheffield, UK: Sheffield Academic Press, 2000), and *Pentecostal Ecclesiology: An Essay on the Development of Doctrine* (Blandford Forum, UK: Deo Publications, 2011); his most recent book, *Grassroots Asian Theology: Thinking the Faith from the Ground Up* (Downers Grove, IL: IVP Academic, 2014) came to my attention too late for me to incorporate his important arguments into the following.

[58]Chan, "The Problem of Transcendence and Immanence in Asian Contextual Theology," *Trinity Theological Journal* 8 (1999): 5-18, and "Problem and Possibility of an Asian Theological Hermeneutic," *Trinity Theological Journal* 9 (2000): 47-59.

much on history and historical processes, resulting in an overemphasis on immanence to the neglect of transcendence in theology. Asian religiosity and
poverty have framed the discourse of Asian theologians, leading to the domination of theological themes such as the cosmic Christ, God's suffering, and
the God of the poor. Chan responds, however, that there is "an irreducible
transcendent reality in the Christian faith,"[59] and it is this transcendent reality
to which the masses who are truly suffering turn. A viable Asian Christian theology must therefore include both social reform and evangelistic proclamation,
both political action and supernaturalistic charismatic empowerment.[60] As
examples of those at the vanguard of such a theological trajectory Chan points
to the work of Vishal Mangalwadi, who has worked among the Dalits in India,
and Wang Ming Dao, an evangelist-reformer among the Chinese churches.
Both recognized the indispensability of social action, but based such on the
proclamation of the gospel (a counterdiscourse to that of the world) and on
church planting and the ecclesial life of the church (a counterculture to that of
their societies). Chan concludes that "those who are so concerned about
making Christ immanent in Asia have ended up making the church powerless
and irrelevant."[61]

In his sequel, Chan takes on the question regarding the theological hermeneutic and methodology of a viable Asian evangelical Christian theology. The
problem with Asian Christian theology (as formulated by nonevangelical
theologians) has been an uncritical acceptance of a modernism that demands
secularization in terms of worldview and requires demythologization in terms
of biblical interpretation. Such moves sit very uncomfortably, Chan suggests,
with Asian forms of thinking. The Daoist worldview, for example, locates
human beings within a wider cosmological context even while it does not
separate human embodiment from that wider environment. Chan goes on to

---

[59]Chan, "Problem of Transcendence," p. 8.

[60]I am ambivalent about Chan's use of "supernaturalism," as it in turn perpetuates the baggage of
Enlightenment dualism. My own proposal is for a triadic-trinitarian construct that goes beyond
the natural-supernatural dichotomy; see Yong, *The Spirit Poured Out on All Flesh: Pentecostalism
and the Possibility of Global Theology* (Grand Rapids: Baker Academic, 2005), §7.3.1.

[61]Chan, "Problem of Transcendence," p. 17. Chan's salvo echoes that of Bruce J. Nicholls, "Salvation
and Humanisation in the Theology of Evangelism," in *Voice of the Church in Asia: Report of Proceedings Asia Theological Association Consultation* (Singapore: Asia Theological Association,
1975), pp. 153-64.

propose that the kind of "body thinking" prevalent among cultures long informed by religious Daoism has a deep affinity with the Christian understanding of truth most clearly embodied in the life of Jesus and in the biblical
narratives.[62] In short, "liberal" Asian Christian theologies may provide astute
social analyses of the pervasive poverty that characterizes the Asian situation,
but they fail to offer religious and spiritual answers that concretely engage the
masses of Asia.[63] On the other hand, unexpectedly, a theological hermeneutic
based on the good news of the incarnation remains plausible in modern Asia,
since it opens up the possibility of meeting the spiritual needs of people in
terms with which they may resonate from the perspective of Asian religious
traditions.[64] In this case, a deeply evangelical reading of Scripture in Asia
would not necessarily be either exclusive of Asian sensibilities or opposed to
making connections with Asian religious perspectives.

The gist of the preceding discussion is that Asian evangelical theologians
are attempting to carve a middle way between two ends of a spectrum. Put in
Sanneh's terms, on the one side are the proclivities toward a global theology,
inevitably articulated in Western terms; on the other side are the contextualizing pressures of a local and vernacular theology, which Asian mission requires but toward which Asian evangelical theological sensibilities are struggling for articulation. The pressures to navigate a viable way forward are
palpable, although in some contexts more than others. More locally friendly
theological constructs are in less demand in quickly Westernizing economies
(such as Singapore),[65] but they remain urgent in the South Asian subcontinent

---

[62]Chan, "Problem and Possibility," pp. 52-56.

[63]Thus it has been said, "Although the Korean liberation theology known as *Minjung* theology has
espoused the concerns of the poor and oppressed, it is to the Pentecostal churches that the poor
and oppressed (the *minjung*) flock for relief"; see Allan Anderson, "The Contribution of Cho
Yonggi to a Contextual Theology in Korea," *Journal of Pentecostal Theology* 12, no. 1 (2003): 85-
105, quotation from p. 103. But cf. Lee Hong Jung, "*Minjung* and Pentecostal Movements in
Korea," in Allan H. Anderson and Walter J. Hollenweger, eds., *Pentecostals After a Century: Global
Perspectives on a Movement in Transition*, Journal of Pentecostal Theology Supplement Series 15
(Sheffield, UK: Sheffield Academic Press, 1999), pp. 138-60.

[64]So evangelical theology would be inclusive of both contextual perspectives and of religious and
pragmatic readings of the Bible, rather than having to opt for one or the other (as Moonjang Lee
seems to suggest); see Lee, "Asian Biblical Interpretation," in Kevin J. Vanhoozer, ed., *Dictionary
for Theological Interpretation of the Bible* (Grand Rapids: Baker Academic, 2005), pp. 68-71.

[65]See, for instance, May Ling Tan-Chow, *Pentecostal Theology for the Twenty-First Century: Engaging
with Multi-Faith Singapore* (Burlington, VT: Ashgate, 2007).

of India and in the Confucian-, Buddhist- and Daoist-dominated ethos of East Asia. It is particularly the case that in the Chinese context, which has long attempted to ward off the specter of Western imperialism and colonialism, the search for an indigenous theology will remain a priority long into the future.[66] In any event, understanding the aspirations and struggles of Asian evangelical theologians provides a lens through which to understand the opportunities and challenges before Asian American Evangelicals as well.

Evangelical Theology as Contextual Theology: Possibilities and Challenges

Before we dive fully into the Asian American evangelical context, however, we need to pause more deliberately on this question regarding the contextuality of theology. As we have already seen, the forces of globalization are inciting two apparently counterdirectional movements: one toward universal homogenization (especially at the market level) and another toward the celebration of local customs, languages and histories (at the cultural level). Christian theology in the twenty-first-century context has been sensitized to the latter, although its biblical commitments and long dogmatic history—especially in the wake of Enlightenment assumptions about the possibility of a universal discourse—leave Evangelicals rather unwilling to jettison crosscultural claims to truth. Sanneh's vernacularization thesis inspires evangelical missional contextualization but raises the question of how this is best accomplished in the Asian context. Yet, as we have seen, the lines between missiology and theology are increasingly blurred. Whereas in a previous generation contextual theology would have been a valid exercise in the former domain, it is now increasingly recognized to be at the heart of all theological discourse. Evangelicals, however, struggle with what this means.

Evangelical contextuality: A case study. We can see the strain exerted on evangelical theology by this development when we look more closely and at some length at the fairly recently published landmark *Cambridge Companion to Evangelical Theology* (*CCET*).[67] The volume begins with an introductory

---

[66]See Richard R. Cook and David W. Pao, eds., *After Imperialism: Christian Identity in China and the Global Evangelical Movement*, Studies in Chinese Christianity 1 (Eugene, OR: Pickwick, 2011).
[67]Timothy Larsen and Daniel J. Treier, eds., *The Cambridge Companion to Evangelical Theology*

essay by Timothy Larsen wrestling with and proposing a working definition of "evangelical" for the project. The remaining seventeen chapters are divided into two parts: the first on "doctrines" has eight chapters (on Trinity, Scripture, Christ, theological anthropology, justification/atonement, Holy Spirit, conversion/sanctification and ecclesiology), while the second on "contexts" has nine chapters (on culture, gender, race, the religions, and evangelical theology in, respectively, Africa, Asia, Britain/Europe, Latin America and North America). The perspectives of eighteen different essayists, including four women, from a range of evangelical backgrounds—Reformed, Wesleyan, Baptist, pentecostal, etc.—are voiced in the book.[68]

One way to read the CCET is as a performative speech act in three keys: a restorative one oriented to the past, a reformative one focused on the present and a renewal one hopeful about the future. Sometimes one of these keys is out of harmony with the other two, but taken together they reflect the opportunities and challenges of the ongoing task of contemporary evangelical theology as a live project, especially when viewed from or through an Asian American lens. Let me explain.[69]

First, the restorative key should come as no surprise for a book on evangelical theology. Given Evangelicalism's institutional emergence from out of the fundamentalist side of the fundamentalist-modernist controversies in the first half of the twentieth century, evangelical theology has always been conservative as opposed to liberal. Our goal here is not to nitpick about the definition of conservative or liberal but to simply observe that, as many of the authors of this book put it, evangelical theology is not first and foremost pro-

---

(Cambridge: Cambridge University Press, 2007). All quotations from and references to this volume will be cited parenthetically in the text by CCET and page number.

[68]Terry Cross, of the pentecostal Church of God (Cleveland, Tennessee), writes the chapter on pneumatology; Veli-Matti Kärkkäinen (of the Finnish Pentecostal Church) writes the chapter on theology of religions; and Simon Chan writes on evangelical theology in the Asian context; understandably for a book on evangelical theology, pentecostal perspectives in these chapters assist in rather than drive the argument.

[69]Some readers might question how representative this volume is for contemporary evangelical theology, especially since a few of its contributors have not published specifically as evangelical theologians. While I am sympathetic to such concerns at one level, there can also be no doubt about the editors' evangelical credentials given their institutional home: Wheaton College in Wheaton, Illinois. I also think that one can identify many of the issues I will be discussing vis-à-vis the CCET in other evangelical theological texts, so resolving this particular matter will affect little the points that I will be making in what follows.

gressive or revisionist but restorationist: looking to retrieve the past, especially the creedal tradition, or the Reformational one, or the revivalist one of the eighteenth century, and so on.[70] As restorationist in this sense, it is reasonable to look to evangelical theology to emphasize remaining faithful to the theological traditions of the past, to restate them and perhaps even to merely repeat them (as would be involved in the recitation of the Nicene confession). This is not to denigrate evangelical theology but to suggest how such restorationism may signal its strength. If so, then to find the *CCET* repeating, or restating, or attempting to restore previous formulations and perhaps give them life for the present time—this is precisely what one would expect.[71]

And this is what we do find both at the structural level and at other levels. Structurally, the volume carries on the tradition of evangelical theology that has become standard in the last hundred-plus years, including the sequence of doctrinal loci in part one that contains relatively few surprises. Yet why divide the volume into the two parts of "doctrine" and "contexts," especially when there are admissions in the first part that evangelical doctrines are already contextually shaped (e.g., *CCET*, pp. 27, 43) as well as the repeated calls in part two to contextualize (in non-Western areas) received doctrines (usually derived from the Western traditions)? No claims are being made here about disbanding with doctrines and forgetting about contextualization. Yet the implicit message conveyed in the structure of the book is that part one constitutes the doctrinal heart of evangelical theology while part two presents its applications, translations and vernacularizations. Alternatively, the present arrangement also communicates, at least implicitly, that part one presents universal truths that have been believed by all Evangelicals everywhere and at all times while part two either provides (merely) historical description or addresses the missional dimension of evangelical theology. In fact, one of the essayists even suggests that evangelical theology can be understood in terms

---

[70]Thus I am using the "restorationist" motif in a general sense rather than in any kind of specific sense such as that embraced by the Churches of Christ or Disciples tradition; the latter involves a specific scriptural hermeneutic—which may be included in the former, but not necessarily so.

[71]In one important respect, this restorationist trajectory is central to pentecostal and charismatic forms of evangelical Christianity precisely because of the renewalist orientation that looks back to the apostolic tradition as providing the template for Christian life in all generations; see my *Renewing Christian Theology: Systematics for a Global Christianity*, with Jonathan A. Anderson (Waco, TX: Baylor University Press, 2014).

of a scriptural or gospel core (the "doctrines") which, as structurally unfolded in the volume itself, can then be packaged and presented in many different ways in various contexts (*CCET*, pp. 215, 218, 222n5).

Finally, at the methodological level, the more traditional evangelical starting point of scriptural reflection is found in at least a few chapters (e.g., on theological anthropology, on justification/atonement and on conversion/sanctification). This is not to dismiss the proposals presented in these essays but rather to simply observe that this is what one would expect in evangelical theological approaches. In fact, it is a wonder that there is not much more of this by others in part one of the volume, and this itself is noteworthy for understanding both the *CCET* in particular and the shape of evangelical theology today in general.

The restoring framework, however, is nicely complemented by a reforming thread. In fact, the efforts to reform evangelical theology in the *CCET* are more substantive than one might anticipate. For example, Kevin Vanhoozer's theodramatic hermeneutic and theological method take seriously the narrative aspects of human understanding, while D. Stephen Long engages with conversations regarding deification and the "new perspective on Paul" in his contribution.[72] There are chapters on such topics as culture, gender, race and religious pluralism that in the previous generation were not engaged in evangelical theological reflection. And the attention to the contextual character of evangelical theology also marks an increasing sensitivity to the reformational task of doing theology.

There are two specific chapters that invite further comment with regard to the reformational thrust of the *CCET*. First, Elaine Storkey's piece at least takes a stand on a disputed issue in evangelical theology: on behalf of an egalitarian view of gender over and against the complementarian perspective.[73] Her approach is not necessarily novel, and her specific strategy—of

---

[72]See also Kevin J. Vanhoozer, *The Drama of Doctrine: A Canonical Linguistic Approach to Christian Doctrine* (Louisville: Westminster John Knox, 2005); and D. Stephen Long and Nancy Ruth Fox with Tripp York, *Calculated Futures: Theology, Ethics and Economics* (Waco, TX: Baylor University Press, 2007).

[73]Storkey is widely published in this area; for other pent-evangelical perspectives, see Estrelda Alexander and Amos Yong, eds., *Philip's Daughters: Women in Pentecostal-Charismatic Leadership* (Eugene, OR: Pickwick, 2009).

appealing to the relationality of the trinitarian identity of God—is itself questioned elsewhere in the volume (e.g., by Vanhoozer's query about whether the turn to relationality itself is a selling of the evangelical soul to another master; *CCET*, p. 34n55). My point is that given how volatile this issue remains across the spectrum of the evangelical theological landscape, as well as the predominantly patriarchal character of much of Evangelicalism in the Global South, this is indeed a reformist stance within the evangelical context (even if such an option may be "old hat" in "liberal" circles since the age of women's suffrage!).

Much more radical is J. Kameron Carter's discussion of race and theology.[74] Carter does not assume theology always proceeds from a core that is then translated into a racialized (or any other) context (as a restorationist approach might argue). Instead, he asks how the experience of race itself emerges out of and then also informs a theological vision—a much more dialectical, and maybe even correlational, conception. More precisely, he explores "how black folks' reception of the religion of their masters represents a counter-performance of American Evangelicalism itself" (*CCET*, p. 178) and argues that "Evangelical belief was received by persons of African descent 'who made Jesus their choice' so as to bear witness to a different, non-triumphalist Christian reality" (*CCET*, p. 190).[75] The genius of this approach is that the good news of the *euangelion* itself is realized only in and through the Holy Saturday of the black evangelical bodily experience of slavery, lynching and death.[76] There is much more to think about here regarding Latino/a and Asian approaches to evangelical theology.

---

[74]Carter's book, *Race: A Theological Account* (Oxford: Oxford University Press, 2008), is a must-read for those interested in the future of evangelical theology in general and in Christian theology in general. See also the work of Willie James Jennings, *The Christian Imagination: Theology and the Origins of Race* (New Haven, CT: Yale University Press, 2011).

[75]For my own views on especially African American pentecostal realities, see Yong, "Justice Deprived, Justice Demanded: Afropentecostalisms and the Task of World Pentecostal Theology Today," *Journal of Pentecostal Theology* 15, no. 1 (2006): 127-47; cf. Estrelda Alexander and Amos Yong, eds., *Afro-Pentecostalism: Black Pentecostal and Charismatic Christianity in History and Culture* (New York: New York University Press, 2011). This present volume should be understood as a complement to the preceding from the Asian American experience and perspective.

[76]Carter's discussion of the Holy Saturday motif is different from that of Hans Urs von Balthasar or Alan Lewis precisely because its dogmatic content is not just merely read from out of the scriptural account but is filled in from out of the palpable encounter of black Christians with the gospel. Compare, e.g., Lewis's *Between Cross and Resurrection: A Theology of Holy Saturday* (Grand Rapids: Eerdmans, 2001).

In her chapter, Storkey suggests that "an evangelical theology of gender can only be developed by unearthing presuppositions in all these areas [i.e., the doctrines of creation, *imago Dei*, sin, redemption, ecclesiology and others]" (*CCET*, p. 167). Her efforts then proceed to sketch, in a very programmatic sense, what kinds of reforming are required for evangelical theology to transition from a complementarian to an egalitarian position. Following out the logic of Storkey's and Carter's contributions would require an equally massive rethinking of central Christian doctrines such as christology, the atonement and soteriology. In fact, these doctrinal categories themselves may not even survive the reformation that ensues in (especially) Carter's train—at least not in the same format or structure as those that the restorationist tradition of evangelical theology would probably seek to preserve.

While Storkey and Carter articulate why and how evangelical theology needs to be reformed—that is, so that evangelical praxis can be better performed—their efforts raise questions about the future of evangelical theology. The *CCET* recognizes not only that Evangelicalism is a global phenomenon but also that there are a multiplicity of voices under that tent, some of which may cause seismic shifts in evangelical theological reflection. While this may be of concern to restorationists, there are some voices that call for a more dialogical approach (*CCET*, p. 45) and insist that "for the full truth, all the genuinely insightful voices must be spoken and heard together" (*CCET*, p. 49n42). Herein lies the recognition that not only should Evangelicalism be counting the numbers in their churches and organizations but also that evangelical theology should be listening to and even internalizing what is being said.

The chapters in part two represent the initial contributions of evangelical perspectives from the Global South, and this, of course, opens up unavoidably into the worldwide renewal movement. Within this framework, parts of the result include a willingness to entertain "new possibilities" for evangelical theology in dialogue with primal traditions (*CCET*, p. 233); an openness to the influence of culture and society in evangelical theology (*CCET*, p. 256); and even the courage to risk the cross-fertilization of Evangelicalism across racial, national, linguistic and cultural lines (*CCET*, p. 271). Renewal herein is understood less in terms of what pentecostal and charismatic movements urge than with regard to what needs to be revisited and reconsidered in light of prevailing global trends. Still, the winds of renewal are clearly discernible. But the question is whether such postures of renewal will enable the reformation of the doctrinal loci represented in part one of the book as well as the new performance of their correlated practices. Does this represent a genuinely forward-looking orientation among evangelical theologians that may, perhaps, get us beyond the conservative/liberal (or restorationist/progressivist) dichotomy?

Even the "dogmaticians" (used here in reference to the authors of the "doctrine" chapters in part one) acknowledge the unfinished and dynamic nature of evangelical theological reflection. Are Evangelicals serious in saying, "The label 'evangelical' is the statement of an ambition—to correspond to the gospel—rather than an achievement. Similarly, 'God of the gospel' names a project, not a finished product" (*CCET*, p. 18)? Is the strategy of asking questions—in some cases many of them in succession (*CCET*, p. 101)—merely a rhetorical ploy or in effect a reflection of a genuine openness, curiosity and quest to renew evangelical theology in anticipation of the time when we shall no longer see through a glass dimly? If the latter, then herein are manifest humble approaches to the theological task.[77]

Hence, these restorationist, reformationist and renewal strands of the *CCET* can be interpreted as representing the conflicted nature of Evangelicalism in general and evangelical theology in particular, or they can be seen to reflect the pluralism within Evangelicalism, which bodes well for those desiring vibrant conversations into its future. As a pent-evangelical theologian, I resonate with how I see other evangelical theologians wrestling with the present task, since my own pentecostal tradition also has restorationist, reformationist and renewal streams. Each is necessary, even if we wish to look ahead while not neglecting to look left, right and to the rear before making a move.

Yet as the preceding shows, it is precisely the complex task of negotiating a way forward amid these various impulses that constitutes both the opportunity and the challenge for contemporary evangelical theology. To ask the question bluntly: how can evangelical theology retain its universalistic thrusts

---

[77]Some would be concerned that too much humility betrays instead a loss of conviction; I would suggest instead that it takes boldness to ask the hard questions of our time. This is precisely what drives what I have elsewhere called a theology of quest; see Yong, *Spirit-Word-Community: Theological Hermeneutics in Trinitarian Perspective* (Burlington, VT: Ashgate, and Eugene, OR: Wipf & Stock, 2002), esp. chap. 1.

while yet being appropriately missional, contextual and local? In terms of San-neh's thesis, how can the gospel be for all, not just for Westerners, yet also be translatable into as many vernacular languages as there are people groups? Considered within the overall parameters of this volume, what does it mean to talk about Asian American theology or about Asian American contribu-tions to theology in a globalizing world?

Roman Catholic missiology: Dialogical possibilities. Before turning ex-plicitly to the Asian American theological scene, however, I want to explore briefly the nature of local or vernacular theology in dialogue with Roman Catholic missionary-theologians and longtime Catholic Theological Union (in Chicago) colleagues Robert Schreiter and Stephen Bevans. Both are aware that the Enlightenment assumptions no longer hold and that theology's uni-versality needs to be argued for rather than presumed. Yet in a post–Vatican II climate, Schreiter and Bevans realize that the charge for Roman Catholic the-ology is precisely to shift from the Latin to the local and the vernacular. Hence, following their efforts will set up a mirror into which evangelical theologians can peer in light of their own efforts. Three moments in Schreiter and Bevans's journey deserve discussion.

First, the task of articulating a methodology and justification for local the-ology is taken up by Schreiter.[78] Yes, local theology is deeply shaped and in-formed by indigenous cultural realities as well as popular religious expressions in all their variety. Simultaneously, local theologies are never only dictated by the contemporary horizon. Rather—and this is Schreiter's important contri-bution in this volume—local theologies are also informed by local ecclesial traditions. In fact, church tradition itself, while often discussed in the singular, can and ought best to be understood "as a series of local theologies."[79] Local theologies thus can be viewed as local articulations and understandings of when traditions are received by new localities. There will be liturgical, prac-tical and doctrinal matters that will need to be negotiated in each instance, not only between the past and present but also between each local present vis-à-vis other local theological projects (each of which, in turn, is also adjudicating between the traditions handed down and local concerns). In short, each local

---

[78]Robert J. Schreiter, *Constructing Local Theologies* (Maryknoll, NY: Orbis, 1985).
[79]Ibid., pp. 93-94.

theological expression can also be understood as a kind of syncretism—understood nonpejoratively within the Catholic theological tradition, the subject of the book's final chapter—although there are more and less viable forms of such vis-à-vis the inherited traditions of the church. Schreiter's point, however, is to highlight how syncretism itself is a dynamic process, one that is no less complicated than that attending to local theological formation.

The fact that, as Schreiter details it, local theologies emerge from out of the various ways in which local theologians receive and interact with other historic local theologies and their doctrines, liturgies, practices and so on, leads Bevans to present a plurality of models for how such local or contextual theologies are constructed.[80] Bevans suggests that there are at least six such models: (1) a translational approach that attempts to carry over from the scriptural and dogmatic traditions into contemporary culture the kernel of the gospel; (2) an anthropological method that presumes that there are seeds of the Logos within every culture and in human hearts that need to be discovered; (3) a praxis orientation that emphasizes the never-ending task of theological construction following the liberative practices of the church; (4) a synthetic mode that underscores the dynamic and dialogical nature of theology; (5) a transcendental framework in which the theologian is attentive to the affective and cognitive operations at work in him or her as a self-transcending subject; and (6) a countercultural type that assumes that culture is always ambivalent if not resistant to the gospel and thereby in need of the latter's prophetic critique.[81] Bevans does not presume these are exclusive styles. He sketches their basic form, provides examples of each model and highlights both their strengths and weaknesses. In the end, of course, he presses the question surely on the minds of readers: is one superior to the others? While granting that in different contexts, one or more may be better or more needed than the others, in the end each has commendable virtues. Thus there "needs to be a healthy pluralism" manifest in these models even as

---

[80]Stephen B. Bevans, *Models of Contextual Theology*, rev. and expanded ed. (Maryknoll, NY: Orbis, 2002).

[81]There are many influences behind Bevans's types; the most distinctly recognizable, correlated with his transcendental type, is that of Bernard Lonergan, especially Lonergan's *Method in Theology* (New York: Herder & Herder, 1972).

theologians need to be all the more attentive to their contexts in theological reflection.[82]

Yet Catholic theologians like Bevans and Schreiter know that they cannot remain forever on the local or contextual ground since they are submitted to a magisterium, including to a Roman bishop whose claims can on occasion be infallibly uttered. Thus Schreiter has more recently also sought to bridge the gap between the local and the global in his book *The New Catholicity*.[83] Local theological processes are now reconceived in terms of intercultural hermeneutical and methodological exchanges. Schreiter's "new catholicity," then, is not only dynamic but also emergent from the full interculturality of local theologies, considered both diachronically and synchronically. This means that the Christian tradition in all its fullness and historical thickness is engaged, along with Christianity in its worldwide expressions, so that the church's catholicity continues to ebb and flow, shift and change, as communication and dialogue occur. Scripture, tradition, liturgy, praxis and dialogue both ecumenical and with those outside the church—each of these plays ongoing roles in local theologizing within the global context.

Schreiter and Bevans's efforts suggest that the way forward for Christian theology in the third millennium will be a catholicity or universality that is ever-informed by local or contextual dynamics. This response to the perennial challenge of the one and the many attempts to find a middle way between the homogenizing tendencies of Enlightenment rationality and the debilitating pluralism of at least some forms of postmodern thought. So it would seem that evangelical theologians need to carve out a similar way forward in a globalizing world, even as pent-evangelical theology insists that God will enable the many tongues of the Spirit to bear witness to the living Christ. This volume proceeds on the wager that Asian American evangelical perspectives can contribute to this task.

---

[82]Bevans, *Models of Contextual Theology*, p. 139.
[83]Robert J. Schreiter, *The New Catholicity: Theology Between the Global and the Local* (Maryknoll, NY: Orbis, 1997).

2

ASIAN AMERICAN CHRISTIANITY

Wider Trends and Trajectories

This chapter turns specifically to the Asian American context. Its three sections explore the following questions: What would a review of the literature on Asian American religion tell us about the changing face of the Asian diaspora across North America? What characterizes the existing scholarship both on and by Asian Americans? How has Asian American theology intersected or interfaced with the dominant (white) evangelical culture? Discussion of these questions uncovers a vibrant field of Asian American studies and even scholarship *on* Asian American Evangelicalism from inter- and multidisciplinary perspectives that contrasts with a relatively weak and anemic Asian American evangelical theological frontier (discussed in chapter three).

A number of caveats, however, need to be noted. First, the field of Asian American religion is a burgeoning one. Hence I have opted to conduct a select review of the literature rather than to attempt an impossibly exhaustive survey. Similarly, the discipline of Asian American studies and other humanities scholarship by Asian Americans has exploded since the 1970s. I will therefore only sketch its overall contours while focusing, in the middle section, on a distinctive Asian American philosophical movement, that of Boston Confucianism. Finally, the broader Asian American conversation is no less diverse than the pluralism of Asian theologies we encountered in the previous chapter. The following intends to do no more than delineate the major trends in Asian American historical, philosophical and theological scholarship for the sake of appreciating the emerging shape of Asian American evangelical theological consciousness.

THE ASIAN AMERICAN RELIGIOUS EXPERIENCE: A SELECT REVIEW OF THE LITERATURE

A few years ago, I attempted to assess the state of the question on the scholarly literature on Asian American religiosity as it existed at the beginning of the third millennium.[1] The following expands slightly on that discussion. I survey five distinct genres of the literature: two introductory texts (Yoo; Iwamura and Spickard), two predominantly social-scientific texts (Min and Kim; Carnes and Yang), two comparative transnationalistic analyses (Ebaugh and Chafetz), two congregational ethnographies (Yang and Alumkal) and three more recent developments (Jeung, Ecklund and Kim). This discussion will interweave studies on Asian American Evangelicalism into the mix, thus highlighting how its various guises are part and parcel of Asian American realities and yet also distinctive in many ways amid wider Asian American religious currents.

Introductory texts. David Yoo is a historian by training, and his collection, appearing on the eve of the twenty-first century, approaches Asian American religions through various means.[2] Besides nine academic essays derived from American studies, American history, religious studies and Asian American studies, *New Spiritual Homes* includes three poems (combining a range of religious themes), one memoir (of an Indian Muslim's loss and then recovery of faith, the latter during his time as a student in the United States) and one short story (of race and colonialism from the first Jesuit journeys east to the recent Asian American immigration experience). The scholarly essays describe and analyze the following: the Chinese Protestant experience during the 1880s through 1920s, especially the appropriation of Christian ideas in the service of Chinese national identity; Filipino folk spirituality as manifest in the Filipino Federation of America, founded in 1925 and directed toward addressing the concerns of both Filipino national freedom and Filipino immigrant experiences; Sikhs engaging the American court system in defense of their religious right to wear *kirpans* (ceremonial knives) in public schools in

---

[1]See my "Asian American Religion: A Review Essay," *Nova Religio: The Journal of Alternative and Emergent Religions* 9, no. 3 (2006): 92-107.
[2]David K. Yoo, ed., *New Spiritual Homes: Religion and Asian Americans* (Honolulu: University of Hawaii Press, 1999).

California, and the questions these events raise about the meaning of "multi-culturalism" in the twenty-first century; the Chinese Buddhist experience in California; Asian American evangelical college students;[3] shamanism as a syncretistic religiousness par excellence, bridging cultures and religions from East and West; and Korean American evangelical women's experiences. The last is an important topic that highlights the gendered nature of much of Asian American evangelical Christianity even as it lifts up its paradoxical potential for liberating women within patriarchal cultures.[4] Throughout the volume, concerns about Asian ethnicity vis-à-vis the processes of assimilation and Americanization are viewed through the religious practices and beliefs of Asian American immigrants. *New Spiritual Homes* thus calls attention to how religion functions as a "cultural broker" that introduces, preserves and even enables the flourishing of Asian ethnicities in the United States on the one hand, even as it helps ethnic Asians adapt to American culture on the other. Asian American forms of religious belief and practice "betwixt and between" Asia and America emerge as neither fully one nor fully the other.[5]

Yoo's book was shortly followed by another edited volume derived from the joint sponsorship of the Asian and Pacific Asian Religion Research Initiative and the Asian North American Religions, Culture and Society group of the American Academy of Religion.[6] The collection is framed according to the orientation and direction of research on Asian American religions and is structured by particular aspects of their religious lives: spirit, context, practice, identity, community, reflection, legacy and texts. There are at least two chapters devoted to discussion of each of these aspects (except that of "reflection," which has only one). "Spirit" includes discussions of the back-and-

---

[3]This is an increasingly noticeable phenomenon, to which we will return shortly in the discussion of Rebecca Kim's book.

[4]See Jung Ha Kim, "The Labor of Compassion: Voices of Churched Korean American Women," in Yoo, ed., *New Spiritual Homes*, pp. 202-17. While many studies of Asian American Evangelicalism are attentive to the theme of gender, to my knowledge no book-length analysis has so far appeared.

[5]I get this phrase from Peter C. Phan, "Betwixt and Between: Doing Theology with Memory and Imagination," in Peter C. Phan and Jung Young Lee, eds., *Journeys at the Margin: Toward an Autobiographical Theology in American-Asian Perspective* (Collegeville, MN: Liturgical Press, 1999), pp. 113-33; see also Irene Lin, "Journey to the Far West: Chinese Buddhism in America," in Yoo, ed., *New Spiritual Homes*, pp. 134-69, at p. 148.

[6]Jane Naomi Iwamura and Paul Spickard, eds., *Revealing the Sacred in Asian and Pacific America* (New York: Routledge, 2003).

forth between indigenous and folk islander (Hawaiian, more precisely) spirituality and Mormon faith, and the living out of compassionate faith among
second-generation older Nisei Japanese (Buddhist and Christian) Americans.
"Context" unfolds the religious and public role of a Taiwanese American Buddhist temple in Southern California, and profiles the grimmer and darker
sides of racialized identification experiences by Asian Pacific Islanders.[7]
"Practice" includes two chapters on Hindu American life: one comparative
with Korean American Christianity, and one diachronic in exploring religious
transitions between first- and second-generation South Asian immigrants.
"Identity" discusses Cambodian American dual religious practices (Buddhist
and Christian) on the one side and Korean American essentialist self-
understandings that equate Korean and Buddhist identities on the other.
There is one chapter on the "Reflection" motif: on how non-Christian religious building projects, in particular that of Hindu temples in the United
States, are attempts to redefine American religiosity in rather public and spec-
tacular ways. "Legacy" examines the shifting fortunes of Chinese American
Evangelicals[8] and revisits the religious dimensions of the horrific Japanese
internment episodes during the Second World War that still stain American
history. Finally, "Texts" looks at Japanese American Protestant spiritual auto-
biographies and a Korean American woman's memoir for insight. This volume,
along with Yoo's, highlights the dynamism and pluralism of Asian American

---

[7]The author, Carolyn Chen, has also expanded her argument into a monograph: *Getting Saved in America: Taiwanese Immigration and Religious Experience* (Princeton, NJ: Princeton University Press, 2008). Her thesis, that Taiwanese immigrants negotiate their transition to the United States in part by becoming religious, is elaborated against the backdrop of conversions both to evangelical Christianity and to a broad form of Mahayana Buddhist teaching and practice. In both cases, how-ever, converts understand their Americanization in terms of breaking with Taiwanese tradition—ironically, from traditional aspects of Confucian culture for Buddhists on the one hand, and from superstitious forms of Confucian-Daoist-Buddhist religiosity for Evangelicals on the other—and forming new otherworldly narratives that simultaneously enable the cultivation of disciplines and practices that are instrumental for middle-class survival in the new land. Throughout, Chen applies her sociological craft judiciously, engaging where appropriate with the dominant theories and lit-erature in the sociology of religion but always coming back to provide detailed ethnographic data and analysis. *Getting Saved in America*, while limited in terms of its geographic focus, regional scope and ethnic sample, is suggestive regarding the kind of comparative sociological studies that are needed and helpful for illuminating the complex and dynamic forces of globalization, immigration and transnationalism at work in contemporary Asian America.

[8]The author here is Timothy Tseng, one of the foremost authorities on Asian American evangelical history and whose work we will have ample opportunity to cite in the rest of this volume.

religion, even for those in the second generation, who are assumed to be more assimilated than their parents.

Social-scientific analyses. The volumes by Min and Kim and by Carnes and Yang total twenty-five essays—nine in the former and sixteen in the latter—written primarily although not exclusively by sociologists. *Religions in Asian America: Building Faith Communities* (Min and Kim) includes two historical essays on the Japanese American and Filipino American experiences alongside Min's invaluable review of the sociological literature on Asian American religions and other social-scientific analyses of Southeast Asian refugee experiences, and other articles on Chinese, Korean (Protestant) and Indian (Hindu) religiousness.[9] In the chapter on Chinese immigrants, the author observes the diversity of Buddhist, Christian and folk religious practices.[10] Russell Jeung's concluding chapter on Asian American pan-ethnic organizations in the San Francisco Bay Area introduces the emergence of churches that are negotiating the crossing of ethnic boundaries—especially Chinese, Korean, Southeast Asian and, to a lesser extent, Japanese—but are less intent on bridging class differences or the boundaries that separate the first from the one-and-a-half and second generations. We return to the themes of Jeung's essay momentarily.

Asian American Religions: The Making and Remaking of Borders and Boundaries (Carnes and Yang) is divided into four parts and is introduced by two chapters (one on religious demographics).[11] Highlights of part one on symbols and rituals includes coverage of the intriguing phenomenon of South Asian Muslim taxi drivers in New York City (primarily Bangladeshi, Pakistani and Indian, although there are also a smaller number of Malaysian and Indonesian drivers) who are carving out liminal spaces of prayer that are neither fully private (often in busy, public places) nor fully corporate (prayer is offered at the prescribed times of the day, but often alone), and therefore perhaps

---

[9]Pyong Gap Min and Jung Ha Kim, eds., *Religions in Asian America: Building Faith Communities* (Walnut Creek, CA: AltaMira, 2002).

[10]The Korean immigrant experience is just as complex; see Ho-Youn Kwon, Kwang Chung Kim and R. Stephen Warner, eds., *Korean Americans and Their Religions: Pilgrims and Missionaries from a Different Shore* (University Park: Pennsylvania State University Press, 2001), and Su Yon Park, Unzu Lee, Jung Ha Kim and Myung Ji Cho, *Singing the Lord's Song in a New Land: Korean American Practices of Faith* (Louisville: Westminster John Knox, 2005).

[11]Tony Carnes and Fenggang Yang, eds., *Asian American Religions: The Making and Remaking of Borders and Boundaries* (New York: New York University Press, 2004).

contributing to the development of a "pan-Islamic" identity. The volume also reports on different Hindu temples, also in New York City, each derived from a separate sect of the tradition but functioning cooperatively in various respects, and therefore contributing to the development of a larger Hindu culture that may have been impossible anywhere except in the United States in our time. Part two, titled "Boundaries of Time: Events, Generations, and Age," discusses intergenerational transitions through analyses of the emergent Asian American evangelical subculture, gender issues and the experience of aging senior immigrants. Part three, on political boundaries, includes two survey-driven essays that are heavily statistical and focused on political trends among immigrants. The last part, "Transcending Borders and Boundaries," includes another piece by Jeung (on a specific pan-ethnic congregation), one on intermarriage, interraciality and interreligiousness in Silicon Valley,[12] and one on social aspects of Asian American religion, specifically the annual bowling tournaments among Filipino Christians in northern California. Along with the two more general introductions (by Yoo and by Iwamura and Spickard) discussed above, these more sociologically oriented analyses highlight the multidimensionality of Asian American religious life. Any theological reflection will require interdisciplinary approaches in order to be adequately informed by and engaged with not only the peculiarities of Asian American religion but also its interface with the broader American landscape.

Transnational studies. The volumes by Ebaugh and Chafetz expand on the horizons of Asian American religiousness by exploring its transnational dimensions.[13] Both are University of Houston sociologists who began by conducting close analyses of Hispanic and Asian immigrant religions in the Houston, Texas, area. In most cases, Hispanics connected with Latin American countries and Asians with those across the Pacific Rim, but in a few instances, Asian immigration to Latin America has produced a Hispanic Asian diaspora

---

[12]Of interest is not just the intermarriage of Thai Theravada Buddhist women and Anglo (primarily) Roman Catholic men but the fact that they are raising their children as distinctively Buddhist and Catholic without attempting to develop a synthetic (or, some would say, syncretistic) religion. For more on such dual Buddhist and Christian identities, see Rose Drew, *Buddhist and Christian? An Exploration of Dual Belonging* (New York: Routledge, 2011).

[13]Helen Rose Ebaugh and Janet Saltzman Chafetz, *Religion and the New Immigrants: Continuities and Adaptations in Immigrant Congregations* (Walnut Creek, CA: AltaMira, 2000), and idem, eds., *Religion Across Borders: Transnational Immigrant Networks* (Walnut Creek, CA: AltaMira, 2002).

with resulting ongoing migration, bringing these agents into the North American region as well. Case studies in the initial volume zero in on a Hindu temple, a Vietnamese Buddhist center, a Chinese evangelical church, two Catholic parishes, a pentecostal church and a Greek Orthodox congregation. Insofar as "transnationals" are "people with feet in two societies,"[14] these authors explore the religious practices of persons, communities and even institutions that are enacted both in the United States and in one or more Asian countries. By setting Asian American religious experiences in international context, the connections, influences and exchanges of ideas, practices, materials and even personnel to and from various nations in Asia are considered.

In their follow-up book, Ebaugh and Chafetz provide three levels of transnational analysis. First, they include three case studies of American-Asian transnationalism: Vietnamese Buddhists and Vietnamese Catholics; Chinese evangelical Christians; and immigrants from Fuzhou (a southeastern coastal region on mainland China) to New York City. Second, they compare and contrast Asian American religious transnationalism with Hispanic American religious transnationalism, including four case studies of the latter focused on evangelical and Catholic connections to sites in various parts of Latin America and Europe.[15] Third, given that their American case studies are all, with the exception of Kenneth Guest's discussion of New York City Fuzhounese (to which we return in chapter six), located in the Houston metropolitan area, they are better able to control the variables of their transnational analyses, and therefore to generalize from more specific empirical data sets within a socioeconomic and political region.

So, while the introductory chapter lays out the methodological parameters of their book, Ebaugh and Chafetz's conclusion is a richly textured theoretical analysis informed by comparative ethnography accomplished stateside (especially in Houston) and abroad. They thereby identify transnational connections at three levels: between individuals, between organizations (e.g.,

---

[14]Helen Rose Ebaugh and Janet Saltzman Chafetz, "Introduction," in Ebaugh and Chafetz, eds., *Religion Across Borders*, pp. 1-14, at p. 1.

[15]Ebaugh and Chafetz generalize from both the Hispanic American and the Asian American case studies. Hence my summary of their findings in the next paragraph does not break down the differences. Suffice it to say that, from my reading, the major difference of analysis is that the Hispanic American connections stretch over three continents. The forces of globalization will soon require that analyses of Asian American religions will need to include Asian communities in Europe and Latin America as well.

churches, temples, nongovernmental organizations) and between macrolevel institutions (such as the Roman Catholic Church), with various kinds of intersections between all three levels. Material and social resources are imported from the home countries when immigrants start out in the host nation. Then later, after immigrants become more established, the same kinds of resources, along with normative theological ideas, values and beliefs (e.g., books), and various religious practices (e.g., devotional objects and other religious items) flow in both directions. Ties are more personal, and exchanges occur at higher rates of intensity according to various factors: the proximity of home and host communities (the more proximate, the more interpersonal; the less proximate, the more interinstitutional); the availability of human capital, level of socioeconomic status, and access to telecommunication (the more of each, the "thicker" the density of network interactions); the capacity to travel home (in terms of resources and legality); and the presence of religious persecution suffered by minority religious persons at home (the more persecution, the more institutionalized the mode of charitable donations). Finally, Ebaugh and Chafetz observe that transnational links gradually weaken during second and later generations, especially if the rates of immigration also decrease.

Congregational ethnographies and other trends. Fenggang Yang's and Antony Alumkal's ethnographies of Chinese and (in Alumkal's case) Korean American Evangelicalism represent a more traditional yet still relevant approach to the study of religion: congregational analysis. Negotiating the opportunities and challenges of being a participant-observer at the Chinese Christian Church of Greater Washington, D.C. (Yang was baptized in this church midway through his course of graduate studies), Yang's *Chinese Christians in America* explores immigrant and second-generation Chinese evangelical beliefs and practices.[16] As a social scientist, however, Yang is also interested in various social processes, specifically those surrounding the assimilation of immigrants to the dominant culture, and the role of ethnicity and religion in the immigrant experience. Hence the heart of this volume focuses on the various strategies that are developed for deconstructing the immigrant Chinese identity and reconstructing an "adhesive" Chinese American

---

[16]Fenggang Yang, *Chinese Christians in America: Conversion, Assimilation and Adhesive Identities* (University Park: Pennsylvania State University Press, 1999).

Christian identity that is simultaneously "an evangelical Protestant identity, a conservative American identity, and a cosmopolitan and cultural Chinese identity."[17] In this way, the religious, social and biological-cultural dimensions are integrated without losing distinctive characteristics of each domain. In the process, Yang also asks how evangelical Christian conversion facilitates this kind of social process—that is, why were Chinese immigrants drawn to this kind of Christianity?—and suggests that there is not only a compatibility between certain Confucian and conservative Christian values, but also that the evangelical identity provides a universal ground for accepting or rejecting either Chinese or American cultural traditions (unavoidable tasks in the assimilation process) as seen fit for the new social context.

Asian American Evangelical Churches was written by Alumkal as both an "outsider"—of Filipino-Indian extraction with membership in the more mainline Episcopal Church—and a participant-observer at a nondenominational (independent) Chinese congregation and at a Korean Presbyterian church in New York City.[18] Many of Yang's findings are here traced among second-generation Chinese and Korean American evangelical congregations. Drawing from Bakhtin's model of "heteroglossia," which identifies how a social group employs a multiplicity of discourses that intersect with and condition one another depending on the situation at hand,[19] Alumkal describes how second-generation Asian American Evangelicals fluidly shift or move between discursive identities as appropriate. For example, Chinese and Korean Americans are ethnic minorities subject to social and racial discrimination, even as they prefer to emphasize their evangelical (read: Christian) minority-identity, leading to an expectation that they will be persecuted for their faith by the dominant majority. Further, Chinese and Korean Americans are discussed according to the "model minority" stereotype, as unhelpful as that is (discussed above in the introductory chapter); this allows for emphasis on certain East Asian values such as hard work and discipline even while these gifts and talents are manifest in school or the workplace as part of their

---

[17]Ibid., p. 187.

[18]Antony W. Alumkal, *Asian American Evangelical Churches: Race, Ethnicity, and Assimilation in the Second Generation* (New York: LFB Scholarly Publishing, 2003).

[19]Alumkal references Mikhail Bakhtin, *The Dialogic Imagination: Four Essays*, ed. Michael Holquist, trans. Caryl Emerson and Michael Holquist (Austin: University of Texas Press, 1981).

Christian stewardship. Finally, second-generation Chinese and Koreans do not become more egalitarian in the assimilation process but rather shift their legitimization of gender hierarchy from Confucian-based arguments to ideals drawn from conservative evangelical interpretations of the Bible that emphasize male headship in the home and the church. This is especially intriguing in the Korean case wherein congregants manifest a distinctive dissonance from the parent Presbyterian Church (USA) denominational position, which affirms the ordination of women. Throughout, Alumkal is careful to engage, modify and even challenge previous sociological theories of race, ethnicity and assimilation in light of his observations of and interviews with second-generation Chinese and Korean American Evangelicals.

Before moving on, we briefly observe trends particularly but not exclusively among Asian American evangelical communities. First, there are the phenomena of multiethnic and pan-Asian churches, including some attaining megachurch status (over 2,000 adherents on any given Sunday morning).[20] The former is often multiracial, including not only Asian but also white and African American members, sometimes in significant numbers, while the latter often includes numerous blends of Asian American groups, which provides venues for cross-Asian solidarity yet also enables interface with majority (especially evangelical) subcultural norms.[21] Second, Asian American and Asian American evangelical congregations are increasingly sensitive to, present among and engaged with civic life.[22] Even for those who remain in ethnic-specific evangelical churches and communities, there is emerging a much wider range of civic and even public (political) self-understandings among Asian Americans in second and later generations than existed among their forebears. This suggests an unpredictability about the development of second-generation ethnic Evangelicalism and how various groups, each one reflecting a plurality of cultural backgrounds, might shape—even diversify—the next generation of evangelical

---

[20]Russell Jeung, *Faithful Generations: Race and New Asian American Churches* (New Brunswick, NJ: Rutgers University Press, 2004). For further social analysis, see Yen Le Espiritu, *Asian American Panethnicity: Bridging Institutions and Identities* (Philadelphia: Temple University Press, 1992).

[21]See also the landmark study by Curtiss Paul DeYoung, Michael O. Emerson, George Yancey and Karen Chai Kim, *United by Faith: The Multiracial Congregation as an Answer to the Problem of Race* (Oxford: Oxford University Press, 2003).

[22]See Elaine Howard Ecklund, *Korean American Evangelicals: New Models for Civic Life* (Oxford: Oxford University Press, 2006).

discursive practices vis-à-vis civic life. Last but not least, there is the growing phenomenon of what might be called the "Asian Americanizing" of evangelical Christian groups on public college and university campuses.[23] These run parallel with the formation of multiethnic and pan-Asian congregational communities but also perpetuate the "model minority" myth. More interestingly, this opens up questions about the future of Asian American assimilation not only with regard to American life in general but also with regard to the dominant (white) evangelical subculture. In each case, there are clearly identifiable paths of assimilation but also just as distinct markers highlighting the desire to maintain ethnic segregation and solidarity. Whither Asian American evangelical theology amid these oftentimes competing developments?

ASIAN AMERICAN SCHOLARLY CURRENTS: EMERGING DISCOURSES

The following segues into the discussion of Asian American theology through a brief introduction to scholarship on Asian America and by Asian Americans. After overviewing this domain of Asian American studies, broadly defined, we move into a more focused assessment of developments in the humanities in general and in the discipline of philosophy particularly. These forays enable us to chart the major trajectories engaged in the wider scholarly and academic arenas, which will assist in our tracking with Asian American theologians later.

Asian American studies. Asian American studies, along with other ethnic studies, was catalyzed out of the Asian American movement that emerged from the 1960s civil rights era.[24] It is an interdisciplinary field of inquiry—deploying historical, sociological, cultural, political, literary, gender theory and other methods and analytical tools—focused on the experiences of people with Asian ancestry in the United States. Historians working within the field, of course, have attempted not only to reconsider the history of Asian Americans from their various perspectives but also to resituate the American historical narrative in light of Asian American experiences.[25] Yet the point of

---

[23]E.g., Rebecca Y. Kim, *God's New Whiz Kids: Korean American Evangelicals on Campus* (New York: New York University Press, 2006).

[24]William Wei, *The Asian American Movement* (Philadelphia: Temple University Press, 1993).

[25]E.g., Ronald Takaki, *Strangers from a Different Shore: A History of Asian Americans* (Boston: Little, Brown, 1989), and Franklin Odo, ed., *The Columbia Documentary History of the Asian American Experience* (New York: Columbia University Press, 2002).

Asian American studies is not just to retell a more complete story, as important as that is, but to address the challenges before Asian American life, in particular what has been said to be a betwixt-and-between identity (as both "model minority" and "perpetual foreigners") in an increasingly capitalistic transnational and global world order.[26]

This betwixt-and-between-ness is a constant and pervasive theme in Asian American scholarly literature. Surely there is no denying the profound otherness represented by at least some Asian American immigrant experiences, in particular those uprooted as refugees and exiles due to war and other disrupting international realities. On this end of the spectrum, Asian Americans struggle in ethnic communities—some say enclaves or even ghettoes—hopeful for assimilation yet clinging desperately to whatever continuities are maintainable given their adverse (immigration-related) circumstances.[27] Yet there is also no minimizing the gradual and irrepressible forces accomplishing what some observers have called the "Asianization" of the United States.[28] Everywhere we turn, we see Asian influence: in what we eat, in architecture, film, music, literature, scholarship, in the professional working class and so on. Some see these trends as evidence of Asian assimilation, however. What might be called the "emergence of an American people" from one perspective[29] might be feared as the loss of Asian American identity from another. From a third vantage point, even if Asian Americans were successful in their efforts to ascend the social ladder and assimilate to American culture, this would fuel the "model minority" myth and exacerbate presumption that other ethnic minorities are not working as hard, which thereby ignores the systemic racism within which all Americans exist.[30]

Many working in the field of Asian American studies, then, have sought to

---

[26]See David Palumbo-Liu, *Asian/American: Historical Crossings of a Racial Frontier* (Stanford: Stanford University Press, 1999), pp. 387-93.

[27]Danling Fu, *"My Trouble Is My English": Asian Students and the American Dream* (Portsmouth, NH: Boynton/Cook Publishers and Heinemann, 1995), and Wendy Walker-Moffat, *The Other Side of the Asian American Success Story* (San Francisco: Jossey-Bass, 1995).

[28]See the last chapter of Warren I. Cohen, *The Asian American Century* (Cambridge, MA: Harvard University Press, 2002).

[29]Halen Zia, *Asian American Dreams: The Emergence of an American People* (New York: Farrar, Straus and Giroux, 2000).

[30]Mia Tuan, *Forever Foreigners or Honorary Whites? The Asian Ethnic Experience Today* (New Brunswick, NJ: Rutgers University Press, 1999), pp. 162-63.

find a middle way between these currents.[31] In Asian American literary and cultural studies, for instance, the identification of various genres (memoir, poetry, fiction, drama) has been foregrounded, as well as elaboration on multiple (not just a few) major themes and motifs. Yes, the expected issues are discussed: acculturation/assimilation, heritage/identity, homeland/nostalgia, intergenerational dynamics, immigrant/diaspora, racism, stereotypes, refugee experiences, war/violence, postcolonial realities and so on. Simultaneously, aspects common to the human species are also being lifted up, albeit refracted through the range of Asian American lenses: childhood, community, conflict, creativity, freedom and responsibility, love/relationships, sensuality, sexuality, gender and so on. In the mix are certainly self-critical assessments of the American dream,[32] not as if negatively judging the United States from an Asian point of view but as contributing to its refinement from a perspective also desiring of a stronger and more just American future. In addition, however, there are also creative second- or third-generation immigrants whose self-critical perspectives are countercultural and subversive of the Asian American genres and discourses that they have inherited.[33]

The point is that Asian American voices are cutting in multiple directions. They are neither wholly passive, as if subjected under the dominant (white) other, nor wholly active, as if mounting their own resistance to and broadside against the majority culture.[34] Instead, it could be said that Asian Americans inhabit multiple subjectivities across the full spectrum between Asia and the United States. More precisely these are also dynamic subjectivities and postures, reflecting not only generational but also relational, political and other

---

[31]Shirley Geok-lin Lim and Amy Ling, eds., *Reading the Literatures of Asian America* (Philadelphia: Temple University Press, 1992); King-Kok Cheung, ed., *An Interethnic Companion to Asian American Literature* (Cambridge: Cambridge University Press, 1997); Shirley Geok-lin Lim and Cheng Lok Chua, eds., *Tilting the Continent: Southeast Asian American Writing* (Minneapolis: New Rivers, 2000); Rajini Srikanth and Esther Y. Iwanaga, eds., *Bold Words: A Century of Asian American Writing* (New Brunswick, NJ: Rutgers University Press, 2001).

[32]I will return in chapter six to address the unspoken assumptions at the interface of theology and economics undergirding the "American dream."

[33]See Maria Hong, ed., *Growing Up Asian American: An Anthology* (New York: William Morrow & Company, 1993).

[34]E.g., Robert G. Lee, *Orientals: Asian Americans in Popular Culture* (Philadelphia: Temple University Press, 1999); Sheng-Mei Ma, *The Deathly Embrace: Orientalism and Asian American Identity* (Minneapolis: University of Minnesota Press, 2000); and Tina Chen, *Double Agency: Acts of Impersonation in Asian American Literature and Culture* (Stanford: Stanford University Press, 2005).

contextual shifts. Individual and group identities, in other words, are flexible in adapting to and engaging with different constituencies, realities and demands. The reality is that Asian Americans are no different from other groups, even the majority culture, in having to negotiate multiple domains and contexts. So instead of reducing Asian American experiences to either end of the spectrum—that of "perpetual foreigner" or of "model minority"—perhaps their lives and communities open up alternative sites of material, aesthetic and cultural production, and agency. From these liminal spaces, Asian Americans may be able to both interrogate and shape not just "Americanism" but, more importantly, globalizing, transnationalizing and internationalizing trends.[35] In short, when we peer beneath the surface, "Asian America" opens up to the variety, diversity and plurality of Asian America*s* that reflect a two-way exchange between the two worlds across various frames of reference and partially overlapping axes.

Asian American philosophical developments: Boston Confucianism. In the remainder of this section, I want to take a brief tour into philosophical territory, in particular the movement known as Boston Confucianism, for three interrelated reasons. First, it provides one venue for us to drill deeper into the broad area of Asian American studies in order to get further traction on our thesis regarding the multiplicity of its discourses. Second, the emergence of Boston Confucianism as a philosophical movement anticipates the theological considerations we will take up with regard to the transportability of an Asian tradition into the Western academy. Third, insofar as philosophy perennially has been considered the handmaiden of theology, to that degree considering this specifically philosophical conversation may aid in theological reflection. If indeed portable, the question of why would or should contemporary philosophers welcome Boston Confucianism into the discussion can also be asked by theologians. Seeing how that project has fared may thus be illuminating for the Asian American evangelical theological enterprise.

The Confucian tradition, of course, even before its adaptation by Bostonians (to which we return in a moment), is, like other philosophical and religious

---

[35]Lisa Lowe, *Immigrant Acts: On Asian American Cultural Politics* (Durham, NC: Duke University Press, 1996).

traditions, a complicated and even contested one.[36] At its fount is the Chinese philosopher-sage Confucius (Kongzi, lit. "Master Kong," 551–479 B.C.). His teachings became the official ideology of the Han Dynasty (206 B.C.–A.D. 220) and after the disintegration of the Han government were suffused with Buddhist and Daoist elements and practices. Yet the Master's doctrines were revised during the Tang period (618–907) and then adopted as the basis for imperial examinations by scholar officials during the Song era (960–1279). The fortunes of the tradition have waxed and waned in the last millennium, albeit its basic themes—the triadic relation of heaven-earth-humanity; emphases on *ren* (humaneness) and *li* (ritual etiquette and actions) as shaping human relations; unity of heart-mind as guiding human experience in the world; filial piety and social harmony as fundamental cultural orientations; *zhèngmíng* or the "rectification of names" as ordering human thought and action; and so on—have persisted even if in a variety of configurations over time.

The label "Boston Confucianism" originally emerged as an oxymoron, an insider's joke, so to speak, among attendees of the Second Confucian-Christian Dialogue Conference at Berkeley, California (1991), who recognized the increasing number of participants, compared to the first conference (1988), hailing from Boston.[37] The three Bostonians there were all affiliated with Boston University: Robert Cummings Neville, dean of the School of Theology; John H. Berthrong, a transplanted Canadian Sinologist, and associate dean and professor of comparative theology; and Chung Chai-Sik, a Korean scholar and social ethicist who later became the Walter G. Muelder Professor of Social Ethics. Absent from the second conference but involved in its planning and present at the first and third conferences—the latter in Boston (1994)—was Chinese-born and American-naturalized Tu Wei-Ming, then professor of Chinese history and philosophy at Harvard University, across the Charles River from Boston University, and later director of the Harvard-Yenching Institute and first chair-holder of the Harvard-Yenching Professorship of Chinese History and Philosophy and of Confucian Studies. While

---

[36]See, e.g., the introductory chapter to John H. Berthrong, *Transformations of the Confucian Way* (Boulder, CO: Westview Press, 1998).

[37]An overview of the first two conferences is provided by John H. Berthrong, *All Under Heaven: Transforming Paradigms in Confucian-Christian Dialogue* (Albany: State University of New York Press, 1994), pp. 5-8.

others have come and gone from Boston over the years, and still many more have been students of the Confucian tradition under them, these four have been at the center of this trend in contemporary Confucian philosophy.

Neville, in particular, has been responsible for promoting Boston Confucianism as a viable philosophical movement, with the publication of his book by that title in 2000.[38] At the heart of the Confucianist experiment in its Boston form is the conviction that philosophy in global context necessarily involves the great philosophical traditions of the East, one of which is the Confucian with its East Asian roots. More precisely, just as Asian philosophers engaging the Western academy have had to become adept conversationalists in Western philosophical traditions, and have even made original contributions to these discussions, so also in our contemporary global situation should Western philosophers develop facility in Asian philosophies. Put alternatively, Asian philosophies no longer belong to those of Asian provenance, nor are the latter solely responsible for the fortunes of Asian traditions on the world philosophical stage.

But this raises the question: how does the Confucian tradition belong in contemporary philosophical conversation? Neville's *Boston Confucianism* responds to this question at three levels. (1) The Confucian tradition has perennially addressed matters that are of ongoing discussion including, but not limited to, philosophy of culture, conceptions of selfhood, social and political philosophy, and, most relevant for theology, the philosophy of religion;[39] Western philosophers should at least consider the classical and present debates among Confucians rather than remaining exclusively Western-focused in an a priori manner, especially since ancient Confucian philosophies of ritual interaction have the potential to contribute to the rebuilding of a contemporary world fragmented by religious, ethnic and ideological strife.[40] (2) Confucian thinkers over the past two millennia have also

---

[38]Robert Cummings Neville, *Boston Confucianism: Portable Tradition in a Late-Modern World* (Albany: State University of New York Press, 2000).

[39]The Bostonians south of the Charles River, all teaching at a theological seminary, have consistently addressed religious and theological issues from the Confucian tradition. But those north, at Harvard, have also done so, as we shall see soon in the thought of Tu Wei-Ming.

[40]Neville has since developed his ideas on these topics in his *Ritual and Deference: Extending Chinese Philosophy in a Comparative Context* (Albany: State University of New York Press, 2008).

grappled with the classical Western metaphysical and ontological questions regarding being, transcendence, and the relationship between the one and the many; once again, if Western philosophers would begin paying attention to the Confucian arguments, they would not merely find parallels in how the issues are negotiated but perhaps also derive new resources from their Confucian interlocutors to rethink matters, particularly since the Confucian tradition has not generally operated with a concept of divine transcendence. (3) Most challenging, however, has been the conservatism of the Confucian tradition, whether articulated in terms of the patriarchal subordination of women or in the classical terms related to filial piety and ritual propriety; yet even here, the Boston Confucians, in dialogue with their East Asian counterparts, point to major resources internal to the tradition—for example, the Neo-Confucian "principle" in each individual, male or female, that enables both personal grounding and communal harmonization; or the notion of filial piety as holy duty; or of ritual propriety (*li*) as involving an appropriateness that is sensitive to new times, places and conditions—that can be drawn upon to leverage against such conservative tendencies and therefore also contribute to the ongoing discussion of these matters in the contemporary world philosophical arena. In each of these ways, then, the argument is that Confucianism is a portable intellectual tradition, and that its Boston guise is one manifestation of its viability in global context.

Neville's work, of course, has been deeply informed by the work of his Confucian colleague from north of the Charles River, Tu Wei-Ming. In the Boston area since the early 1980s, Tu has consistently built on his earlier historical explorations of Confucian philosophy in order to articulate a viable New Confucian posture for the modern world.[41] New Confucianism is a twentieth-century intellectual movement within the Confucian tradition that is informed by the Neo-Confucianism of the Song and Ming dynasties but updated, as it were, for China's interface with the modernity.[42] The critique of the Confucian tradition, from the beginning of the twentieth century even

---

[41]See especially Tu Wei-Ming, *Neo-Confucian Thought in Action: Wang Yang-Ming's Youth* (Berkeley: University of California Press, 1976); *Humanity and Self-Cultivation: Essays in Confucian Thought* (Boston: Asian Humanities Press, 1978); and *Confucianism in Historical Perspective* (Singapore: Institute of East Asian Philosophies, 1989).

[42]See Berthrong, *Transformations of the Confucian Way,* esp. chap. 7.

through the Cultural Revolution era in China (1966–1976), was its putatively backward-looking worldview that perpetuated the ancient and outdated classical tradition. Tu's argument (along with that of other New Confucianists), now running to almost forty years, is that the Confucian sage of old ought now to be the Confucian intellectual for the contemporary world.[43] Confucian thought, ethics and philosophy, especially when refracted through the New Confucian paradigm, are not only adaptable but also essential for human flourishing at the beginning of the third millennium.[44]

We can see more clearly the gist of Tu's position when we examine his view of Confucian religiosity.[45] As the Confucian tradition is not explicitly theistic (nor explicitly non- or antitheistic), Confucian religiousness is best characterized as an overall spirituality or orientation to life rather than a theocentric posture. Confucian self-cultivation is ultimately intertwined with the family and the community, even as it has implication for the world as a whole. To be properly adjusted as a person involves proper orientation to others and to the world, with moral and cosmic implications and even consequences. In other words, there is what might be called an "anthropocosmic vision" in the Confucian tradition that sees heaven, earth and humanity bound up indissolubly.[46] The creative transformation of the self thus involves a spiritual dimension of proper alignment with heaven as well as a moral coordination of ritual relationship to others, even the world. Transcendence is not denied, although that is never cut off from the human and environmental domains.[47]

---

[43]Tu has authored and edited numerous works along these lines; the former include Tu Wei-Ming, *Confucian Ethics Today: The Singapore Challenge* (Singapore: Federal Publications, 1984); *Confucian Thought: Selfhood as Creative Transformation* (Albany: State University of New York Press, 1985); and *Way, Learning, and Politics: Essays on the Confucian Intellectual* (Albany: State University of New York Press, 1993). Edited works include *China in Transformation* (Cambridge, MA: Harvard University Press, 1994); *The Living Tree: The Changing Meaning of Being Chinese Today* (Stanford: Stanford University Press, 1994); and *Confucian Traditions in East Asian Modernity* (Cambridge, MA: Harvard University Press, 1996). See also William Theodore De Barry and Tu Wei-Ming, eds., *Confucianism and Human Rights* (New York: Columbia University Press, 1998).

[44]I attempt to develop a Confucian-evangelical pedagogical and educational paradigm in my "Evangelical *Paideia* Overlooking the Pacific Rim: On the Opportunities and Challenges of Globalization for Christian Higher Education," *Christian Scholar's Review* 42, no. 4 (2013): 393-409.

[45]Tu Wei-Ming, *Centrality and Commonality: An Essay on Confucian Religiousness* (Albany: State University of New York Press, 1989).

[46]Ibid., p. 102.

[47]See also Rodney Taylor, *The Religious Dimensions of Confucianism* (Albany: State University of

While much more can and should be said, space constraints and the major tasks related to this chapter require us to step back from the details of the Boston Confucian project and reengage the larger theological issues that it touches on. Of first importance is the question concerning the reception of the movement and its views. The reviews of Neville's *Boston Confucianism* have on the whole been positive.[48] Tu's work, understandably, has been relatively neglected by theologians, with the exception of Jung Sun Oh, who has sought to construct a viable (Nevillean) Christian theological anthropology in creative dialogue with (Tu-inspired) Confucian thought.[49] For Oh, there is a transcendental aspect to filial piety that, properly nurtured, organically interrelates human beings with one another, the world and heaven, and this New Confucian view of human nature has theological implications and potential.

Of course, other responses are possible, such as ignoring, shouting down or marginalizing the newcomers to the philosophical party. None of these appears to have occurred, although it is difficult to imagine such reactions given the stature of these Boston protagonists in philosophical and religious studies circles. It would appear Asian traditions are here to stay on the global philosophic conversation, even if Confucianism in its specifically Bostonian dress were to finally limp off into the sunset.

From philosophy to theology. Looking backward and looking ahead, then, what is the relevance of Boston Confucianism to our quest for an Asian American theology in general and an Asian American evangelical theology

---

New York Press, 1990), and Tu Wei-Ming and Mary Evelyn Tucker, eds., *Confucian Spirituality*, 2 vols. (New York: Crossroad, 2003–2004).

[48]See the reviews by Jay Goulding, in *Dao* 4, no. 1 (2004): 193-96; Patsy Rahn, in *Nova Religio* 7, no. 3 (2004): 105-6, and Liu Shuxian, "Confucianism as World Philosophy: A Response to Neville's *Boston Confucianism* from a Neo-Confucian Perspective," in *Journal of Ecumenical Studies* 40, nos. 1-2 (2003): 59-73. Consult also John H. Berthrong, "Boston Confucianism: The Third Wave of Global Confucianism," *Journal of Ecumenical Studies* 40, nos. 1-2 (2003): 26-47. The most critical review is by a Sinologist, one who seems to think of Confucianism less as a philosophical than a cultural tradition—see Bryan W. Van Norden, review in *Philosophy East and West* 53, no. 3 (2003): 413-17, plus Neville's clarifying and corrective "Response to Bryan W. Van Norden's Review of *Boston Confucianism*," in *Philosophy East and West* 53, no. 3 (2003): 417-20.

[49]Jung Sun Oh, *A Korean Theology of Human Nature: With Special Attention to the Works of Robert Cummings Neville and Tu Wei-Ming* (Lanham, MD: University Press of America, 2005). There is also an extensive Confucian-Christian dialogue and comparative theological enterprise, one of the most recent volumes of which is Paulos Zhanzhu Huang, *Confronting Confucian Understandings of the Christian Doctrine of Salvation: A Systematic Theological Analysis of the Basic Problems in the Confucian-Christian Dialogue* (Leiden: Brill, 2009).

more particularly? Let me make two general comments in this regard. First, as a philosophical movement informed by "the rationalist egalitarianism of the European Enlightenment mixed with vigorous ethnic and minority communities from all over the world"—Neville's description of Boston's "primal culture"[50]—the Confucianism on both banks of the Charles River is admittedly elitist, even "brahminist," as Neville confesses Bostonians have been considered.[51] This may be as it should be since Boston Confucianism is a philosophical "school" (here loosely considered), not a mass movement. In that sense, the trajectory that charts its emergence and its anticipated trends may be said to correspond to the historical role played by the Reformed tradition in Evangelicalism especially, which has certainly been much more dominant theologically than the pietist movement, whether following through Wesley or other streams. As the Bostonians are leading the charge to take seriously Confucianism in world philosophical discourse, so also have Reformed Evangelicals traditionally been major players at the helm of the evangelical theological enterprise.

From a broader Asian American perspective beyond the evangelical world, however, the Boston Confucian project needs translation so that it can be made more relevant beyond the circle of the philosophically initiated elite. Filial piety and ritual propriety, for example, are important and central themes not only for East Asians but also for Asian Americans and, if Tu, Neville and company are right, for the world. In that case, the expansion of such notions into global philosophical context requires an additional step, one that involves the possibility of its trickling down to the wider masses. Granted, philosophy is intrinsically an elitist discourse, so in that sense, to think or talk about any "democratization" of either Boston Confucianism or Asian American philosophical inquiry may be hoping for too much. At the same time, perhaps what could be expected is either expansion from Boston (to include other forms of North American Confucian philosophical discourse) or of the Confucian or East Asian conversation (to include other Asian philosophical discussions). Asian American theologians concerned about rethinking Asian traditions in global context may have much to learn from the development of Boston Confu-

---

[50]Neville, *Boston Confucianism*, p. xxiv.
[51]Ibid., p. xxi.

cianism on this matter, even as specifically theological perspectives can also augment and extend what is being developed in the philosophical discussion. In short, the philosophical dialogues generated "from above"—that is, from the intellectual high ground of Boston Brahmin life—need to be complemented by a Confucianism "from below," one that takes into more substantive consideration life as negotiated around the world by Confucians and others asking questions about filial piety, ritual propriety and so on. If so, then perhaps that discussion can also accompany and inform the theological conversations "from above" emanating from the various citadels of the North American theological academy. What might such an Asian American theology look like?

ASIAN AMERICAN THEOLOGIES: THE STATE OF THE QUESTION

Any survey of Asian American theology within the space constraints of this section will necessarily have to be selective, charting the most important developments. Fortunately, Jonathan Tan's recent book has already overviewed the field,[52] which frees us to focus on those currents that are most pertinent to our own constructive theological task later. Three trajectories deserve comment.

Mainline Protestant voices. We begin with Asian American theologians in mainline Protestant circles. There have been a few in the last generation who began their theological work focused on "accepted" theological tasks and topics, rather than on articulating a specific Asian American theological vision. Most prominent here has been Korean American Sang Hyun Lee, who achieved his reputation as a Jonathan Edwards scholar and has taught since 1980 at Princeton Theological Seminary.[53] Although Lee has published a number of articles and essays on Asian American theological issues over the years, by and large his contributions have been in Edwardsian scholarship. In general, Lee is better known as a Reformed theologian who happens to be Asian American rather than as an Asian American theologian who does Reformed theology.[54] More recently, his book on Asian American theology high-

---

[52]Jonathan Y. Tan, *Introducing Asian American Theologies* (Maryknoll, NY: Orbis, 2008).

[53]Sang Hyun Lee, *The Philosophical Theology of Jonathan Edwards* (Princeton, NJ: Princeton University Press, 1988).

[54]This is exemplified in Lee, "Jonathan Edwards's Dispositional Conception of the Trinity: A Resource for Contemporary Reformed Theology," in David Willis and Michael Welker, eds., *Toward*

lights the themes of marginality and liminality, central to the Asian American experience.[55] It is here that Lee's Asian American identity comes to the forefront, even if one might ask what is unique to the Asian American experience of either marginality or liminality from that of other ethnic groups in our age of globalization. Yet it may also be precisely insights into marginality and liminality that enable Lee to contribute as an Asian American to a discourse with wider theological purchase beyond his ethnic community, especially when engaged multidimensionally across economic and political arenas.[56]

Parallel to Lee in the Reformed tradition (serving as president of the World Alliance of Reformed Churches from 1997 to 2004) but moving in a very different direction has been the Taiwanese American Choan Seng Song. Song began with a doctoral dissertation on Karl Barth and Paul Tillich (Union Theological Seminary, 1965) but gradually was convinced of the need to theologize more explicitly and intentionally from Asian sources. By the time he arrived to teach at the Pacific School of Religion—a multidenominational divinity school in Berkeley, California, with formal affiliations with the United Church of Christ, the United Methodist Church and the Christian Church (Disciples of Christ)—in 1985 (with which he continues to remain affiliated), he was firmly committed to a research and writing program that involved the retrieval and appropriation of Asian traditions for the theological task.[57] For Song, however, that does not mean that his theological work is relevant only in Asian contexts. Rather, Song emphasizes the importance of local or contextual theologies that are pertinent across the Asian diaspora in a globally

---

the Future of Reformed Theology: Tasks, Topics, Traditions (Grand Rapids: Eerdmans, 1999), pp. 444-55. Otherwise, Lee has published a handful of essays on Asian American theology, one of which has been reprinted variously: "Pilgrimage and Home in the Wilderness of Marginality: Symbols and Context in Asian American Theology," Princeton Seminary Bulletin 16, no. 1 (1995): 49-64.

[55]Sang Hyun Lee, From a Liminal Place: An Asian American Theology (Minneapolis: Fortress, 2010).

[56]See Anselm Kyongsuk Min, "The Political Economy of Marginality: Comments on Jung Young Lee, Marginality: The Key to Multicultural Theology," Journal of Asian and Asian American Theology 1 (1996): 82-94.

[57]Song has written many books, including Christian Mission in Reconstruction: An Asian Analysis (Madras: The Christian Literature Society, 1975; repr., Maryknoll, NY: Orbis, 1977), Tell Us Our Names: Story Theology from an Asian Perspective (Maryknoll, NY: Orbis, 1984), Theology from the Womb of Asia (Maryknoll, NY: Orbis, 1986) and Third-Eye Theology: Theology in Formation in Asian Settings, rev. ed. (Maryknoll, NY: Orbis, 1991). Song's theological trilogy will no doubt constitute his legacy: C. S. Song, Jesus, the Crucified People (New York: Crossroad, 1990; repr., Minneapolis: Fortress, 1996), Jesus and the Reign of God (Minneapolis: Fortress, 1993) and Jesus in the Power of the Spirit (Minneapolis: Fortress, 1994).

shrinking world, while also insisting that Asian sources invite a narrative hermeneutical and methodological approach to theology that is applicable not
only to the formulation of Asian theology but also to the theological enterprise as a whole.[58] In other words, Song has never understood his working
with Asian materials and ideas as thereby circumscribing his audience. Instead,
the what and the how of Asian theological reflection is relevant both to Asian
Americans and to the wider theological conversation. The response to Song's
oeuvre so far, however, has been mixed: some are appreciative of his efforts to
think consistently and deeply from out of Asian sources while others are leery
about what they feel are uncritical deployments of such for Christian theological reflection.

A third theologian has turned more explicitly to imagining an American
future constituted by many voices. Fumitaka Matsuoka, the Robert Gordon
Sproul Professor of Theology emeritus at Pacific School of Religion, argues
that American peoplehood has been forged historically upon the anvil of
learning about new cultures and languages, that this has been marginalized or
lost over time, and that Asian American epistemological perspectives can re-
invigorate both the discussion about and quest for American identity in the
globalizing era of the twenty-first century.[59] He urges a hybridized or "am-
phibolous faith," one defined by a plural epistemology and consciousness that
is commensurate with a view of reality as multiple—a "non-singular vision of
a web of relationships," as one section title puts it.[60] While writing as a
Christian theologian, Matsuoka strives in this volume to reflect the amphiboly
he calls for so that, for instance, he urges consideration of whether and how
the monotheistic foundations of American religious life might be recon-
figured either in nontheistic (thus intersecting more directly with Asian traditions) or at least multitheistic terms. To avoid a debilitating relativism,
however, a normative telos of such a religious and political vision is required.
Matsuoka suggests that the goal is less a destination than the relational and
dynamic shape of the path required to be taken by many people groups with

---

[58]E.g., C. S. Song, *The Believing Heart: An Invitation to Story Theology* (Minneapolis: Fortress, 1999).
[59]Fumitaka Matsuoka, *Learning to Speak a New Tongue: Imagining a Way That Holds People Together—An Asian American Conversation* (Eugene, OR: Pickwick, 2011).
[60]Ibid., p. 97.

different value systems who now must have an implicit trust in others even as all yearn for belonging within an always-altering landscape. His political point is that the building of any nation is never complete, even as the religious perspective aligned to this also presumes that faith is always *in via*. I would insist that from a pent-evangelical Christian perspective, the *whereto* dimension of the question always has to be asked: Christian theology is inextricably teleological, normed according to the biblical revelation of God in Christ, even if always also tentative in anticipating the coming reign of God.

Many other Asian American Protestants have also begun registering specifically Asian perspectives in their theological work. Jung Young Lee, Andrew Sung Park and others from ecumenical perspectives, and Rita Nakashima Brock and her colleagues from a feminist perspective—all have brought distinctively Asian voices into the theological arena, in the process proposing that the Christian theological tradition as a whole has much to gain from engaging Asian viewpoints.[61] Fumitaka Matsuoka and Eleazar S. Fernandez's edited book *Realizing the America of Our Hearts* provides representative windows into contemporary Asian American theological trends: those that relate to the reflective aspects of religious belief and to the normative dimensions of religious praxis.[62] So their book is at once a theological and a religious text. Some essayists reflect theologically out of the depths of their Asian American experiences (e.g., through the internment of Japanese Americans during World War II, the refugee experiences of South Asian Americans, or the rioting that targeted Korean American shops during the racial uprising in Los Angeles in 1992), while others attempt theological reconstruction in dialogue with primordial symbols of the Asian religious consciousness (e.g., a

---

[61]E.g., Jung Young Lee, *The Theology of Change: A Christian Concept of God in an Eastern Perspective* (Maryknoll, NY: Orbis, 1979), *Marginality: The Key to Multicultural Theology* (Minneapolis: Fortress, 1995) and *The Trinity in Asian Perspective* (Nashville: Abingdon, 1996); Andrew Sung Park, *The Wounded Heart of God: The Asian Concept of Han and the Christian Doctrine of Sin* (Nashville: Abingdon, 1993), *Racial Conflict and Healing: An Asian-American Theological Perspective* (Maryknoll, NY: Orbis, 1996) and *Triune Atonement: Christ's Healing for Sinners, Victims, and the Whole Creation* (Louisville: Westminster John Knox, 2009); and Rita Nakashima Brock, *Journeys by Heart: A Christology of Erotic Power* (New York: Crossroad, 1988) and, with Jung Ha Kim, Kwok Pui-Lan and Seung Ai Yang, *Off the Menu: Asian and Asian North American Women's Religion and Theology* (Louisville: Westminster John Knox, 2007).
[62]Fumitaka Matsuoka and Eleazar S. Fernandez, eds., *Realizing the America of Our Hearts: Theological Voices of Asian Americans* (St. Louis: Chalice, 2003).

theology of *Tao*-ology [a theology of "the way"], or a theology of *han* [a theology of "brokenheartedness"[63]]). Prevalent throughout, however, are themes, metaphors and images birthed out of the immigrant experience: theology in quest of, journey theology, diaspora theology, theology of hospitality, theology "betwixt and between" (neither Asian nor American), theology of homelessness, theology of hybridity, theology at/over the boundary and so on.[64] In the process, readers catch a direct glimpse of how the nature of Christian theology is transformed in light of Asian American religious experiences and, by extension, get a sense of how other religious beliefs and ideas are also transformed as a result of immigration (e.g., both the "Americanization" of Buddhism and the "Buddhification" of Christianity).

Roman Catholic articulations. Beyond Protestant Asian American theology, a few comments should be made about Asian American theologians in the Roman Catholic tradition. Here we find Korean Americans such as Anselm Min, who teaches at Claremont Graduate School, sitting across the ecumenical table from those like Sang Lee. While Lee's focus has been on Edwards, Min, nurtured in a classical Roman Catholic theological education, is as comfortable with philosophers like Hegel as he is with "magisterial" philosophical theologians like Aquinas. Nevertheless, Min brings these major voices of the tradition to bear on questions and issues most relevant to the Catholic Church's global experience, such as development and liberation, globalization, and religious pluralism.[65]

Perhaps the most prominent, and certainly the most prolific, Asian American Catholic theologian today is Peter C. Phan, a native of Vietnam and

---

[63]The Korean concept of *han* is notoriously difficult to translate into English. At one level, *han* refers to the pain experienced by Koreans in their history of subjugation under foreign conquerors—hence a theology of *han* is also a theology of brokenheartedness or of captivity. Andrew Sung Park's essay, "A Theology of Tao (Way) Han, Sin, and Evil," in Matsuoka and Fernandez (pp. 41-54), talks about *han* as "a critical wound generated by unjust psychosomatic, social, political, economic, and cultural repression and oppression" (p. 42), and uses this concept as a springboard to rethink the Christian doctrine of sin as individual, collective and structural realities (see also earlier note on Park's work).

[64]A previous volume sounding similar notes is Eleazar S. Fernandez and Fernando F. Segovia, eds., *A Dream Unfinished: Theological Reflections on America from the Margins* (Maryknoll, NY: Orbis, 2001).

[65]Anselm Kyongsuk Min, *Dialectic of Salvation: Issues in Theology of Liberation* (Albany: State University of New York Press, 1989), *The Solidarity of Others in a Divided World: A Postmodern Theology After Postmodernism* (New York: T & T Clark, 2004) and *Paths to the Triune God: An Encounter Between Aquinas and Recent Theologies* (Notre Dame, IN: University of Notre Dame Press, 2005).

current Ignacio Ellacuria Chair of Catholic Social Thought at Georgetown University. Like other senior Asian American theologians, Phan also cut his theological teeth on the major thoroughfares of the tradition, writing his first books on the church fathers and important contemporary theologians.[66] Upon establishing himself, however, he has gradually turned his gaze to Asia, beginning with a study of Christian/Catholic theological enculturation in his homeland.[67] In the last decade, Phan has increasingly written on Asian and Asian American theological issues, traversing fluently between Asia and the United States, between the theological tradition and its contemporary horizon, between Catholic and ecumenical environments, between global and local contexts, and, in terms of theological disciplines, between missiology and systematic theology.[68]

From an Asian American theological perspective, Phan's work is pathbreaking precisely because of his ability to cross what to most others would be insurmountable chasms. This can be appreciated from his essay "The Dragon and the Eagle: Toward a Vietnamese American Theology,"[69] wherein he provides phenomenological depth and existential richness to the interstitiality and liminality that characterize the immigrant experience, and wherein he is able to give voice to the exilic sense of journeying between two cultures, two churches and two continents. Thus the theological themes that surface tap into Asian cosmological intuitions on the one hand (e.g., with the themes

---

[66]Phan's books in the 1980s were *Social Thought*, Message of the Fathers of the Church 20 (Wilmington, DE: Michael Glazier, 1984), *Grace and the Human Condition*, Message of the Fathers of the Church 15 (Wilmington, DE: Michael Glazier, 1988), *Culture and Eschatology: The Iconographical Vision of Paul Evdokimov*, American University Studies Series VII: Theology and Religion 1 (New York: Peter Lang, 1985) and *Eternity in Time: A Study in Karl Rahner's Eschatology* (Selinsgrove, PA: Susquehanna University Press, 1988).

[67]Peter C. Phan, *Mission and Catechesis: Alexandre de Rhodes and Inculturation in Seventeenth-Century Vietnam* (Maryknoll, NY: Orbis, 1998).

[68]E.g., James H. Kroeger and Peter C. Phan, *The Future of the Asian Churches: The Asian Synod and Ecclesia in Asia* (Quezon City, Philippines: Claretian Publications, 2002); Peter C. Phan, ed., *The Asian Synod: Texts and Commentaries* (Maryknoll, NY: Orbis, 2002); Peter C. Phan, *Vietnamese-American Catholics* (New York and Mahwah, NJ: Paulist, 2005); and Peter C. Phan, ed., *Christianity in Asia* (Oxford: Wiley-Blackwell, 2010). Phan has also written a trilogy: *Christianity with an Asian Face: Asian American Theology in the Making* (Maryknoll, NY: Orbis, 2003), *In Our Own Tongues: Perspectives from Asia on Mission and Inculturation* (Maryknoll, NY: Orbis, 2003) and *Being Religious Interreligiously: Asian Perspectives on Interfaith Dialogue* (Maryknoll, NY: Orbis, 2004).

[69]See Phan, *Christianity with an Asian Face*, chap. 11.

of heaven-earth-humanity playing a central role), while sketching a christology that bridges traditional concepts with those drawn from the Asian and immigrant experiences on the other hand (e.g., Jesus Christ the Son of God now viewed also as the marginal immigrant, elder brother and the divinely incarnate ancestor). The result, at least in part, calls for a contemplative spirituality suitable for the Asian American mind and heart, a liturgical inculturation relevant to transnational and globalization trends as these are being played out especially in the North American context, and a reign of God ecclesiology that nurtures hope and anticipation without minimizing the importance of the church in the present time. In each of these ways, Phan models how Asian American themes are relevant not only for Asians, nor only for Asian Americans, but also for the enrichment of the church C/catholic—all the while without denying the distinctiveness and particularity of the Vietnamese American experience.

Asian American biblical studies. A third area of Asian American theology consists of advances made in biblical scholarship. Here I will only very briefly mention the major contributions.

- The work of established and senior biblical scholars such as K. K. Yeo (who is Chinese American), while not intended to be limited specifically to Asian American issues, has implications not only for crosscultural biblical scholarship but also for the Asian American evangelical theological endeavor more specifically;[70]

- Collections of essays produced by those working within the orbit of the Society of Biblical Literature are currently at the vanguard of what is happening among Asian American biblical scholars;[71]

---

[70]Yeo has been a very productive scholar—e.g., Khiok-Khng Yeo, *Rhetorical Interaction in 1 Corinthians 8 and 10: A Formal Analysis with Preliminary Suggestions for a Chinese, Cross-cultural Hermeneutic* (New York: Brill, 1995); *What Has Jerusalem to Do with Beijing: Biblical Interpretation from a Chinese Perspective* (Harrisburg, PA: Trinity Press International, 1998); *Chairman Mao Meets the Apostle Paul: Christianity, Communism, and the Hope of China* (Grand Rapids: Brazos, 2002); *Navigating Romans Through Cultures: Challenging Readings by Charting a New Course* (New York: T & T Clark, 2004); and *Musing with Confucius and Paul: Toward a Chinese Christian Theology* (Eugene, OR: Cascade, 2008).

[71]E.g., Tat-Siong Benny Liew and Gale A. Yee, eds., *The Bible in Asian America*, Semeia 90-91 (Atlanta: Society of Biblical Literature, 2002); Mary Foskett and Jeffrey Kah-Jin Kuan, eds., *Ways of Being, Ways of Reading: Asian American Biblical Interpretation* (St. Louis: Chalice, 2006).

- A number of younger scholars working at the interface of biblical studies and postcolonial studies or at the intersection of biblical studies and Asian American studies particularly have begun to produce monographs in conscious dialogue and substantial engagement with the Asian American experience;[72]

- A growing number of works on homiletics, in particular by those trained in biblical studies, highlights the recognition that Asian American preaching is not only an important subfield of inquiry but also that it is informed by rigorous biblical scholarship—both of which are so important for maturing Asian American congregations and ecclesial communities;[73]

- There have also been a good number of Asian American Evangelicals who have earned their PhDs in biblical studies but who have not yet begun to publish explicitly from an Asian American perspective;[74] I turn momentarily to consider this lack of interaction with Asian American perspectives among these and other evangelical scholars.

Insofar as biblical studies inevitably informs theological reflection, those interested in the evolution of Asian American theology should pay close attention to the work that is being done by Asian American biblical scholars. This is especially important since the lines between biblical scholarship and theological thinking are increasingly blurred and since few Asian American biblical scholars see their work as limited to the exegetical issues of "what the text meant" as opposed to the more theological tasks of deciphering "what the text means."

The preceding does no more than highlight some of the major developments in the field of Asian American theology. Depending on how one defines "evangelical," the achievements noted above have involved some scholars with

---

[72]E.g., Uriah Y. Kim, *Decolonizing Josiah: Toward a Postcolonial Reading of the Deuteronomistic History* (Sheffield, UK: Sheffield Phoenix, 2005) and *Identity and Loyalty in the David Story: A Postcolonial Reading*, Hebrew Bible Monographs 22 (Sheffield, UK: Sheffield Phoenix, 2008); and Tat-Siong Benny Liew, *What Is Asian American Biblical Hermeneutics? Reading the New Testament* (Honolulu: University of Hawaii Press, 2008).

[73]See Mary F. Foskett, *Interpreting the Bible: Approaching the Text in Preparation for Preaching* (Minneapolis: Fortress, 2009) and, earlier, Eunjoo Mary Kim, *Preaching the Presence of God: A Homiletic from an Asian American Perspective* (Valley Forge, PA: Judson Press, 1999).

[74]Leading the way here are the biblical studies faculty at Logos Evangelical Seminary (Silas Chan, Hing Wong, John Wu, Jeffrey Lu and Chloe Sun) and International Theological Seminary (Kyu Sam Han), both in El Monte, California, among others.

evangelical sympathies if not commitments. Yet institutionally speaking, the major steps forward have taken place in mainline Protestant and Roman Catholic environments. In effect, the cumulative thrust of these theological developments can be understood as providing a range of responses to the rhetorical question: "What if Paul had gone to China (instead of to Rome)?"[75] although in reality here the Asian diaspora has returned to the Western world.

Set within the wider context of Asian American philosophy, especially as expressed in the Boston Confucian discussion, and Asian American studies, it is also fair to say that there is a noticeable pluralism of interpretive frames of reference in Asian American theology. Some might consider such diversity to be debilitating, although others opt to approach the theological task as having many resources that can generate further conversation. At one level, it may well be that this multiplicity of voices and perspectives simply represents the postmodern, post-Western and postcolonial academy. At another level, of course, it represents the many cultures, languages and traditions of Asia as well as the globalizing forces that move people across oceans and national borders in our time. These have been, perennially, marginal and marginalized voices, but perhaps precisely for such reasons, they are well positioned in the present time to echo the marginalized person and message of God in Christ.[76]

From a theological perspective, then, I want to argue that the many soundings from the Asian American diaspora to be trumpeted in this volume reflect the many tribes, peoples and languages that are intended to manifest the coming reign of God. I will earnestly attend to this argument in chapter four. For now, however, we need to focus specifically on trends in Asian American evangelical theology, both in light of the preceding discussion and in anticipation of the one to come.

---

[75]I adapt here the title of the essay by Gerald R. McDermott, "What If Paul Had Been from China? Reflections on the Possibility of Revelation in Non-Christian Religions," in John G. Stackhouse Jr., *No Other Gods Before Me? Evangelicals and the Challenge of World Religions* (Grand Rapids: Baker Academic, 2001), pp. 17-35.
[76]This is the thesis of Lee, *Marginality*; see esp. his chap. 4.

3

THE LEGACY OF EVANGELICAL THEOLOGY

Asian American Reception and Interrogations

In this chapter, we drill deeper into the inner logic of Asian American evangelical theology. Why has the Asian American nature of evangelical theology been relatively underplayed when compared to Asian evangelical theology and to Asian American theology in mainline Protestant and Roman Catholic circles? This chapter argues that there are many reasons for this and that they relate both to the legacy of the (white) North American evangelical endeavor as a whole and to how this tradition has been received and internalized by Asian American Evangelicals.

The three sections to come introduce the whence of Asian American evangelical theology and its largely conservative ethos, explore how this conservatism is the result of internalizing the theo-logic of the dominant (Western) evangelical culture, and conclude by urging Asian American Evangelicals to live more intentionally into and out of the particularity, sociality and historicity of their experiences. While Asian American evangelical theology has been by and large consonant with that of the (white) evangelical establishment, it has not found much of its own voice. Part of the goal is to clarify why and how the current generation of Asian American Evangelicals faces a fork in the road: to allow nonethnic (read: white) Evangelicals to continue to set the theological agenda that minimizes or marginalizes their perspectives, or to assert why the historicity and particularity of the Asian American history and experience is important not only for Asian American evangelical theology specifically but also for the evangelical theological task as a whole.

If the first two chapters have attempted to map the broader global and wider Asian American theological landscapes, this chapter conducts a self-critical analysis of aspects of Asian American evangelical thinking. While there is more diversity underneath the Asian American evangelical label than many think, there is also some justification for discussing it in terms I present. This chapter probes some of these taken-for-granted features of the Asian American evangelical mentality that have inhibited creative and constructive theological reflection. Note, however, that the point is not to merely be critical of the white evangelical theological establishment; rather, the point is to highlight how, in our contemporary global context, the evangelical tradition can be expanded, renewed and developed in dialogue with non-Euro-American conversation partners. Positively put, then, the following intends to open up a way forward for the pent-evangelical theological path that chapters four and following chart.

ASIAN AMERICAN EVANGELICAL THEOLOGY: WHENCE AND W(H)ITHER?

It is fair to say that we are still at the very beginning stages of Asian American evangelical theologizing.[1] As we shall see, we can only speak about Asian American evangelical theology if understood in a very broad sense. The following sketches three streams of such reflection, which enables comprehension of its largely conservative instincts.

Particularly for Asian Americans from an East Asian background, the Confucian emphasis on filial piety plays out in their evangelical spirituality. Some of the earliest works on Asian American evangelical theology, therefore, were focused on how especially second-generation Asian Americans could honor their parents while following Christ.[2] This was and remains an especially important matter if the immigrant generation were non-Christians. Beyond this is the pressure of perfectionist expectations by parents, not to mention having also to live into the "model minority" stereotype outside the home.

---

[1]One of the few forays into the question remains Young Lee Hertig, "Why Asian American Evangelical Theologies?" *Journal of Asian and Asian American Theology* 7 (2005–2006): 1-23.

[2]See Jeanette Yep, ed., *Following Jesus Without Dishonoring Your Parents: Asian American Discipleship* (Downers Grove, IL: InterVarsity Press, 1998), and Nikki A. Toyama and Tracey Gee, eds., *More Than Serving Tea: Asian American Women on Expectations, Relationships, Leadership and Faith* (Downers Grove, IL: IVP Books, 2006).

When combined with the deferential East Asian posture, many Asian Americans develop a self-inferiority complex—devastating within a culture of shame—particularly when having also to confront linguistic challenges in navigating through school and then a career.

The ecclesial or congregational domain is also one where Asian American Evangelicals have expended some effort. This is to be expected given the long history of ethnic churches and the many debates, not to mention challenges, related to assimilation to the dominant culture. Within the literature on Asian American Evangelicalism, we find works on pastoral ministry (designed to equip ministers to cross generational, cultural, ecclesial, gender and other divides),[3] congregational health and effectiveness (which provide models for ethnic-dominant, bilingual and even mixed ecclesial communities),[4] and even a growing number of pan-Asian or pan-ethnic visions of the future (which often deal with the issues of race and racialization within an evangelical paradigm).[5] Asian American Evangelicals have focused some of their energies on these ecclesiological matters. What can be hoped for is that these more practical, ministerial and missional emphases will also translate, in due course, into more robust ecclesiological and theological reflection.

Recent developments in Asian American evangelical theology. It is at the more properly understood theological level that Asian American Evangelicals can be said to be barely out of the starting gate. Still, even in these gestational times, some potential routes for development can be discerned. One is a collection of essays that appeared in 2006.[6] Published by the L2 Foundation, an organization devoted to Asian American leadership and legacy development, this is the first book to appear on the topic of Asian American *evangelical* theology. The six essayists reflect

---

[3]E.g., Ken Uyeda Fong, *Pursuing the Pearl: A Comprehensive Resource for Multi-Asian Ministry* (Valley Forge, PA: Judson Press, 1999), and Russell Yee, *Worship on the Way: Exploring Asian North American Christian Experience* (Valley Forge, PA: Judson Press, 2012).

[4]See Peter Cha, S. Steve Kang and Helen Lee, eds., *Growing Healthy Asian American Congregations* (Downers Grove, IL: IVP Books, 2006), and M. Sydney Park, Soong-Chan Rah and Al Tizon, eds., *Honoring the Generations: Learning with Asian North American Congregations* (Valley Forge, PA: Judson Press, 2012).

[5]Elizabeth Conde-Frazier, S. Steve Kang and Gary A. Parrett, *A Many-Colored Kingdom: Multicultural Dynamics for Spiritual Formation* (Grand Rapids: Baker Academic, 2004), and Kenneth A. Mathews and M. Sydney Park, *The Post-Racial Church: A Biblical Framework for Multiethnic Reconciliation* (Grand Rapids: Kregel Academic, 2011).

[6]D. J. Chuang and Timothy Tseng, eds., *Conversations: Asian American Evangelical Theologies in Formation* (Washington, DC: L2 Foundation, 2006).

the diversity of the AAE community. David Yoo, a historian at Claremont McKenna College, surveys (with two collaborators) the pre–World War II histories of Japanese and Korean American Christians and urges that religion needs to be factored into immigration and race analyses of these communities, even as Tim Tseng, a historian of American Christianity and founder of the Institute for the Study of Asian American Christianity, exposes the "color blindness" of American church history and provides some hermeneutical options for moving beyond orientalist or assimilationist models of the Asian American Christian experience. A practical theologian at Trinity Evangelical Divinity School, Peter Cha, discusses the challenges involved in identity formation among second-generation Korean Americans. An intriguing chapter is missiologist James Zo's (affiliated with Logos Evangelical Seminary in El Monte, California) insightful analysis of how structural and power issues complicate the assessment of racism, prejudice and discrimination on both sides of the American and Asian American equation. For a volume on evangelical theology, the two explicitly theological contributions are by historical theologians: Paul Lim (who specializes in early modern England, has taught at Gordon-Conwell Theological Seminary and now is, as of the time of this writing, at Vanderbilt University) reveals the importance of biography in the construction of any Asian American evangelical theology, and Jeffrey Jue (a post-Reformation historian at Westminster Theological Seminary) seeks a way beyond both modernist experientialism and postmodernist subjectivism by returning to the gospel. The conversational approach of each chapter in the volume invites others to join in the discussion.

A second line of development lies with Asian American evangelical women, many of whom are also working in the area of biblical studies.[7] A recent volume includes ten chapters, most springing off female biblical characters, all set within what Young Lee Hertig calls a "yinist paradigm" that is neither merely feminist (nor womanist nor mujerista) nor yet acquiescent to the patriarchal structures dominant within Asian American Evangelicalism in particular and (white) evangelical theology in general.[8] *Mirrored Reflections* is thus a groundbreaking and

---

[7]See Young Lee Hertig and Chloe Sun, eds., *Mirrored Reflections: Reframing Biblical Characters* (Eugene, OR: Wipf & Stock, 2010).

[8]See Hertig's lead chapter, "The Asian American Alternative to Feminism: A *Yinist* Paradigm," in Hertig and Sun, eds., *Mirrored Reflections*, pp. 3-14.

paradigmatic book not only for Asian American theology but also for evangelical biblical hermeneutics. It opens up space for Asian American women's readings of the Bible without mimicking other feminist agendas; it embraces reader-response approaches while honoring the scriptural horizon; it boldly explores a countercultural contextualism, polyphonous multivocalism, and intersubjective perspectivism without lapsing into relativism; and it insists on the need for us to come to terms with pluralism, globalization and transnationalism in the pursuit of faithful Christian discipleship in our time. Arguably, this is biblical interpretation and theological reflection at its best: engaging, subversive, transformative and salvific—for women and men.[9] Such paths opened up by Asian American evangelical women may well be what is most generative and productive for Asian American evangelical theology in the longer run.

The contributions of Hertig and company run parallel to other Asian American evangelical voices that find themselves betwixt-and-between the center of the evangelical movement and the mainline Protestant communities. Soong-Chan Rah's work mediates these spaces as representative of a promising path in contemporary Asian American evangelical theology.[10] The potency of Rah's argument is that he speaks not only to Asian American Evangelicals but also to the evangelical theological establishment as a whole. This is because his is a call for the church to let go of its individualism, consumerism, materialism and racism—all effects of Western culture—in order to be freed from its cultural captivity.[11] Rah's analysis, however, can find deeper Asian American traction, particularly if wedded to the uncompromising call for living into the Asian American identity by theologians such as Jonathan Tran.[12] The latter empowers a distinctive Asian American voice,

---

[9]Perhaps in contrast to the dominant strands of Asian American evangelical biblical interpretation that have swallowed Western hermeneutical methods almost hook, line and sinker; see Andrew Yueking Lee, "Reading the Bible as an Asian American: Issues in Asian American Biblical Interpretation," in Viji Nakka-Cammauf and Timothy Tseng, eds., *Asian American Christianity: A Reader* (Castro Valley, CA: The Institute for the Study of Asian American Christianity, 2009), pp. 60-69.

[10]Soong-Chan Rah, *The Next Evangelicalism: Freeing the Church from Western Cultural Captivity* (Downers Grove, IL: IVP Books, 2009).

[11]From a hermeneutical perspective, see the similar argument of E. Randolph Richards and Brandon J. O'Brien, *Misreading Scripture with Western Eyes: Removing Cultural Blinders to Better Understand the Bible* (Downers Grove, IL: IVP Books, 2012).

[12]See Jonathan Tran, "A Few Things I Want from Asian American Evangelicals," in Nakka-Cammauf and Tseng, *Asian American Christianity*, pp. 243-51; cf. also Tran, "Identity as Missiology," *SANACS Journal* 1 (2009): 29-40.

albeit one that is not parochial since it addresses larger ecclesial (and perhaps even social) concerns.[13]

The fact of the matter is, however, that there is little else available on Asian American evangelical theology and that Asian American Evangelicals are still a long way off from thinking theologically as Asian Americans. Part of the reason is that many Asian American Evangelicals, even those who are theologically trained, have basically replicated the majority evangelical (white) approaches to Scripture. Further, many second-generation Asian Americans have adopted the assimilationist experience as their model and have presumed that an "American universalism" maps onto a biblical universalism.[14] The result is the subordination of their racial and ethnic identities and modes of thinking. Among the many reasons for this is the dominant conservatism of Asian American culture, especially within ecclesial communities of East Asian descent (e.g., Chinese, Korean, Japanese and Vietnamese churches). As such, Asian Americans are content to persist with the status quo of evangelical theology inherited from their (white) evangelical teachers.

Asian American evangelical conservatism. The phenomenon of East Asian or Confucian cultural conservatism is, of course, a complicated one to untangle. On the one hand, there is something to the stereotype of East Asian Confucianism as essentially androcentric (in subordinating women to men), patriarchal (sustained by the tradition's emphasis on filial piety) and authoritarian (preserved in the king-subject and older-younger brother aspects of the "fivefold relations"). On the other hand, like most extended cultural traditions, Confucianism has been neither static nor free from dissenting trends that have attempted to retrieve, reappropriate and, when necessary, jettison these tradi-

---

[13]Matthew Soerens and Jenny Hwang, *Welcoming the Stranger: Justice, Compassion and Truth in the Immigration Debate* (Downers Grove, IL: IVP Books, 2009) is another example of Asian American Evangelicals speaking into wider conversations, precisely the thrust of this book and part of its goal in terms of motivating Asian American evangelical theological inquiry. I will return to discuss the proposals of this volume in more depth in chapter six.

[14]This is my way of putting what other Asian American scholars have also observed; see both Antony W. Alumkal, "The Scandal of the 'Model Minority' Mind? The Bible and Second-Generation Asian American Evangelicals," and Timothy Tseng, "Second-Generation Chinese Evangelical Use of the Bible in Identity Discourse in North America," both in Tat-siong Benny Liew, *The Bible in Asian America: Semeia 90-91* (Atlanta: The Society of Biblical Literature, 2002), pp. 237-50 and pp. 251-67, respectively.

tional doctrines for the late modern world.[15] Certainly, in the North American context, there are progressive forces at work especially among second and later generations of Asian Americans, but equally certainly, the weight of portable cultural and philosophical traditions like Confucianism (see chapter two) means that change occurs slowly.

Within the Asian American evangelical community, the gradual transformation of the inherited cultural conservatism is certainly being played out, even if at a much slower pace than in nonevangelical contexts. One the one side, the gospel is understood as providing a critical perspective on culture— on which I will say more momentarily; on the other side, however, there are certain biblical themes such as honoring of parents and the submission of women (read off the surface of some Pauline texts) that resonate with the filial piety of especially Confucian cultures, and these have inevitably become central issues for the forging of Asian American identities.[16] Hence Asian American immigrants who are attracted to Christianity are often drawn to evangelical Protestantism because it provides a similarly conservative worldview, one that enables their acculturation into American society. For these reasons, Confucian conservatism morphs, among Asian American Protestants, into a form of evangelical conservatism.

To be sure, the exact role of Confucianism behind Asian American evangelical conservatism might be debated among scholars, particularly since the appropriation of the Confucian tradition across the Asian American diaspora is not all of one stripe. At the same time, even if other Asian traditions were to be factored into the matrix of Asian American life, many are informed by a kind of patriarchal, hierarchical and authoritarian conservatism that functions similarly in East Asian Confucian culture. In short, perhaps the "model minority" stereotype, as contested as might be such a designation, that characterizes much of the Asian American experience contributes to the conservatism that permeates Asian American Evangelicalism.

North American evangelical conservatism and its implications. But high-

---

[15]See here Daniel A. Bell, *China's New Confucianism: Politics and Everyday Life in a Changing Society* (Princeton, NJ: Princeton University Press, 2008), chap. 3.

[16]E.g., Tom Lin, *Losing Face and Finding Grace: 12 Bible Studies for Asian Americans* (Downers Grove, IL: InterVarsity Press, 1996), esp. part 1.

lighting East Asian conservatism tells only one side of the story about why Asian Americans tend to be contented with and passive recipients of the theology of the dominant evangelical culture. The other half of this tale has to do with North American conservatism as well. Of course, historically, North American Evangelicalism was formed out of a long history of reaction to mainline Protestant liberalism. By definition, to be conservative means to resist the forces of change insofar as such changes are thought to compromise the received values of a particular tradition. So while some changes have been embraced, evangelical conservatives have long resisted what are perceived as adjustments to historic Christian orthodoxy foisted upon the North American church by their liberal counterparts.[17] More recently, Evangelicals have also entered into the culture wars in defense of traditional family values and other aspects of the agenda of the Republican Party.

Over time, then, Evangelicals have been led to develop theological arguments for their conservative stances. Most relevant for the Asian American experience is how the dominant evangelical culture has accepted, while slightly redefining, at least more recently, the basic categories of the classical *Christ and Culture* study of H. Richard Niebuhr.[18] Yet historically, Evangelicals have embraced the "Christ against culture" stance, albeit more recently shifting toward the "Christ transforming culture" posture. This involves either, at worst, the rejection of culture, which has traditionally characterized evangelical sectarianism (especially among fundamentalists, the close cousins of Evangelicals),[19] or at best, an ambiguous relationship with culture, one featuring what might be called a cultural hermeneutic of suspicion that is always concerned about syncretism with the world. Culture, in popular evangelical parlance, is almost equivalent to the world, and in that sense, is what humans need to be saved from rather than partake of.

---

[17]There are many versions of this story; my own telling is here: "The Word and the Spirit, or the Spirit and the Word? Exploring the Boundaries of Evangelicalism in Relationship to Modern Pentecostalism," *Trinity Journal* 23, no. 2 (2002): 235-52.

[18]See H. Richard Niebuhr, *Christ and Culture* (1951; repr., San Francisco: Harper Torchlight, 1956); cf. Glen H. Stassen, D. M. Yeager and John Howard Yoder, *Authentic Transformation: A New Vision of Christ and Culture* (Nashville: Abingdon, 1996).

[19]I.e., as manifest in missionary and evangelistic strategies that called on converts to abandon their cultural beliefs and practices in following Christ—e.g., Birgit Meyer, *Translating the Devil: Religion and Modernity Among the Ewe in Ghana* (Trenton, NJ: Africa World Press, 1999).

So how has this played out in Asian American evangelical communities? Most pointedly, Asian American Evangelicals have traditionally understood their Christian conversion to involve either a turning away from their Asian cultural roots or a minimizing of such aspects of their identity. That Christian conversion actually involves Americanization is quite prevalent across the Asian American scene. In my own case growing up, as already indicated in the prologue, we never talked about the importance of Chinese culture; the emphasis at home (my parents were first-generation converts to Christianity) was always on embodying Christian culture. Many Asian Americans thus tend to view their Asian historical and cultural legacies in binary terms: food, dress and music might be retained, because they concern the outward aspects of life, which are incidental anyway to true human identity; but literary, philosophical and religious ideas are to be cautiously approached (at best) since they are probably representative of "the world" and thus antithetical to the gospel.

This confluence of Confucian and evangelical conservatism has been strengthened through the process of theological education. Asian American Evangelicals tend to attend solidly evangelical seminaries because of their conservative commitments. So whereas mainline Protestant seminaries are much more focused on corporate identities, evangelical seminaries, and their curricula, focus more on personal identities, particularly the formation of spiritual lives in relationship to Christ.[20] What this means is that ethnic identities are minimized as having no more than biological significance, and historical and cultural aspects of Asian identity are accepted only as accidental to identity in Christ. Asian American Evangelicals are first and foremost Christians, and only secondarily, if at all, Asians (although, interestingly, the prevalence of nationalism among Evangelicals means that American identity is much more important than evangelical rhetoric usually lets on). Evangelical theological education thus provides the philosophical and theological apparatus to make sense of such modes of identity construction.

---

[20]Russell Jeung, "Evangelical and Mainline Teachings on Asian American Identity," in Liew and Yee, *Bible in Asian America*, pp. 211-36, reprinted in Nakka-Cammauf and Tseng, *Asian American Christianity*, pp. 197-216.

THE BURDEN OF EVANGELICAL THEOLOGY: A MINORITY REPORT

In the following, I highlight the major epistemological, hermeneutical, methodological and doctrinal aspects of (white) evangelical theology embraced by many Asian American Evangelicals. I argue not that these are the only ways in which Asian American Evangelicals have accommodated to the dominant (white) evangelical subcultural worldview, nor that Asian American evangelical theology can be reduced to these features. I suggest however that these provide some explanation for how many Asian American evangelical theologians view the *Asian* dimension of their work in contextual terms but do not also understand the dominant white theological constructs similarly. The result is that Asian American concerns are not only subordinated but also effectively silenced in many cases. In the following I critically assess this dominant view from the marginal horizons of the Asian American experience.

A (putatively) global epistemology. I begin with the Enlightenment epistemology and its quest for, or presumption to have attained, *the* universal perspective. In their battle against liberalism, Evangelicals have highlighted the importance of developing a biblical worldview.[21] Worldview construction is inevitably an intellectual exercise.[22] What most Evangelicals do not often interrogate is how rooted the worldview quest is in the Enlightenment project. As such, evangelical worldview formulation operates epistemologically according to modernist canons of rationality. This is reinforced in evangelical seminary education variously, not least in the embrace of some form of foundationalism characteristic of the Enlightenment quest for certainty thought to secure evangelical claims to universal truth.[23]

Foundationalism, classically understood, is the view that all beliefs can be justified directly (founded upon) sense experience or reason available to all—hence, universal—rather than inferred from other (subjectively held) beliefs.[24] While Evangelicals are philosophically just as sophisticated as anyone

---

[21] Thus InterVarsity Press has just published, in 2009, the fifth edition of James Sire's *The Universe Next Door: A Basic Worldview Catalog,* a testimony to its popularity at evangelical colleges and universities.

[22] Another popular text among Evangelicals notes its conceptual nature: David K. Naugle, *Worldview: The History of a Concept* (Grand Rapids: Eerdmans, 2002).

[23] As reflected in another popular evangelical textbook: J. P. Moreland and William Lane Craig, *Philosophical Foundations for a Christian Worldview* (Downers Grove, IL: InterVarsity Press, 2003).

[24] Note that the dualism between objectivity and subjectivity is itself a modernist construction; I discuss these matters as well as evangelical forms of foundationalism in my "The Demise of Foun-

else in their defense of foundationalism,[25] more often than not they are epistemological foundationalists for two reasons. Negatively put, epistemic foundationalism is a deterrent to what they see as the threatening alternative of epistemological skepticism, philosophical, if not moral, relativism, and religious and theological pluralism. Positively put, the foundations of Christian knowing are given in the Bible. I will return in a moment to address the hermeneutical issues involved with such an appeal. For the moment, however, I simply note that evangelical foundationalism, in whatever its guise, buttresses its claims to have access to a universal standpoint for (theological) knowledge.

Such a universal vantage point is, of course, related to the Enlightenment quest for certain knowledge. Hence the undermining of foundationalism opens up to perspectivism. Evangelicals resist epistemic perspectivism for the same reasons that they defend foundationalism: because that is felt to be the only way to secure rationally the stability of truth claims. Opening the door to perspectivism invites the multiplicity of views that characterizes the relativism of the postmodern situation. Conservative Evangelicals are thus very concerned about the ascendency of the postmodern agenda.[26]

What does this have to do with Asian American Evangelicalism? My claim is that Asian Americans educated at conservative evangelical seminaries have unwittingly embraced not only the foundationalist epistemology of their teachers but also its attendant applications. In order to ward off epistemic skepticism, moral relativism and theological pluralism, Asian American Evangelicals have also uncritically rejected the perspectivism central to postfoundationalist epistemology.[27] More to the point, the defense of foundationalism is also the defense of the status quo: the universal frame of reference claimed by evangelical

---

dationalism and the Retention of Truth: What Evangelicals Can Learn from C. S. Peirce," *Christian Scholar's Review* 29, no. 3 (Spring 2000): 563-88.

[25]E.g., J. P. Moreland and Garrett DeWeese, "The Premature Report of Foundationalism's Demise," in Millard J. Erickson, Paul Kjoss Helseth and Justin Taylor, eds., *Reclaiming the Center: Confronting Evangelical Accommodation in Postmodern Times* (Wheaton, IL: Crossway, 2004), pp. 81-107.

[26]Thus part 2 of Millard J. Erickson, *Postmodernizing the Faith: Evangelical Responses to the Challenge of Postmodernism* (Grand Rapids: Baker Books, 1998), is titled, "Negative Responses to Postmodernism" and discusses a number of contemporary and recent defenders of classical evangelical faith: David Wells, Thomas Oden and Francis Schaeffer.

[27]As argued, e.g., by Stanley J. Grenz and John R. Franke, *Beyond Foundationalism: Shaping Theology in a Postmodern Context* (Louisville: Westminster John Knox, 2001); the critical, and apologetic, response has been the recognition that this takes us "beyond Evangelicalism"—see Steven Knowles, *Beyond Evangelicalism: The Theological Methodology of Stanley J. Grenz* (Burlington, VT: Ashgate, 2009).

theology. Simultaneously, so the argument goes, the abandonment of foundationalism opens the door to perspectivism and pluralism. And if the latter are problematic, so are their ideological movements, especially and including multiculturalism (with some advocates of such having reinterpreted Christian teaching in light of a politics of identity instead of vice versa).[28] Asian American Evangelicals are thus armed foundationally to confront, engage and resist the perils of cynicism, relativism and pluralism. Unbeknownst to them, however, this not only undercuts the ideology of multiculturalism but also assails the basis upon which they can reclaim their own historical and cultural identities. Of course, Evangelicals have more recently recognized, at least in general, the importance of embracing the diversity of cultures, even of celebrating them, but only so long as doing so does not threaten the foundations of evangelical certitude.

An (allegedly) a-cultural hermeneutic. This presumption of having a universal perspective, while undergirded as biblical rather than recognized as founded on an Enlightenment paradigm, bleeds over into evangelical hermeneutics. In the Asian American evangelical landscape, such hermeneutical presuppositions bracket Asian America, whether intentionally (more often) or not. In this way, Asian American Evangelicals have imbibed not only the foundationalism of their classical seminary education but also the biblical hermeneutic that works to secure such an epistemic stance. Unsurprisingly, at the heart of the evangelical interpretation of Scripture is another instrument from the modernist toolkit: that of historical criticism. This time, however, such a hermeneutical approach is deployed to access the authorial intent of the Scriptures, and it is this that is central (foundational!) to identifying the biblical message, which in turn enables the Bible to serve as the unshakable norm for Christian belief.

There is much to unpack in the preceding brief description of evangelical hermeneutics, classically considered. But I want to focus instead on the principles of biblical exegesis as emphasized in evangelical seminary education.[29] The goal of exegesis is to draw out of or to cull from the Bible what the original authors meant to communicate. This involves understanding first and

---

[28]Thus have some Evangelicals harangued against multiculturalism as an ideology, for example—
Dennis McCallum, ed., *The Death of Truth: What's Wrong with Multiculturalism, the Rejection of Reason and the New Postmodern Diversity* (Minneapolis: Bethany House, 1996).

[29]E.g., Walter C. Kaiser, *Toward an Exegetical Theology: Biblical Exegesis for Preaching and Teaching* (Grand Rapids: Baker Books, 1998).

foremost how the biblical authors were understood by their initial audiences in the ancient context. Exegesis accesses these primordially intended biblical principles. What the Bible means today is thereby a secondary issue, dependent primarily on what it originally meant to the first hearers and readers of the Scriptures. Contemporary application thus involves identification of the original and, for some, single meaning of the biblical texts.[30]

The flip side of the emphasis on exegesis, then, involves the rejection of *eisegesis*, the insertion of contemporary perspectives into the meaning of the biblical text. If the burden of biblical hermeneutics is to take away from the Scriptures what its authors intended to communicate, the bane of evangelical interpretation is to read into the Bible whatever our present viewpoints may dictate. This, of course, is a violation of the cardinal rule of evangelical hermeneutics: readers should leave their prejudices and biases at the door and allow the Bible to inform them instead. Otherwise, the concern is that the reader will find whatever he or she is looking for, and this infects, contaminates, skews and distorts the pristine message of the Bible.[31]

The problem here is not just that the lines between exegesis and eisegesis are much more blurred than Evangelicals usually acknowledge,[32] but that the persistent application of such an approach to the Bible dictates that evangelical readers intentionally bracket, or at least attempt to hold in abeyance, their own histories, experiences and perspectives as being of secondary import, if of any relevance at all, for their reading of Scripture. Now I am certainly not suggesting that we all willy-nilly insert our biases in appropriating the biblical text. Simultaneously, I urge that the cost of such hermeneutical bracketing is too high for

---

[30]See Robert L. Thomas, *Evangelical Hermeneutics: The New Versus the Old* (Grand Rapids: Kregel, 2002), chap. 6, titled, "The Principle of Single Meaning," which argues that the pluralism, polyphony and plurivocity of meaning advocated by recent progressive Evangelicals reflects more the effects of humanity's fall into sin than it does the classical assumptions of evangelical biblical interpretation. For a counterargument, one that I am largely sympathetic with, see James K. A. Smith, *The Fall of Interpretation: Philosophical Foundations for a Creational Hermeneutic* (Downers Grove, IL: InterVarsity Press, 2000).

[31]For evangelical concerns regarding reader-response hermeneutics, see Norman R. Gulley, "Reader-Response Theories in Postmodern Hermeneutics: A Challenge to Evangelical Theology," in David S. Dockery, ed., *The Challenge of Postmodernism: An Evangelical Engagement* (Wheaton, IL: Victor Books, 1995), pp. 208-38.

[32]In mainline Protestant circles, of course, there has long been recognition that the traditional line between exegesis and eisegesis is much blurrier than previously thought; see Jay G. Williams, "Exegesis-Eisegesis: Is There a Difference?" *Theology Today* 30, no. 3 (1973): 218-27.

ethnic minorities who are Evangelicals since this in effect rejects their questions
and concerns as pertinent to their engagement with the Bible. In addition, such
presumptive bracketing blinds white Evangelicals to the fact that their own horizons and perspectives are involved in any reading of ancient texts, and this lack
of awareness makes it doubly difficult to recognize, moderate or correct.

I would urge instead that we recognize and embrace the tension involved
in the fusion of biblical and contemporary horizons, but do so in a way that
both allows contemporary readers to enter into the world of the Bible on the
one hand ("this is that") and for the Bible to map onto our contemporary lives
on the other hand ("that is this").[33] This not only allows for an Asian
American reading of the Bible, something that is barred in the evangelical
environment; it also invites, even encourages, such an approach, and this in
turn gives Asian Americans—all people, actually—permission to read the
Bible as if it really mattered to their lives.

A (presumably) biblical-theological method. Enlightenment assumptions
thus inform not only Asian American evangelical epistemology and hermeneutics but also theological method, and they do so in ways that marginalize
Asian America. This is consistent with the general evangelical fear of licensing
what they see as merely subjective readings of the Bible, for the same reasons
that they are wary about enabling theological methodologies that consciously
acknowledge the role of experience. In other words, the status quo in evangelical approaches to the Bible (with its accentuation of exegesis and rejection
of eisegesis) has its counterpart in evangelical approaches to theological reflection: this time with the emphasis on the Bible as the primary, if not sole,
source for theology, over and against history, tradition, culture and experience.

At one level, the *sola scriptura* commitments of Reformation traditions have
a very specific history and should be understood according to the nuances
with which this idea has developed in the past five hundred years.[34] At another

---

[33]I explicate some aspects of the "this is that" hermeneutic from a Pentecostal perspective in my
"Reading Scripture and Nature: Pentecostal Hermeneutics and Their Implications for the Con-
temporary Evangelical Theology and Science Conversation," *Perspectives on Science and Christian
Faith* 53, no. 1 (2011): 1-13.

[34]Reflecting developments from the publication of *The Fundamentals* to the "Chicago Statement on
Biblical Inerrancy" (1978), many conservative North American Evangelicals—e.g., from Norman
L. Geisler, *Inerrancy* (Grand Rapids: Zondervan, 1980) to James R. White, *Scripture Alone* (Min-
neapolis: Bethany House, 2004)—have seen and continue to see both *sola scriptura* and the doc-

level, however, conservative Evangelicals also sometimes tend to oppose *sola scriptura* to any theological methodology that they feel allows for too much input from other sources.[35] In the evangelical world, the chief competitors to the primacy of Scripture are usually either what has come to be known as the Anglican triad—Scripture, tradition and reason—or the Wesleyan quadrilateral, which adds the role of experience.[36] To be sure, as the history of theology reveals, all too often tradition has muted the voice of Scripture, and rationalism has "explained away" whatever has not seemed appropriate to contemporary sensibilities. And certainly, the perspectives we bring to the Bible informed by our life histories and experiences often may lead us to conclusions that are (at best) harmless extrapolations from the Scripture but may also be (at worst) illegitimate defenses of morally harmful activity. But after recognizing the potential abuse of allowing tradition, reason and experience to inform our interaction with the Bible, we might come to see how recognition of such factors actually helps us to control for their illicit operations and how they may even be helpful for illuminating aspects of the biblical text that were previously unnoticed.[37] Yet while an increasing number of Evangelicals have come to recognize the important roles that these sources play for the theological task,[38] in conservative circles Evangelicals have long emphasized the primacy of Scripture in ways that subordinated these other elements.[39]

---

trine of inerrancy as central for evangelical theology. Yet the World Evangelical Fellowship's statement of faith is silent about both matters, preferring the more accepted (even ecumenical) language of, "the Holy Scriptures as originally given by God, divinely inspired, infallible, entirely trustworthy" (worldevangelical.org/wea/statement.htm).

[35]E.g., R. C. Sproul, *Scripture Alone: The Evangelical Doctrine* (Phillipsburg, NJ: P&R, 2005).

[36]Ross Thompson, *Is There an Anglican Way? Scripture, Church and Reason—New Approaches to an Old Triad* (London: Darton, Longman and Todd, 1997); Donald A. D. Thorsen, *The Wesleyan Quadrilateral: Scripture, Tradition, Reason and Experience as a Model of Evangelical Theology* (Grand Rapids: Zondervan, 1990); and W. Stephen Gunter et al., *Wesley and the Quadrilateral: Renewing the Conversation* (Nashville: Abingdon, 1997).

[37]So I argue in Yong, *Spirit-Word-Community: Theological Hermeneutics in Trinitarian Perspective* (Burlington, VT: Ashgate, and Eugene, OR: Wipf & Stock, 2002).

[38]As reflected in John G. Stackhouse Jr., ed., *Evangelical Futures: A Conversation on Theological Method* (Grand Rapids: Baker Books, 2000), and Vincent Bacote, Laura C. Miguélez and Dennis L. Ockholm, eds., *Evangelicals & Scripture: Tradition, Authority and Hermeneutics* (Downers Grove, IL: InterVarsity Press, 2004).

[39]This is part of the legacy of the Princeton theology of Charles Hodge and B. B. Warfield during the nineteenth and at the turn of the twentieth century, as documented by Mark A. Noll, ed., *The Princeton Theology, 1812–1921: Scripture, Science, Theological Method from Archibald Alexander to Benjamin Breckinridge Warfield* (Grand Rapids: Baker Book House, 1983).

The problem, however, is that Asian Americans have rarely, if ever, questioned more rigid applications of this methodological norm for evangelical theology. Rather they have internalized the evangelical bias against history, tradition and experience, thus silencing the role that particular perspectives might play in the theological task. If we appeal to our experience at all, we must do so apologetically, as if admitting that such theological interpretations are at best parochial concerns of a community not yet assimilated to the dominant culture, or at worst signaling our theological immaturity and need to grow up from or transcend the "backwardness" representing our history and experience before our life in Christ. Ironically, however, such intentional marginalization of the Asian American experience, not to mention Asian American philosophical ways of thinking and reasoning, does not call into question how the predominantly Anglo- and Euro-American experiences of modernity have shaped evangelical theology. As a result, Asian American Evangelicals have adopted what is claimed to be a biblical worldview and theological framework, supposedly shorn of the subjective biases of historically situated human interpreters. But these are surely devoid of their own experiential and contextual (Asian American) locations and yet uncritically naive in thinking that Euro-American historical accidents have been adequately "Christianized."

So far, I have suggested that epistemologically, hermeneutically and methodologically, Asian Americans have rarely questioned the modernist, Enlightenment, and Anglo- and Euro-American presuppositions of the evangelical theological endeavor. And since this undertaking has never acknowledged the cultural contexts and perspectives of the predominantly white framers of the evangelical theological tradition,[40] the assumption is that ethnicity plays little, if any, role in the work of theology. Not surprisingly, then, Asian American theologians have been reticent to suggest that ethnicity, culture and historicity count in theological reflection. By extension, the theological and doctrinal

---

[40]My point is not that white perspectives have distorted the gospel; this itself assumes a sort of a-cultural gospel that needs contextualization—a point that needs to be addressed and nuanced, which we will do momentarily. My point is that such white viewpoints are not only unrecognized but that they are then presumed to be normative for nonwhites. It is part of the goal of this chapter to call Asian American theologians to attend to this assumption, and to find ways to intentionally address and subvert it.

results have been formulated and transmitted as biblically funded and universally applicable, regardless of contextual considerations.

A (supposedly) universal doctrinal framework. One example of how North American evangelical theology has proceeded with universalistic assumptions and thereby overlooked, if not intentionally ignored, other cultural perspectives has to do with the doctrine of the atonement and what it addresses. Put crassly, humankind suffers from one overall problem, that of sin against God, and that one problem demands basically one solution, the substitutionary atonement of the Son's death on the cross.[41] Now I realize that it is unfair to depict evangelical views regarding the atonement in such homogeneous terms since the matter itself is still being contested.[42] But the fact is that in some evangelical circles, departure from the substitutionary view of the atonement is considered deviation from evangelical orthodoxy.[43] From this position, other biblical aspects and alternative interpretations are either subsumed under the doctrine of penal substitution or argued to be flawed in some respect.

Of course such a viewpoint minimizes the role of medieval feudalism and the jurisprudential background of some of the Reformers in the emergence and establishment of this understanding of the atonement in the evangelical tradition, just as it really does not question the basically Augustinian anthropology presumed in this process. Now, I am not a historical determinist who believes that context leads inexorably to our theological ideas, just as I do not think that allowance for historical contextual factors relativizes the truth of theological claims or produces doctrinal heterodoxy. Rather, without denying

---

[41]The World Evangelical Alliance's Statement of Faith affirms: "We believe in . . . Our Lord Jesus Christ, God manifest in the flesh, His virgin birth, His sinless human life, His divine miracles, His vicarious and atoning death, His bodily resurrection, His ascension, His mediatorial work, and His Personal return in power and glory. The Salvation of lost and sinful man through the shed blood of the Lord Jesus Christ by faith apart from works, and regeneration by the Holy Spirit" (see worldevangelical.org/wea/statement.htm; emphases original).

[42]See James Beilby and Paul R. Eddy, eds., *The Nature of the Atonement: Four Views* (Downers Grove, IL: IVP Academic, 2006), and Derek Tidball, David Hilborn and Justin Thacker, eds., *The Atonement Debate: Papers from the London Symposium on the Theology of the Atonement* (Grand Rapids: Zondervan, 2005); cf. J. Denny Weaver, *The Nonviolent Atonement* (Grand Rapids: Eerdmans, 2001); and Hans Boersma, *Violence, Hospitality and the Cross: Recovering the Atonement Tradition* (Grand Rapids: Baker Academic, 2004).

[43]See S. Lewis Johnson Jr., "Behold the Lamb: The Gospel and Substitutionary Atonement," in John H. Armstrong, ed., *The Coming Evangelical Crisis: Current Challenges to the Authority of Scripture and the Gospel* (Chicago: Moody Press, 1996), pp. 119-38.

the importance of the biblical and theological theme of substitution for the doctrine of the atonement, I am simply suggesting that other cultural perspectives and even assumptions might highlight and emphasize other biblical metaphors regarding Christ's salvific work.

But to pursue the question onto Asian American terrain, what difference will it make if we recognize that some Asians and Asian Americans live and exist in a shame rather than guilt culture? How might evangelical thinking about the atonement be adjusted, revised and maybe even transformed if Christ's work not only assuaged the guilt of sin from human lives but also removed the shame in human hearts?[44] My point is that evangelical theological tendencies generally urge a universalistic standpoint, and in this paradigm there is no need to attend to the particularities of or articulate Asian, Asian American or other cultural perspectives since these are all subsumed within the biblical framework read in an evangelical way. In this case, there isn't even a need to ask whether traditional evangelical theologies and doctrines, like those regarding the atonement, may need to be revisited and rearticulated in light of other historical, cultural and experiential dynamics. In fact, Asian Americans are both too shameful and too shy to even consider asking about these matters.

I have argued so far in this section that Asian American Evangelicals, formed theologically according to the sensibilities of the dominant evangelical culture in North America, have internalized the white evangelical worldview and in that sense mostly do not see the need to think explicitly from an Asian American vantage point. Asian American evangelical views are therefore, at best, no more than a minority theological perspective. Two related summary consequences have followed Asian American acquiescence to the majority culture. First, methodologically and materially, evangelical theology has been understood to be a-historical, a-cultural and even a-contextual. The assumption is that the Bible addresses all human beings, so any plain reading of the Scripture will or should be able to access the Word of God at any and all times and places. Traditionally formulated and framed evangelical doctrines derived from an inductive study

---

[44]Asian Americans are beginning to do just this, however—e.g., Rachel Y. Lei, "Saving Significance of the Cross in the Asian American Context," *SANACS Journal* 1 (2009): 95-116; cf. Mark D. Baker and Joel B. Green, *Recovering the Scandal of the Cross: The Atonement in New Testament and Contemporary Contexts* (Downers Grove, IL: InterVarsity Press, 2000), chap. 6, "Removing Alienating Shame: The Saving Significance of the Cross in Japan."

of Scripture thus form the undisputable and unrevisable core of the gospel. There is little recognition of the historical, cultural and contextual perspectives that have contributed to the articulation of such evangelical beliefs.

What this means is that there still remains a core set of evangelical doctrinal achievements, and these remain valid across space and time, although they may be supplemented by or translated into local, contextual and situational perspectives and idioms. As we saw previously (chapter one), the recent *Cambridge Companion to Evangelical Theology* reflects precisely this mindset.[45] The *Companion*, we know, is divided into two parts. The first is titled "Evangelicals and Christian Doctrine," and this includes eight chapters on the foundational doctrinal matrix of evangelical beliefs: the Trinity, Scripture, christology, theological anthropology, justification/atonement, pneumatology, conversion/sanctification and ecclesiology. Part two, "The Contexts of Evangelical Theology," then provides another nine chapters, and these cover issues related to culture, gender, race and pluralism, and include five chapters on evangelical theology in African, Asian, European, Latin American and North American contexts. This structure of the *Companion* communicates a twofold message: that evangelical doctrine is a-contextually derived (part one), and that various historical contexts (part two) can add at most parochial truths that will not upset the doctrinal superstructure of the evangelical theological landscape. In short, basic theological and doctrinal truths of the Christian faith have already been formulated and can be found in any other evangelical systematic theological text quite apart from Asian American or any other more specified perspectives.

Put more pointedly, if Asian Americans (or any other ethnic or cultural group) were to write their own theologies, these would be provincial undertakings, with marginal relevance for the wider evangelical community. These would be of value only for "those" people (maybe immigrants, refugees or exiles) who have not yet been assimilated into the broader American evangelical culture. Little wonder, then, that few Asian Americans have ventured into theological territory.

The second summary consequence of internalizing the dominant

---

[45]Timothy Larsen and Daniel J. Treier, eds., *The Cambridge Companion to Evangelical Theology* (Cambridge: Cambridge University Press, 2007).

worldview—that evangelical theology, at least in its dogmatic and systematic configurations, is by and large a finished project with minimal input needed from Asian American or other perspectives—is that Asian Americans with theological education have turned, in general, to work in the historical and social scientific disciplines.[46] There certainly remains important work to be done by those working across the disciplines, so I am not decrying such efforts. Yet the fact that historical, sociological or other disciplinary explications of Asian American life are published by university presses communicates to Asian Americans that their role is to shed new light on the Asian American experience. At the same time, the prevalence of these analytical approaches amid the lacuna of explicitly theological works suggests that the former is of minimal value, at least for the "real" theological work of dogmatics and sys-tematics. Further, that these scholarly publishers do not feature texts on Asian American evangelical *theology* confirms this division of labor (white Evangelicals write *real* theology, Asian American Evangelicals do history, sociology, etc.). At the end of the day, evangelical theology's assumption remains undisturbed: that there are core doctrines that only need to be contextualized—that is, translated and made relevant—around the world. In this framework, Asian Americans can contribute not to the former theological formulation but only to the latter translation and dissemination task.[47]

---

[46]E.g., the work of Timothy Tseng and David Yoo in history, Fenggang Yang and Rebecca Kim in sociology, and Russell Jeung in Asian American studies, among others; see also my "Asian American Religion: A Review Essay," *Nova Religio: The Journal of Alternative and Emergent Religions* 9, no. 3 (2006): 92-107.

[47]One could argue that a parallel yet distinct motivation drives Latin American or Hispanic evangelical theology in a similar direction. If Asian Americans are cautioned against thinking theologically from out of ethnic, historical and contextual lives because of their uncritical embrace of white evangelical assumptions, Hispanic Evangelicals may have adopted similar commitments albeit for slightly different reasons related to the Latin American context. The dominance of the Roman Catholic Church, along with its theological and folk traditions, in the latter environment may be behind Hispanic evangelical suspicions about the role of history and culture in the doing of theology. The anti-Catholic sentiment in historic Evangelicalism no doubt is attractive to Latino/as on the migrant trail (from Latin America to the United States), although such accommodation has brought with it the theological costs elaborated in the preceding pages. For further discussion and other angles on these issues, see Oscar Garcia-Johnson, *The Mestizo/a Community of the Spirit: A Postmodern Latino/a Ecclesiology* (Eugene, OR: Wipf & Stock, 2009); Sammy Alfaro, *Divino Compañero: Toward a Hispanic Pentecostal Christology* (Eugene, OR: Pickwick, 2010); Juan Martínez, "'Outside the Gate': Evangelicalism and Latino Protestant Theology," in Jeffrey Greenman and Gene L. Green, eds., *Global Theology in Evangelical Perspective: Exploring the Contextual Nature of Theology and Mission* (Downers Grove, IL: InterVarsity Press, 2012), pp. 179-94; and

THE MANDATE OF ASIAN AMERICAN EVANGELICAL THEOLOGY

The preceding analysis raises self-critical awareness for Asian American Evangelicals and invites them, in dialogue with other Evangelicals, to consider whether their minority status is problematic and what, if anything, can and ought to be done about it. Now I am aware that there are developments within the evangelical theological tradition, broadly construed, that have moved beyond some of the strictures identified in the preceding section. Progressive Evangelicals, the evangelical left and postconservative Evangelicals denote just a few of the trends, among others, percolating on the margins of evangelical theology.[48] But that is precisely part of the problem: these are movements that, except for a small minority, remain outside the evangelical mainstream and have also, by and large, been ignored by Asian American evangelical scholars and theologians. I believe that productive ways forward can be charted via Asian American Evangelicals in dialogue with some of these ideas, although at the end of the day, such conversations will only be productive as Asian American Evangelicals formulate a platform on which they can bring something substantive to the discussion. This latter task is part of the present challenge, and burden of the present book.

Insofar then as I am interested in the question of what Asian Americans can contribute to evangelical theology, not just historically or sociologically but at a theological level, my claim is that pursuit of these matters, ironically, also involves taking seriously the historicity and particularity of Asian American cultures, experiences and perspectives. In this final part of this chapter, I do no more than suggest, in broad strokes, how to go about such an undertaking.

Realities of the Asian American diaspora. Part of "the problem of evangelical theology" can be clarified if we situate Asian American evangelical theology amid the broader Asian American diasporic, historical and social realities described in part at the beginning of chapter two. Doing so enables the stark realization that Asian American Evangelicals are composed by a wide range of experiences on the one hand and pressure to assimilate to

---

Juan F. Martínez and Lindy Scott, eds., *Los Evangélicos: Portraits of Latino Protestantism in the United States* (Eugene, OR: Wipf & Stock, 2009).

[48]Many of these are discussed in Roger E. Olson, *Reformed and Always Reforming: The Postconservative Approach to Evangelical Theology* (Grand Rapids: Baker Academic, 2007).

American culture on the other. While Asians have lived in North America since the founding of the republic and had even contributed to the building of the American empire during the nineteenth century, the 1965 Immigration Act that repealed the Oriental Exclusion Act of 1924 reopened the door to a new wave of Asian migration. During the last generation, Asian American life has been further transformed by the forces of globalization: diasporas created by modernization, industrialization and urbanization; refugee populations displaced by war, famine and climate changes; movement enabled by the emergence of a worldwide market economy, advances in technology and mass communication; the cross-fertilization of ideologies; and shifts in international relations.[49] The result, as saw in the previous chapter, is the appearance of a wide range of Asian American communities across North America. Life in such communities is fluid, affected by migration patterns, socioeconomic pressures and the strength of relations with those "back home." The stronger the transnational ties between Asian immigrants in the West and their families, organizations and institutions (religious and otherwise) in their homeland, the more intense and longer-lasting the exchange of religious goods and ideas (in the form of books, periodicals and various forms of telecommunication).

Unsurprisingly, then, first-generation immigrants often deepen the religious commitments that they held or practiced perhaps more nominally before moving. Sometimes immigrants convert to the more dominant religion of their new home. In either case, religious affiliation often serves to secure social networks, confer status otherwise difficult to come by for immigrants, and strengthen ethnic, cultural and linguistic bonds and identities. But for the 1.5 generation (those born in Asia but who grew up at least in part in the United States, like myself), the process of assimilation is well under way. In these cases, the ethnic enclave will develop English-speaking sections, as well as social organizations, school clubs and Christian congregations.

For young adult Asian American Evangelicals, however, there is often a

---

[49]For an overview of these issues, see Wanni W. Anderson and Robert G. Lee, eds., *Displacements and Diasporas: Asians in the Americas* (New Brunswick, NJ: Rutgers University Press, 2005). I discuss further the implications of globalization for Christian theology in Amos Yong and Peter Heltzel, "Robert Cummings Neville and the Global Future of Theology," in Yong and Heltzel, eds., *Theology in Global Context: Essays in Honor of Robert Cummings Neville* (New York: T & T Clark, 2004), pp. 29-42, esp. pp. 30-34.

keen sense that their own ethnically organized congregations or groups are somehow less religiously and theologically legitimate because they do not have the more "universal" appeal of white or multicultural evangelical churches or parachurch organizations.[50] The result is either the transition of ethnic congregations into pan-ethnic congregations or movement from their "home" congregation to other less ethnically defined church environments.[51] By the time the second generation attains adulthood, the remaining cultural or linguistic barriers to full assimilation into American society are practically overcome, often to the dismay of parents and grandparents.[52]

What does such assimilation consist of? Certainly speaking English, participating in the market economy and adapting to the options provided by American secularity and politics are minimal adjustments. But perhaps assimilation also requires abandoning the norms of the immigrant culture in favor of American norms for family and gender relations, and engaging with the public square on its terms. If so, would this not lead to an evangelical self-understanding deeply formed by American culture, politics and economics? Would this not result in a subordination and even deformation of all that is Asian except for the biological phenotype? It would appear, then, that becoming American would more easily facilitate the embrace of evangelical Christianity—if such is defined as a suburban, Midwestern, white, middle-class religious phenomenon with Wheaton, Illinois, as its veritable "Mecca"—but this brings with it the cost of losing one's Asianness. Does this mean that full acceptance of Evangelicalism

---

[50]See, e.g., Rebecca Y. Kim, "Negotiation of Ethnic and Religious Boundaries by Asian American Campus Evangelicals," in Tony Carnes and Fenggang Yang, eds., *Asian American Religions: The Making and Remaking of Borders and Boundaries* (New York: New York University Press, 2004), pp. 141-59, and Rudy V. Busto, "The Gospel According to the Model Minority? Hazarding an Interpretation of Asian American Evangelical College Students," in David K. Yoo, ed., *New Spiritual Homes: Religion and Asian Americans* (Honolulu: University of Hawaii Press, 1999), pp. 169-87.

[51]See Russell Jeung, *Faithful Generations: Race and New Asian American Churches* (New Brunswick, NJ: Rutgers University Press, 2004).

[52]As can be discerned by reading between the lines of the Bible studies in Tom Lin's *Losing Face and Finding Grace*. This appears to be the case whether the second generation intentionally attempts to distinguish its ethnic congregational life from that of the first immigrant generation, or whether the second generation becomes absorbed into nonethnic or even multiethnic congregations; on this point, see Elaine Howard Ecklund, "Models of Civic Responsibility: Korean Americans in Congregations with Different Ethnic Compositions," *Journal for the Scientific Study of Religion* 44, no. 1 (2005): 15-28.

includes "repentance" from Asia and "conversion" to Americanism?[53]

That this is not the case seems to be borne out by the sociological literature, which confirms that ethnicity remains just as important as religion in the formation of Asian American identity.[54] But if so, evangelical theology has not even begun to wrestle with the importance of ethnicity and race, not to mention their theological implications. Second-generation Korean Americans, for instance, seem to be intuitively drawn to churches and parachurch ministries that foreground their Korean cultural identity,[55] but they have developed few theological rationales for such forms of social organization; more to the point, their own theological presuppositions mitigate against such activity, which may explain their identity conflictedness.

Unsurprisingly, then, Asian American evangelical theology has yet to get off the ground even at the beginning of the twenty-first century. Asian American Evangelicals getting degrees from institutions of higher education have had to wrestle with/against this assimilative impulse, to struggle with the question of whether they are or should be doing (descriptive) sociology rather than theology (as normative reflection), and to articulate an apologetic for doing *Asian American* evangelical theology rather than just *evangelical* theology. For too many Asian American Evangelicals, their status "betwixt and between"—on the one hand belonging to Asia and to the United States in some respects, but on the other hand being a stranger to both Asia and the United States in other respects—puts them in a unique position to interrogate evangelical theology but (to date) leaves them outside the formal organizational and institutional structures to critique effectively and transform the evangelical theological tradition.

---

[53]One could also make the reverse argument, however, that Evangelicalism in the United States has already been molded by its social, cultural and historical context to the extent that the very features that mark the American way of life—i.e., individualism, experientialism, pragmatism, even consumerism—have also come to characterize evangelical Christianity. For an insightful analysis of the oftentimes uncritical conflation of Evangelicalism and Americanism, and of the forces that have also resisted such accommodations, see D. G. Hart, *That Old-Time Religion in Modern America: Evangelical Protestantism in the Twentieth Century* (Chicago: Ivan R. Dee, 2002).

[54]See Jerry Z. Park, "The Ethnic and Religious Identities of Young Asian Americans" (PhD diss., University of Notre Dame, 2004).

[55]See Sharon Kim and Rebecca Y. Kim, "Second-Generation Korean American Christians' Communities: Congregational Hybridity," in Carolyn Chen and Russell Jeung, eds., *Sustaining Faith Traditions: Race, Ethnicity, and Religion Among the Latino and Asian American Second Generation* (New York: New York University Press, 2012), pp. 176-93.

Moving trajectories of theological reflection. Of course, if Asian Americans hope to climb the ranks of the North American evangelical theological academy, they can only do so on the terms established by their hosts. And rather than responding to sociopolitical factors, the evangelical theological guild has always understood itself primarily in theological terms and seen its charge as defending historical orthodoxy, whether that be against liberalism's denial of biblical supernaturalism, against neo-orthodoxy's ambiguous stance on Scripture, against mainstream science's theory of evolution, against open theism's doctrine of God, and so on.[56] If evangelical theology has never before entertained ethnic perspectives in its discursive construction, why now undermine the (its presumed) universal framework and applicability by adding the *Asian* or *Asian American* qualifiers?

While in a sense this entire book provides a set of responses to this question, here I suggest three reasons that can motivate such a theological path forward. First, the Asian diaspora in the United States is now in a situation to reflect substantively on its experience of migration. While there are tremendous challenges to migration,[57] some Asian Americans have achieved a level of upward social mobility so that they are now in the position of producing scholarship informed by such experiential perspectives. Since the memory of migration among Asian Americans is more recent than those of their Caucasian colleagues, such perspectives might be helpful to identify how the migration from the European continent has shaped the evangelical theological enterprise as a whole. If Asian Americans can help their evangelical colleagues identify the historical impact of old to new world migration on the beliefs and practices of North American Evangelicalism, that in itself will open up possibilities for considering afresh Asian American histories and their contributions to the wider conversation.

Second, Asian Americans are forced to think about race and ethnicity in a way unlike most of their white brothers and sisters, although their reflections

---

[56]Evangelical theology's many internal and external battles are documented by Jon R. Stone, *On the Boundaries of American Evangelicalism: The Postwar Evangelical Coalition* (New York: St. Martin's Press, 1997).

[57]Some of these are documented by Kenneth J. Guest, *God in Chinatown: Religion and Survival in New York's Evolving Immigrant Community* (New York: New York University Press, 2003), whose work we will return to in chapter six.

can also mediate perspective in an otherwise white-and-black demarcated world. Race and ethnicity are undeniable aspects of Asian American history and experience. The import of this is at least twofold. First, Asian Americans are positioned to engage the discussion opened up by black evangelical theologians regarding contemporary theology—even in its evangelical guises—as reflecting the ascent of white perspectives in the early modern period at the expense of Jewish and other nonwhite cultural realities. Asian American perspectives on race and ethnicity will open up new vistas on the racial and ethnic dimensions of the biblical world.[58] In other words, the marginalized histories and perspectives of Asian American Evangelicals have much to contribute to contemporary biblical interpretation and theological explication. The dominant forms of evangelical theology forged in part out of the hegemony of Christendom are in need of critical analysis and dialogical revision.

Last but not least, central and ongoing elements of Asian American history are part of the present experiences of transnationalism and globalization. The issues here are complex.[59] One matter that needs to be addressed is the interwoven character of the global economy and how it affects people around the world differently depending on various social, political and cultural circumstances. In addition, with regard to the Asian American side of this equation, there remain difficult issues related to how the question of assimilation or acculturation is being negotiated and adjudicated. First-, second- and third-generation perspectives differ, sometimes momentously, and this does not even factor in the perspectives of the 1.5 generation. If theology is to engage the historical realities of real flesh-and-blood human beings, it must engage such questions in our contemporary world. Asian American Evangelicals can lead the way in thinking theologically about such things, and this will benefit not only Asian

---

[58]Asian Evangelicals thus need to build from the insightful readings of mainline Protestant biblical scholar Tat-Siong Benny Liew, *What Is Asian American Biblical Hermeneutics? Reading the New Testament* (Honolulu: University of Hawaii Press, 2008), regarding the ethnic dynamics underneath Jewish-Gentile relations in the New Testament. To be sure, Liew's mainline Protestant assumptions may be rather distant from evangelical ones, so some critical dialogue and perhaps correction may also be in order. Yet the strength of Liew's book is to suggest how Asian American experiences of ethnic marginality can illuminate the disputes between Jewish and Gentile followers of the Messiah in the first century. This is an issue worth substantial engagement from an evangelical perspective.

[59]E.g., Neil J. Ormerod and Shane Clifton, *Globalization and the Mission of the Church* (New York: T & T Clark, 2011).

American communities but also those of other ethnic, racial and cultural groups who are also wrestling with life in the twenty-first-century global context.

Evangelical theology today will need to heed more intentionally than it has before factors of migration, ethnicity, globalization and transnationalism. Asian American Evangelicals can assist with these matters, if they will arise to the occasion. This does not detract from the universality of the gospel message. On the contrary it addresses questions of universal significance that are otherwise neglected or engaged from or within only one (dominant, centrist) set of perspectives.

Reconnecting to the broader evangelical theological tradition. Before concluding this chapter, however, an important caveat ought to be sounded. None of the preceding should be read as denying either Asian American indebtedness to the evangelical tradition or the interrelatedness of Asian American and other evangelical efforts in the contemporary theological task. The preceding might suggest that Asian Americans are only pointing accusing fingers at their white evangelical friends. Without taking away anything from the seriousness of the foregoing discussion, I also realize that white Evangelicals in particular and Americans in general have been welcoming to Asians and that we have made it this far on our diasporic journey only with the help of such friends.

Beyond such ecclesial collegiality, however, I would grant that Asian Americans are in various respects beholden theologically to American Evangelicals as well. In particular, American evangelical commitments to Christ-centeredness, biblical faithfulness and missionary zealousness are important elements of Christian belief and practice in the twenty-first century. Asian American Evangelicals should embrace and live out such commitments not only for themselves but also for other Evangelicals and even for the world.

Yet my claim is precisely that such a posture enables Asian American Evangelicals to contribute theologically to the formation of an evangelical belief and praxis relevant to the twenty-first century. For this to happen, however, Asian American Evangelicals must embrace not only the *evangel* but also the historicity of their diasporic experiences. The incarnation of the Son of God consisted, after all, of taking on the concreteness, palpability and temporality of human, Jewish and first-century Palestinian flesh, and the outpouring of the Spirit of God on the Day of Pentecost involved the redemption of the diversity of human tongues, languages and cultures so that they might bear witness to the wondrous works of God (Acts 2:11). This pentecostal theme—related to Acts 2 first and foremost, albeit refracted unavoidably through the lens of my modern pentecostal ecclesial sensibilities—will inform the deep structure of the argument in the remainder of this volume, yet achieved within a pent-evangelical rather than merely charismatic frame of reference. My point going forward, however, is that in light of these theological and trinitarian commitments, Evangelicals should be the first to embrace the diversity of their historical particularities rather than shy away from them. Traditionally, of course, Evangelicals have subordinated the vicissitudes of history, and with that their anxieties about the flux and subjectivities of experience, to the surety and foundationalism of the Word of God as revealed in the Scriptures. My proposal, however, is that work of God in Christ and by the Spirit redeems us amid, with and through the specificities of our historical and cultural experience (rather than saving us from out of such altogether) and thus that the Word of God speaks into such realities (rather than that we have to deny them or reject them as part of who we are).

In short, Asian American Evangelicals do not need to be apologetic about their lives, experiences and perspectives. Rather, by following the path of the Son of God into the far country, by receiving the infilling of the Spirit of God poured out on all flesh, and by faithfully attempting to live out such a Christ-centered and Spirit-empowered faith in the footsteps of their evangelical forebears and ancestors, Asian Americans may then be able to bring their theological gifts to the conversation table, gifts that will challenge the discussion while simultaneously enriching the fare for all those concerned about the *euangelion* in the present time. It is time to theologize as Asian Americans, not just as Evangelicals, in order that Evangelicalism itself can be renewed and invigorated for the sake of the gospel and in anticipation of the reign of God.

4

PENTECOSTAL VOICES

Toward an Asian American Evangelical Theology

Beginning in this chapter, I want to suggest that an Asian American contribution to evangelical theology ought also to resound with pentecostal voices. To be clear, the goal of this volume is neither an Asian American evangelical theology for its own sake, nor a pentecostal theology (Asian American or not) distinct from the evangelical theological enterprise. Rather, it is a contribution to evangelical theology in global context as refracted through Asian American lenses. In particular, such an Asian American evangelical theological contribution inflects pentecostal perspectives. I will begin to mount the argument here and sustain it for the rest of the volume. The result, one might say, is a pent-evangelical theology for the twenty-first century sounded from the Asian American diaspora.

There are various reasons for this dialogical approach, some already noted in the preceding and others to be articulated at length in the following. For the moment, however, I note ecclesial, sociological and theological motivations. Ecclesially, many observers have followed the gradual yet undeniable "evangelicalization" of Pentecostalism on the one hand and also the simultaneous "pentecostalization" or "charismatization" of Evangelicalism on the other hand.[1] Many congregations flow back and forth between these dif-

---

[1] For the former, especially in the North American context, see the work of Margaret Poloma, particularly her *The Assemblies of God at Crossroads: Charisma and Institutional Dilemmas* (Knoxville: University of Tennessee Press, 1989). On the latter, see, e.g., Cephas Omenyo, "From the Fringes to the Centre: Pentecostalization of the Mainline Churches in Ghana," *Exchange* 34, no. 1 (2005): 39-60; Gastón Espinosa, "The Pentecostalization of Latin American and U.S. Latino Christianity," *Pneuma* 26, no. 2 (2004): 262-92; Damaris Seleina Parsitau, "From the Periphery to the Centre:

ferent liturgical modalities so that visitors may not be able to easily discern what kind of church they are attending. Sociologically, in the Latin American world especially, many Pentecostals self-identify as *evangelicos*, which highlights the fluid and intertwined nature of Latin American Pentecostalism and Evangelicalism. Last but not least, as already denoted (in chapter one), Pentecostals embrace the Bebbingtonian marks of Evangelicalism. For these and other reasons to be postulated, I will present in this volume the possibilities of such a pent-evangelical theological front,[2] albeit one slanted from an Asian American point of view.

We begin this chapter in the Asian context and ask about the what of Asian pentecostal theology and how its fortunes also may be threatened before full birth. The middle part unfolds the theological underpinnings of an Asian and Asian American pent-evangelical theological vision. The final section transitions to the Asian American situation and considers how a currently barren theological landscape might be opened up in dialogue with Asian pentecostal and evangelical perspectives. The goal is to explore the soundscape of an Asian American evangelical theological voice with pentecostal intonations.

One caveat is in order. As should be obvious from the preceding, our discussion proceeds primarily theologically, but this potentially obscures historical questions regarding the development of pentecostal theology itself. The issues here are complex, in part related to the contested questions of pentecostal historiography and in part related to the implications of these historiographical matters for pentecostal theology. In brief, the argument divides on whether modern Pentecostalism originated more on American soil or whether it has more diffused impulses from various revival centers across the Global South (see chapter one above). While I am partial to the latter thesis, there is also no denying the important role of North American pentecostal missions and their influence in the growth and expansion of what we now

---

The Pentecostalisation of Mainline Christianity in Kenya," *Missionalia* 35, no. 3 (2007): 83-111; and Douglas L. Rutt, "The 'Pentecostalization' of Christianity," *Concordia Theological Quarterly* 70, nos. 3-4 (2006): 371-73.

[2]Already but very preliminarily articulated by such luminaries as J. Rodman Williams, *Renewal Theology: Systematic Theology from a Charismatic Perspective*, 3 vols. (Grand Rapids: Zondervan, 1996); Larry D. Hart, *Truth Aflame: Theology for the Church in Renewal*, 2nd ed. (Grand Rapids: Zondervan, 2005); and Terry Tramel, *The Beauty of the Balance: Toward an Evangelical-Pentecostal Theology* (Franklin Springs, GA: Lifesprings, 2012).

consider global Pentecostalism. For our purposes, however, these debates need not be adjudicated since the scope of our argument will need to link both American and at least Asian pentecostal voices. While it is certainly justifiable to proceed discursively from the American to the Asian context in the following, I have opted for the reverse trajectory largely to parallel the framework established in chapters one and two above.

ASIAN PENTECOSTAL THEOLOGY: WHAT AND W(H)ITHER?

The following discussion pursues the what and whither of Asian pentecostal theology. I take them up in order to provide a programmatic sketch of an argument for the importance of Asian pentecostal theology for evangelical theology in particular and for Christian theology in general. The parenthetical *h* in the section title and the question mark at the end are suggestive of the vulnerable nature of Asian pentecostal theology in general and Asian American pentecostal and pent-evangelical theology in particular. In all cases, subservience to certain Western (white) evangelical trajectories of thinking may threaten the emergence of these theological voices and perspectives so that these eventually wither instead of blossom and flourish. What happens and whether Asian pentecostal or Asian American pent-evangelicals emerge with their own theological contributions remains to be seen. The following expands on the discussion of the previous chapters by overlaying pentecostal perspectives onto the Asian evangelical theological map.

What is Asian pentecostal theology? Any answer to the query What is Asian pentecostal theology? requires both a survey, however brief, of existing formulations and an attempt to unpack the qualifiers "Asian" and "pentecostal" in the question. If we begin with the latter, the problem is that Asia itself is not a monolithic region. As we have already seen in our discussion of the recent three-volume *Asian Christian Theologies*, the varieties of Christian enculturation or contextualization in Asia have produced a diversity of theologies forged in dialogue with the many historical, social, cultural, political, philosophical and religious movements and traditions of Asia.[3] Some have proposed that Asia is characterized by poverty, cultural diversity and reli-

---

[3]John C. England et al., eds., *Asian Christian Theologies: A Research Guide to Authors, Movements, Sources*, 3 vols. (Maryknoll, NY: Orbis, 2002–2004).

gious pluralism, and the Asian Catholic bishops have therefore suggested
that Asian theology must be informed by a liberative praxis focused on the
widespread poverty afflicting the masses of Asia, by a wide range of cultural
experiences and sensibilities, and by a commitment to the interreligious dialogue.[4] Asian theologians of note operating at least in part within this overarching framework include Kosuke Koyama (Thailand and Japan), Aloysius
Pieris (Sri Lanka), M. M. Thomas (India), Choan-Seng Song (Taiwan), Peter
Phan (Vietnam), and Chung Hyun Kyung, Jung Young Lee and Anselm Min
(Korea), among many others.

From the pentecostal point of view, however, the trajectories opened up by
these Asian theologians are less promising than apparent at first blush. As already indicated (chap. 1), Singaporean pentecostal theologian Simon Chan,
for example, has argued that these Asian theologians have focused too much on
history and historical processes, resulting in an overemphasis on immanence
to the neglect of transcendence in theology. Precisely because Asian religiosity
and poverty have framed the discourse of Asian theologians, leading to the
domination of theological themes such as the cosmic Christ, God's suffering
and the God of the poor, Asian theology has not been able to engage what he
calls the "irreducible transcendent reality in the Christian faith."[5] Further,
these Asian Christian theologians have too uncritically accepted a modernism
that demands secularization in terms of worldview, and demythologization in
terms of biblical interpretation. Such moves sit very uncomfortably, Chan
suggests, with Asian forms of thinking. The Daoist worldview, for example,
locates human beings within a wider cosmological context. Rather than separate human embodiment from that wider environment, the kind of "body
thinking" prevalent among cultures long informed by religious Daoism has a
deep affinity with the Christian understanding of truth most clearly embodied

[4]On the Asian Catholic bishops, see Thomas C. Fox, *Pentecost in Asia: A New Way of Being Church* (Maryknoll, NY: Orbis, 2002), chap. 12; Peter C. Phan, *In Our Own Tongues: Perspectives from Asia on Mission and Inculturation* (Maryknoll, NY: Orbis, 2003), pp. 213-14; and James H. Kroeger and Peter C. Phan, *The Future of the Asian Churches: The Asian Synod and Ecclesia in Asia* (Quezon City, Philippines: Claretian, 2002). For an example of a liberation theology emergent out of a multicul- tural and interreligious dialogue, see Michael Amaladoss, *Life in Freedom: Liberation Theologies from Asia* (Maryknoll, NY: Orbis, 1997).
[5]Simon Chan, "The Problem of Transcendence and Immanence in Asian Contextual Theology," *Trinity Theological Journal* 8 (1999): 5-18, quotation from p. 8.

in the life of Jesus and in the biblical narratives. Whereas liberal Asian Christian theologies may provide astute social analyses of the pervasive poverty that characterizes the Asian situation, they fail to offer religious and spiritual answers that concretely engage the masses of Asia. On the other hand, unexpectedly, a theological hermeneutic based on the good news of the incarnation remains plausible in modern Asia since it opens up the possibility of meeting the spiritual needs of people in terms with which they may resonate from the perspectives of Asian religious traditions. In this case, a deeply evangelical reading of Scripture in Asia would not necessarily be either exclusive of Asian sensibilities or opposed to making connections with Asian religious orientations or viewpoints. Beyond this, of course, a viable Asian Christian theology must include both social reform and evangelistic proclamation, both political action and supernaturalistic charismatic empowerment.[6]

Other pentecostal scholars and theologians also have begun to ask the question about Asian pentecostal theology. In the inaugural issue of the *Asian Journal of Pentecostal Studies*, the lead article, by the journal's coeditor, was Wonsuk Ma's "Toward an Asian Pentecostal Theology."[7] While trained in the Hebrew Bible, Ma has nevertheless been at the forefront of thinking about the pentecostal theological enterprise. Central to Ma's proposal is to argue for the importance of the Asian pentecostal theological project given the assumption that the task of Asian pentecostal theology is to serve as a bridge between divine revelation (in this case, understood in terms of pentecostal truths and distinctives) and the human situation (in this case, understood in terms of the Asian context in general and the spiritist and animist layer of Asian religiosity in particular).

Two responses to Ma's essay have subsequently been published in the same venue. In the next volume, Reuben Gabriel pointedly notes that spiritism alone does not exhaust the Asian context, but he does not proceed to further elaborate on what these other features of the Asian context might be.[8]

---

[6]As previously mentioned (see p. 55 n. 60), I would argue that modernity's dichotomy between what is "natural" and "supernatural" is inconsistent not only with Asian cultural perspectives but also with biblical thought; see Yong, *The Spirit of Creation: Modern Science and Divine Action in the Pentecostal-Charismatic Imagination* (Grand Rapids: Eerdmans, 2011).

[7]Wonsuk Ma, "Toward an Asian Pentecostal Theology," *Asian Journal of Pentecostal Studies* 1, no. 1 (1998): 15-41.

[8]Reuben Louis Gabriel, "A Response to Wonsuk Ma's 'Toward an Asian Pentecostal Theology,'" *Asian Journal of Pentecostal Studies* 2, no. 1 (1999); 77-85.

Gabriel's response is followed by Mathew Clark's.[9] From his South African perspective, Clark suggests common experiences and challenges between the Asian pentecostal and the African pentecostal contexts, including a holistic worldview, the issue of ancestor veneration, the pervasiveness of indigenous religious traditions and the accompanying threat of syncretism, and the need to formulate local ethical stances and postures. On the other side, there are also differences, particularly in terms of modernization and development trajectories, and the availability of missional, ministry and educational resources (these are more scarce in the African situation). Clark concludes with a call for Asian and African pentecostal partnership toward the construction of "a truly global Pentecostal theology."[10]

Nevertheless, even with these initial proposals, Asian pentecostal theologians cannot avoid grappling with what it means to be Asian and what it means to be global. Practically speaking, insofar as Pentecostalism in Asia has exploded in places such as South Korea, for example, it is to be expected that Asian pentecostal theology will be most developed among Korean Pentecostals.[11] At the same time, insofar as Pentecostalism is also growing throughout the rest of the Asian continent, there is gradually emerging a wide range of Asian pentecostal theological voices, including those informed by the experiences of Korean women (such as Julie Ma), Indian (and Dalit) Pentecostals (such as Paulson Pulikottil), the Filipino Roman Catholic charismatic movement (such as Lode Wostyn) and the rural Chinese churches (such as Deng Zhaoming and Edmond Tang), among many others.[12] And once we begin to look across the Asian continent, the question of the meaning of *pen-*

---

[9]Mathew Clark, "Asian Pentecostal Theology," *Asian Journal of Pentecostal Studies* 4, no. 2 (2001): 181-99.

[10]Ibid., pp. 198-99.

[11]Ma is a Korean Pentecostal theological educator. Other Pentecostal theological works are appearing among Korean Pentecostals, including Ig-Jin Kim, *History and Theology of Korean Pentecostalism: Sunbogeum (Pure Gospel) Pentecostalism* (Zoetermeer, The Netherlands: Boekencentrum, 2003); Sung-Hoon Myung and Young-gi Hong, eds., *Charis and Charisma: David Yonggi Cho and the Growth of Yoido Full Gospel Church* (Waynesboro, GA: Regnum Books International, 2003); and Young-Hoon Lee, *The Holy Spirit Movement in Korea: Its Historical and Theological Development* (Eugene, OR: Wipf & Stock, 2009).

[12]See, e.g., Allan Anderson and Edmond Tang, eds., *Asian and Pentecostal: The Charismatic Face of Christianity in Asia* (London: Regnum International, and Baguio City, Philippines: Asia Pacific Theological Seminary Press, 2005), and the contributions to the *Asian Journal of Pentecostal Studies* (1998-).

tecostal will press inexorably upon us. The demographers and statisticians of the *New International Dictionary of Pentecostal and Charismatic Movements* have constructed three categories: classical Pentecostals are those churches and movements connected to the Azusa Street revival; charismatics are those in churches and movements connected to the renewal movement in the mainline, Roman Catholic and Eastern Orthodox churches in the 1960s–1970s; indigenous charismatics and Pentecostals comprise the largest group of pentecostal- and charismatic-type Christians worldwide in terms of their practices of tongues-speaking and embrace of other charismatic manifestations.[13] Many Indian, Chinese and Japanese charismatic-type churches fall into this third category. But the question is whether or not, given their rejection of or obliviousness to the doctrine of glossolalia as the initial evidence of Spirit baptism, for instance, these indigenous Indian, Japanese and Chinese churches would really fit theologically as "pentecostal."[14]

Now if we proceeded to understand Pentecostalism inclusively and broadly, then we would need to provide some sort of account for this wide range of pentecostal-type phenomena. Among the Bible Mission churches in Andhra Pradesh, India, for example, indigenous and Hindu cultures combine in charismatic Christian contexts to produce not only Bhakti-style liturgies but also a guru-mentality that elevates the anointed man-of-God as a charismatic leader. Charismatic gurus like Mungamūri Dēvadās (ca. 1885–1960) claimed to receive revelations from the Holy Spirit through dreams and visions, even as these messages were confirmed through the gift of healings.[15] In the Spirit of Jesus Church and the Holy Ecclesia of Jesus church in Japan, on the other hand, we have ritual chants invoking the presence and activity of God that are phenomenologically analogous to the chanting of the Nembutsu and sutra recitation in Japanese Buddhism. Further, in these and other charismatic churches in Japan, traditional burial practices honoring the ancestors are

---

[13]See D. B. Barrett and T. M. Johnson, "Global Statistics," in Stanley M. Burgess and Eduard M. Van Der Maas, eds., *The New International Dictionary of Pentecostal and Charismatic Movements* (Grand Rapids: Zondervan, 2002), p. 284.

[14]Luke Wesley, *The Church in China: Persecuted, Pentecostal and Powerful* (Baguio City, Philippines: AJPS Books, 2004), illuminates the difficulties attending to this question vis-à-vis the churches in rural China.

[15]See P. Solomon Raj, *A Christian Folk-Religion in India: A Study of the Small Church Movement in Andhra Pradesh, with a Special Reference to the Bible Mission of Devadas* (New York: P. Lang, 1984).

Christianized and legitimated both at the biblical and the theological level, especially with regard to the idea that salvation extends as well to the spirit world.[16] Last (for our purposes) but not least is the Prayer Mountain movement in Korea, which builds on indigenous Korean religious beliefs and practices related to sacred mountain sites. When set within the wider matrix of Korean religious history, charismatic leaders have been likened to shamanic healers even as charismatic spirituality has been compared with popular expressions of Korean Buddhism and Confucianism.[17]

To be sure, any Asian pentecostal theology can choose to either ignore these phenomena or to articulate an apologetic as to why these should not be included in its theological construction. In fact, some would argue that the kind of phenomenological classification deployed by the *New International Dictionary* does not provide a sufficiently common theological platform so that we can or should include these movements in any attempt to develop an Asian pentecostal theology. From this more evangelically oriented perspective, Asian pentecostal theology should be more closely disciplined by classical pentecostal theology, albeit lifting up the importance of the Holy Spirit, the gifts of the Spirit, supernaturalism and worship spontaneity, all of which are more relevant in the Asian context.[18]

Why and whither Asian pentecostal theology? The question Why Asian pentecostal theology? is a more evangelically informed one that needs to be further explored, since it impinges on part of the debate among pentecostal theologians about how to understand the pentecostal theological enterprise in particular as well as the task of Christian theology in general. Put pointedly, does the qualifier of *Asian* in and of itself undermine the coherence of a pentecostal theology specifically or of a pent-evangelical theological as a whole? As we unpack this problematic, we shall see the theo-

---

[16]See Mark Mullins, *Christianity Made in Japan: A Study of Indigenous Movements* (Honolulu: University of Hawaii Press, 1998), and Makito Nagasawa, "Makuya Pentecostalism: A Survey," *Asian Journal of Pentecostal Studies* 3, no. 2 (2000): 203-18.

[17]As suggested by Boo-Woong Yoo, *Korean Pentecostalism: Its History and Theology* (New York: P. Lang, 1988), and Harvey G. Cox, *Fire from Heaven: The Rise of Pentecostal Spirituality and the Reshaping of Religion in the Twenty-First Century* (Reading, MA: Addison-Wesley, 1995), chap. 11.

[18]As articulated, for example, by Hwa Yung, "Endued with Power: The Pentecostal-Charismatic Renewal and the Asian Church in the 21st Century," in Simon Chan, ed., *Truth to Proclaim: The Gospel in Church and Society* (Singapore: Trinity Theological College, 2002), pp. 57-76.

logic of Evangelicalism delineated earlier (chapter three) again on display.

To begin, evangelical theology is about the *euangelion*, the good news. Soteriologically, for instance, and as already alluded to (in the previous chapter), the heart of the gospel as evangelically conceived has historically revolved around the substitutionary atonement of the cross of Christ for the sins of humankind. This conviction empowers the evangelical proclamation of the forgiveness of sin—as Saint Paul puts it, "since all have sinned and fall short of the glory of God" (Rom 3:23)—and the possibility of salvation to all persons. Hence the politics of identity has never been a central feature of evangelical theology. After all, if the assumptions are that none are righteous, not one, and that the gospel is hence equally for all persons regardless of race, ethnicity, gender, class and so on, then evangelical theology itself is universally viable and applicable, without any need for qualifiers such as *Asian* or *American*.

Similarly, of course, pentecostal theology follows evangelical theology on this issue. Many Pentecostals assume the substitutionary theory of the atonement, the universality of sin, and the conviction that the salvation of the world rests on the person and work of Jesus: "I am the way, and the truth, and the life. No one comes to the Father except through me" (Jn 14:6), and "There is salvation in no one else, for there is no other name under heaven given among mortals by which we must be saved" (Acts 4:12). In this scheme of things, it matters little that people are red or yellow, black or white, since anyone who believes in Jesus, regardless of race, ethnicity, gender, class and so on, will have everlasting life (Jn 3:16).

On the flip side, this universalizing logic of evangelical and pentecostal theology contains within itself an individualizing trajectory. The atoning death of Christ opens up the possibility of each individual entering into a personal relationship with God through Jesus Christ. And since God is no respecter of persons, neither does the gospel privilege the categories of race, ethnicity, gender or class. This assumes, of course, that we as individuals are sinners, and that sin is also no respecter of persons. Paradoxically, then, this universalizing-individualizing logic of evangelical and pentecostal theology converges to undermine all other identity qualifiers except those of saint and sinner: all people are either sinners in need of the gospel or saints whose sins have been covered precisely through their reception of the gospel. In this evangelical and pentecostal scheme, qualifying the good news in terms limited to Asia (or any other category) confuses the nature of the gospel at best and needlessly limits its scope at worst.

Finally, the methodological insistence on Scripture as the norming norm also illuminates the superfluity of *Asian* or other qualifiers to evangelical and pentecostal theology. At least as historically conceived, evangelical theology has long featured a robust doctrine of Scripture as the Word of God that judges rather than submits itself to other epistemic authorities, whether that is modern rationalism, liberal experientialism, unquestioning "traditionalism" or an infallible magisterium.[19] The result has been a transformation, especially in the last century, of the Reformational *sola scriptura* into a distinctively articulated doctrine of scriptural inerrancy that continues to serve as the theological, epistemological and hermeneutical foundation for much of conservative evangelical theology. In this methodological framework, evangelical theology is essentially and inherently *biblical*, thus dispensing with the need for other qualifiers.

Similarly, pentecostal theology's biblicism in many ways emerged out of the fundamentalist hermeneutic of the early twentieth century. The difference was that while the fundamentalists insisted that the charismatic manifestations were limited to the apostolic period, Pentecostals were convinced that the gifts of the Holy Spirit had continued throughout the history of the church (albeit sporadically at times) and had been especially infused in these days to empower the church to take the gospel to the ends of the world. Yet both fundamentalists and their distant pentecostal cousins believed in a biblically centered Christian theological enterprise. To even entertain the possibility of an *Asian* theology, for example, is to invite the whole range of confusions attached to the subjective experiences of interpreters defined first and foremost by other factors rather than by the biblical revelation.

From a pragmatic point of view, it is clear that the pentecostal commitment to the Great Commission flows out of the biblical injunction to "Go

---

[19]None of these "isms" are unambiguous, of course, even as each is intertwined with the others at some level. Putting things this way, however, captures some sense of evangelical self-perception vis-à-vis the wider ecumenical discussion of authority in theological method.

therefore and make disciples of all nations, baptizing them in the name of the Father and of the Son and of the Holy Spirit, and teaching them to obey everything that I have commanded you" (Mt 28:19-20). In this framework, what is important is that "all nations" are converted from sin and discipled according to the way of Jesus Christ. Insofar as the Christian theological enterprise emerges from out of the practices of the church, pentecostal theology also emerges out of this commitment to "Go into all the world and proclaim the good news to the whole creation" (Mk 16:15). Adding *Asian* or any other categorical qualifier to pentecostal is incidental and irrelevant at best and distracting and confusing at worst, since local features are subsumed under the universal needs of all human beings. For Pentecostals, then, there may be both puzzlement and resistance to the very exercise of discussing the task of an Asian pentecostal theology.

If the foregoing is correct, then there are at least two major conceptual roadblocks to the construction of an Asian pentecostal theology. On the one side, the very illusion of a meaningful notion of "Asian" is exploded by the fact that there is not one but rather many forms of Asian identities (the *what* question); on the other side, the many forms of Asian identities are not theologically significant when considered against the backdrop that all Asians are nevertheless sinners in need of the gospel (the *why* question). Unless viable responses are forthcoming to these questions, the task of Asian pentecostal theology threatens to either dissipate into many different Asian pentecostal theologies or to evaporate altogether as it is subsumed under the rubrics of either pentecostal theology *simpliciter* or Christian theology in general.

A Pent-evangelical Imagination: Speaking in Many Tongues

How then should we proceed with the articulation of an Asian pentecostal theology, much less an Asian American pent-evangelical one? How then do we retain and legitimate the *Asian* of any evangelical and pentecostal theology? Asked another way, is it possible for a theology to be formulated that draws from Asian traditions and patterns of thought (e.g., as suggested by Simon Chan), speaks to the lives of contemporary Asians and Asian Americans, and is resolutely pentecostal and evangelical? With other pentecostal

theologians,[20] I suggest that Luke's narrative of the outpouring of the Holy
Spirit "upon all flesh" in the second chapter of Acts (Acts 2:17) serves as a
biblical image of a divinely ordered diversity and pluralism.[21] Building on this
idea, I have gone on to argue at length that the many tongues of Pentecost
signify and anticipate not only the multilingual and multicultural character of
the reign of God, but also the potential and possibility of the many cultural
and perhaps even religious aspects of traditions around the world being
caught up in the redemptive work of God in the eschatological long run.[22]

The Day of Pentecost—and today. More particularly, the manifestation of
the Spirit's outpouring on all flesh was that there were "devout Jews from every
nation under heaven living in Jerusalem . . . [and] each one heard them
speaking in the native language of each" (Acts 2:5-6). Acts 2 is central to the
universal vision of the church and the reign of God that extended far beyond
the Jewish self-understanding of a religion centered in Jerusalem.[23] The universality of the gospel is not only announced at the beginning of Luke (Lk
2:31-32) and of Acts (Acts 1:8), but it is also prefigured in the fact that the many
tongues understood on the Day of Pentecost are derived from the ancient
Jewish table of nations and therefore represent all the peoples of the world.[24]
But at the phenomenological level, it is not just the translatability of the gospel
that is miraculous, but the fact that strange tongues can indeed be vehicles of
the gospel and can declare the wonders of God. And given the interconnec-
tions between language and culture, the Pentecost narrative both celebrates
the divine affirmation of many tongues and announces the divine embrace of

---

[20]E.g., Samuel Solivan's discussion of "cultural glossolalia" in his *The Spirit, Pathos and Liberation: Toward an Hispanic Pentecostal Theology* (Sheffield, UK: Sheffield Academic Press, 1998), pp. 112-18, and Frank D. Macchia, "The Tongues of Pentecost: A Pentecostal Perspective on the Promise and Challenge of Pentecostal/Roman Catholic Dialogue," *Journal of Ecumenical Studies* 35, no. 1 (1998): 1-18.

[21]Here I follow Diana Eck's distinction between *diversity* as a descriptive term and *pluralism* as a sensibility or orientation that not only values and respects differences but also seeks to actively engage otherness without eliminating deep commitments; see Eck, *Encountering God: A Spiritual Journey from Bozeman to Banaras* (Boston: Beacon, 1993), esp. pp. 190-99.

[22]For development of the argument, see Yong, *Spirit Poured Out on All Flesh*, esp. chap. 4.

[23]See also Yong, "'As the Spirit Gives Utterance . . .': Pentecost, Intra-Christian Ecumenism, and the Wider *Oekumene*," *International Review of Mission* 92, no. 366 (2003): 299-314.

[24]On this point, see James M. Scott, "Acts 2:9-11—As an Anticipation of the Mission to the Nations," in Jostein Ådna and Hans Kvalbein, eds., *The Mission of the Early Church to Jews and Gentiles*, Wissenschaftliche Untersuchungen zum Neuen Testament 127 (Tübingen: Mohr Siebeck, 2000), pp. 87-123, and Dean Philip Bechard, *Paul Outside the Walls: A Study of Luke's Socio-Geographical Universalism in Acts 14:8-20*, Analecta Biblica 143 (Rome: Editrice Pontificio Istituto Biblico, 2000), chaps. 3-4.

the many cultures of the world. This does not mean that entire cultural traditions are to be uncritically accepted or that every aspect of any particular culture is divinely sanctioned. Rather, languages and cultures need to be discerned, and their demonic elements need to be confronted and purified so that if there is any truth, goodness or beauty in them, such may be redeemed. Hence the outpouring of the Spirit on all flesh preserves, validates and even in this sense redeems the many tongues, languages and cultures of the world, including those of the regions, nations and peoples of Asia. The Pentecost narrative in Acts 2 thus invites Asian Pentecostals in particular, and those across the Asian diaspora in general, to declare and testify in their own tongues and languages about the wondrous works of God.

If at the exegetical level the Pentecost narrative serves as a universalizing motif, not only instantiating the fulfillment of the promise of the Spirit to empower the witness of the gospel to the ends of the earth (Acts 1:8) but also anticipating the actual proclamation of the gospel to all the world, as signified by the arrival of the gospel at Rome, the heart of the empire (Acts 28), at a historical level, the Pentecost narrative has perennially been read as both harmonizing the various tongues confused at Babel on the one hand (e.g., Gregory Nazianzus) and as anticipating the redemption of all languages for the sake of the gospel on the other (e.g., John Calvin).[25] Fast-forward historically to the twentieth century: early pentecostal Christians believed that they were experiencing a "reenactment" of Acts 2 at the Azusa Street revival in Los Angeles, 1906–1908. Since then the further worldwide expansion of the pentecostal-charismatic renewal serves to remind Christians everywhere that the outpouring of the Spirit on all flesh was not just a one-time occurrence in the first century but also a promise for all subsequent generations, "for all who are far away, everyone whom the Lord our God calls to him" (Acts 2:39), even to the present time and beyond.

---

[25]Gregory Nazianzen emphasizes the gift of the Spirit as a harmony that does not undermine the distinctiveness of the various tongues; see Oration 41, "On Pentecost," in *Nicene and Post-Nicene Fathers*, 2nd series, vol. 7: *Cyril of Jerusalem, Gregory Nazianzus*, ed. Philip Schaff and Henry Wace (1894; repr., Peabody, MA: Hendrickson, 1994), pp. 379-85, esp. p. 384. Calvin notes that the Spirit's being poured out on all flesh at Pentecost (Acts 2:17) signifies the gift of God to "an infinite multitude" such that "whereas the diversity of tongues beforehand hindered the gospel from going forth, at Pentecost the diversity of tongues is the means through which the gospel goes forth"; see Calvin, *Commentary upon the Acts of the Apostles* [1585], vol. 1, trans. and ed. Henry Beveridge (1943; repr., Grand Rapids: Baker Book House, 1979), pp. 73-75, 85.

In the pentecostal context, there is widespread consensus that the manifestations of the Spirit were the same as those recorded in the Acts narrative: whereas sons and daughters were said to prophesy in the first century, so also men and women were colaborers in the "harvest field" of Azusa Street and the pentecostal revival in the twentieth century; whereas dreams and visions were characteristic of the first-century Christian experience, so also would dreams and visions be prominent features of the modern pentecostal movement; whereas slave and free were empowered to prophesy by the Holy Spirit in the early church, so also were whites and blacks brought together at Azusa Street, miraculously, in an era of Jim Crow laws.[26] Most importantly for our purposes, just as the Day of Pentecost described in Acts includes the languages of those from many tribes, peoples and nations, so also did modern Pentecostalism almost instantaneously become a global movement involving individuals and people groups from every continent.[27] So because the gift of the Holy Spirit according to the pattern of Acts 2 has been experienced by Asian pentecostal Christians, they are, in turn, not just invited but required to give account of this in their own tongues and languages.[28]

A theology of Pentecost for today. Within these exegetical and historical frames of reference, I suggest a further theological and philosophical rationale for an Asian American pent-evangelical contribution to Christian theology. Whereas critics of an Asian pentecostal and evangelical theological enterprise

---

[26]The most recent history of Azusa Street is Cecil M. Robeck Jr., *The Azusa Street Mission and Revival* (Nashville: Nelson, 2006).

[27]On this point, see Karla Poewe, ed., *Charismatic Christianity as a Global Culture* (Columbia: University of South Carolina Press, 1994); Walter Hollenweger, *Pentecostalism: Origins and Developments Worldwide* (Peabody, MA: Hendrickson, 1997); and Allan H. Anderson and Walter J. Hollenweger, eds., *Pentecostals After a Century: Global Perspectives on a Movement in Transition*, JPTSup 15 (Sheffield, UK: Sheffield Academic Press, 1999).

[28]Here and in the rest of this book, I engage primarily the Lukan corpus within the Christian Testament, and even then focus more on the second volume (Acts) than on the prior Gospel. This is in recognizing the important role of Luke–Acts in the pentecostal hermeneutical imagination and in taking advantage of my own prior exegetical work—see, e.g., Martin W. Mittelstadt, *Reading Luke-Acts in the Pentecostal Tradition* (Cleveland, TN: CPT Press, 2010) and Yong, *Who Is the Holy Spirit? A Walk with the Apostles* (Brewster, MA: Paraclete, 2011). Yet any pent-evangelical theology for the global twenty-first century will certainly need to both engage the full scope of the New Testament and take into account the entirety of the biblical canon, neither of which I attempt in this volume. Hints of a pent-evangelical theology attentive at least to the broad horizon of the Christian Scriptures can be found in Yong with Jonathan Anderson, *Renewing Christian Theology: Systematics for a Global Christianity* (Waco, TX: Baylor University Press, 2014).

have insisted that either the "Asian" disappears in the many local or regional instantiations (the global is the local) or even that the "pentecostal" is subsumed under the more generally evangelical or Christian category (the local is the global), I propose that Asian pent-evangelicalism is both local and global, albeit in important mutual respects. While the category of "Asian" is constituted by various regional constructs, it nevertheless constitutes a coherent category when understood in American and global contexts, alongside non-Asian voices and perspectives. Similarly, "pentecostal-evangelicalism" constitutes a coherent category when understood in global context, alongside Christian voices and perspectives, even if Christian faith is itself constituted by various traditions. In other words, following the logic of Acts 2 and Azusa Street, the one outpouring of the Holy Spirit is manifest in the many tongues; similarly, the project of pent-evangelical theology is itself expressed in the many languages of the world, including those emanating from the regions of Asia. Put philosophically, if the many are constituted by the one and are increased by the one,[29] then pent-evangelical theology is itself constituted, at least in part, by Asia and its diasporic voices and increased by it, even as Asian theology is itself constituted, at least in part, by Indian, Chinese, Japanese and so on, pentecostal and evangelical theologies and increased by them.

It is at this theological level, I suggest, that the divine redemption of human languages involves human cultural realities and human religiousness as these three spheres or domains—the linguistic, the cultural and the religious—are intrinsically bound up one with the others. The retrieval and reappropriation of the Pentecost narrative at this juncture thus provides Evangelicalism with a theological (rather than merely politically correct) rationale for embracing human diversity. Other Asian American theologians have argued similarly. Filipino American theologian Eleazer Fernandez reads the Pentecost narrative as an extension of the Babel story, itself a production of exilic Israel as a counter-discourse to the hegemony of the Babylonian empire.[30] In this postcolonial

---

[29]As phrased by Alfred North Whitehead, *Process and Reality: An Essay in Cosmology* (New York: Harper & Row/Harper Torchbooks, 1960), p. 32.

[30]See Eleazer S. Fernandez, "From Babel to Pentecost: Finding a Home in the Belly of the Empire," in Tat-siong Benny Liew and Gale A. Yee, eds., *The Bible in Asian America*, Semeia 90-91 (Atlanta: Society of Biblical Literature, 2002), pp. 29-50. There is now also the suggestion by other Asian American theologians about the need "to emancipate Western theology from its Babylonian captivity. . . ." Paul M.

reading, the diversity of tongues resists the imperial ideology and praxis that oppose the rule and reign of God. Pentecost then represents the construction of counterprojects aimed at undermining the totalitarian rule of the world (in Fernandez's analysis, the Americanism of Manifest Destiny, *e pluribus unum* and assimilation into the "melting pot"). The result is a plausible vision for Asian Americans that "does not homogenize but allows the flourishing of various colors and narratives."[31]

From a pent-evangelical perspective, I would add two observations. First, I would caution us against an uncritical equation of Babel with any contemporary sociopolitical project in its totality. To be sure, no government is fully righteous, no, not one! At the same time, all governments carry out at least some divinely ordained functions, even if that is accomplished less rather than more righteously. Similarly, all languages and cultures are tainted by human sin, even if they also enable human well-being and flourishing. Discernment is needed to identify when cultures, societies, political structures and even religious traditions are advancing the reign of God versus when they are hindering it. From this, second, discernment leads to prophetic critique and resistance on the one hand, and to dialogical reconciliation and shalom on the other. In the Pentecost narrative, not only did the many tongues testify to God's wondrous deeds, but they also served to introduce the name of Jesus, both Lord and Christ (Acts 2:36). The good news of Pentecost announces the reconciliation of all persons to God in Christ by the power of the Spirit. Such reconciliation includes the judgment of sin according to the norms of the coming reign of God and the redemption of the world for the glory of God. Is it plausible to conceive of Asian American evangelical theology as discerning and even participating in some way in the work of the Spirit to both judge and redeem "Asia" and "America" and thereby herald the world to come?[32]

What I am suggesting is a way forward for evangelical theology read in "pen-

---

Nagano, "Prophetic and Urgent Mission for Today," *Journal of Asian and Asian American Theology* 6 (2003–2004): 14-18, quote from p. 16; cf. also Soong-Chan Rah, *The Next Evangelicalism: Freeing the Church from Western Cultural Captivity* (Downers Grove, IL: IVP Books, 2009).

[31]Fernandez, "From Babel to Pentecost," p. 42.

[32]See Christian T. Collins Winn, "Apocalyptic Pneumatology and the Religions: The Case of Christoph Blumhardt," in Wolfgang Vondey, ed., *The Holy Spirit and the Christian Life: Historical, Interdisciplinary, and Renewal Perspectives*, Christianity and Renewal—Interdisciplinary Studies 1 (New York: Palgrave Macmillan, 2014), pp. 161-77.

tecostal" and "pneumato-theological" key. By this I am referring not only to my own ecclesial location within pentecostal-charismatic Christianity but also to my attempt to read Scripture (e.g., the Pentecost narrative) faithfully as a theologian (in this case through the lens of pneumatological theology). This retrieval and reappropriation of the Pentecost narrative—which I have elsewhere called an exercise in the "pneumatological imagination"—itself participates in the recent renaissance in pneumatology and pneumatological theology.[33] Ironically, while Evangelicalism has always embraced the trinitarian understanding of the divine reality as formulated by the ancient councils, evangelical theology has long participated in a conversation that has been forgetful about the Spirit, perennially the "hidden" or "shy member" of the Trinity.[34]

Karl Barth and pent-evangelical theology. Evangelical theology should take a cue from one of the most influential of twentieth-century theologians, Karl Barth.[35] Barth understood Pentecost to be the revelation of the mystery of how Israel's "borders" are extended to include the world, of how what is far off is now caught up in the near (transforming the near, yet not distorting it),

---

[33]E.g., Miroslav Volf, *Work in the Spirit: Toward a Theology of Work* (Oxford: Oxford University Press, 1991); Michael Welker, *God the Spirit*, trans. John F. Hoffmeyer (Minneapolis: Fortress, 1994); Clark H. Pinnock, *Flame of Love: A Theology of the Holy Spirit* (Downers Grove, IL: InterVarsity Press, 1996); Gary D. Badcock, *Light of Truth and Fire of Love: A Theology of the Holy Spirit* (Grand Rapids: Eerdmans, 1997); D. Lyle Dabney, *Die Kenosis des Geistes: Kontinuität zwischen Schöpfung und Erlösung im Werk des Heiligen Geistes* (Neukirchen-Vluyn: Neukirchener Verlag, 1997); and Veli-Matti Kärkkäinen, *Pneumatology: The Holy Spirit in Ecumenical, International, and Contextual Perspective* (Grand Rapids: Baker Academic, 2002). For more on the pneumatological imagination, see Yong, *Spirit-Word-Community: Theological Hermeneutics in Trinitarian Perspective* (Burlington, VT: Ashgate, and Eugene, OR: Wipf & Stock, 2002), part 2.

[34]See Frederick Dale Bruner and William Hordern, *The Holy Spirit: Shy Member of the Trinity* (Minneapolis: Augsburg, 1984).

[35]Thomas F. Torrance, *Karl Barth, Biblical and Evangelical Theologian* (Edinburgh: T & T Clark, 1990), p. ix, calls Barth "the most powerfully biblical and evangelical theologian of our age," in some ways equating "biblical" and "evangelical," but in other ways understanding "evangelical" in the sense of a generous and ecumenical orthodoxy. For other sympathetic readings of Barth by more established North American evangelical theologians, see Donald G. Bloesch, *Jesus Is Victor! Karl Barth's Doctrine of Salvation* (Nashville: Abingdon, 1976); Gregory D. Bolich, *Karl Barth and Evangelicalism* (Downers Grove, IL: InterVarsity Press, 1980); Bernard Ramm, *After Fundamentalism: The Future of Evangelical Theology* (San Francisco: Harper & Row, 1983); Kurt Anders Richardson, *Reading Karl Barth: New Directions for North American Theology* (Grand Rapids: Baker Academic, 2004); and most recently, Bruce McCormack and Clifford Anderson, eds., *Karl Barth and American Evangelicalism* (Grand Rapids: Eerdmans, 2011). Phillip R. Thorne, *Evangelicalism and Karl Barth: His Reception and Influence in North American Evangelical Theology* (Allison Park, PA: Pickwick, 1995), provides a fine survey of evangelical engagement with Barth, including the very minimal engagement with Barth by pentecostal theologians (pp. 164-65).

and how particularity (of the covenant with Israel) and universality (of the gospel) are somehow conjoined in the gift of the Spirit to all flesh.[36] Yet less well known is that while he was working on the later volumes of his *Church Dogmatics*, Barth wondered about the possibility of a Christian anthropological theology that would be at the same time a theology of the Holy Spirit:

> There is no reason why the attempt of Christian anthropocentrism should not be made, indeed ought not to be made. There is certainly a place for legitimate Christian thinking starting from below and moving up, from man who is taken hold of by God to God who takes hold of man. Let us interpret this attempt by the 19th-century theologians in its best light! . . . One might well understand it as an attempt to formulate a theology of the third article of the Apostle's Creed, the Holy Spirit.[37]

This relatively obscure aspect of Barth's work can be ascribed to the fact that in the *Dogmatics*, Barth worked within a formally trinitarian rather than explicitly pneumatological framework. His concern throughout his life (as our concern should be now) was that unless someone was deeply grounded, both spiritually and theologically, adopting a pneumatological approach would end up where Feuerbach did, turning theology into anthropology.[38] Yet clearly progress has been made, as demonstrated by theologians such as Pannenberg and Moltmann, who have paid greater attention to pneumatology in critical engagement with Barth's legacy, and the way forward to a robustly pneumatological theology is now possible.[39]

---

[36]See Karl Barth, *Church Dogmatics*, trans. G. T. Thomson and Harold Knight (Edinburgh: T & T Clark, 1956), 3:321-23; Barth's discussion of the Pentecost narrative is set in the context of his discussion of human fellowship (§54), not only between male and female and parents and children but most importantly (for our purposes) between "Near and Distant Neighbors."

[37]This comes from Barth's address to the *Goethegesellschaft* in January 1957, which is an expansion of his acknowledgment regarding the plausibility of a theology of the Third Article, first made perhaps in a letter to Rudolf Bultmann written on Christmas Eve 1952; see Barth, "Evangelical Theology in the 19th Century," in his *The Humanity of God*, trans. Thomas Wieser (Richmond, VA: John Knox, 1963), pp. 11-33, quotation from pp. 24-25, and cf. Barth's letter to Bultmann in Bernd Jaspert, ed., *Karl Barth-Rudolf Bultmann: Letters, 1922-1966*, trans. Geoffrey W. Bromiley (Grand Rapids: Eerdmans, 1981), p. 108 (thanks to David Congdon for this latter reference).

[38]This concern was most clearly articulated by Barth in the *Nachwort* he appended in 1968 to his *Schleiermacher—Auswahl* (Eng. trans. by Geoffrey W. Bromiley, *The Theology of Schleiermacher: Lectures at Göttingen, Winter Semester of 1923/24*, ed. Dietrich Ritschl [Grand Rapids: Eerdmans, 1982], esp. pp. 278-79). However, Barth's worries about pneumatology leading to anthropology were also featured in his 1929 lectures at Elberfeld: *The Holy Spirit and the Christian Life: The Theological Basis of Ethics*, trans. R. Birch Hoyle (Louisville: Westminster John Knox, 1993).

[39]Pannenberg's multivolume *Systematic Theology* is pervasively pneumatological, as is Moltmann's work since the mid-1970s.

But beyond this, the turn to the Spirit must be made given the emergence of the pentecostal-charismatic renewal movement in world Christianity. While Barth's cautions will resonate with many evangelical theologians, at the same time, his recognition of the importance of such a project is instructive regarding the possibility of a theological grounding for the renewal of world evangelical theology. As Evangelicals increasingly realize the diversity of cultures and religions that they have to comprehend theologically and engage practically, I suggest that Barth's ruminations regarding an informed pneumatological theology of humanity will provide further *theological* warrant for looking seriously at the "other lights" in a pluralistic world.[40] With an eye on Barth's own course then—from developing a thoroughly trinitarian framework for theology to calling for a theology of the Spirit—contemporary Evangelicals and Pentecostals need to cautiously but urgently engage the project of pneumatological theology.[41]

It is within such a framework that I see possibilities for the reinvigoration of evangelical theology as leavened by the pentecostal-pneumatological imagination. First, the kerygmatic and prophetic dimensions of the gospel would not be compromised (cf. Acts 1:8); rather, they would be conducted by the *many* voices caught up by the Spirit's outpouring on all flesh. Second, this interplay of voices would enrich evangelical theology in a genuinely dialogical direction; this means that evangelical theology will recognize and appropriate the postfoundationalist, postcolonial and postpatriachal perspectives of our time even as pent-evangelical theologians critically engage the more excessive and indefensible aspects of these critiques.[42] Third, the redemption of human

---

[40]And for Barth, such a theology will always be christocentric, as when he discusses the possibility of "other lights which are quite clear and other revelations which are quite real" in his section on Jesus Christ as "The Light of Life" (*Church Dogmatics* 4.3.1, p. 97).

[41]And in the process of doing so, perhaps Evangelicals and Pentecostals can provide additional insight to the debate about Barth as a pneumato-centric theologian (Rosato), as a trinitarian theologian with pervasive pneumatological sensibilities (Thompson), as a pneumatological theologian when understood in eschatological perspective (Hunsinger), etc. E.g., Philip Rosato, *The Spirit Is Lord: The Pneumatology of Karl Barth* (Edinburgh: T & T Clark, 1981); John Thompson, *The Holy Spirit in the Theology of Karl Barth* (Allison Park, PA: Pickwick, 1991); and George Hunsinger, *Disruptive Grace: Studies in the Theology of Karl Barth* (Grand Rapids: Eerdmans, 2000), chap. 7, esp. pp. 173-78.

[42]On Evangelicals and postfoundationalism, see Stanley J. Grenz and John R. Franke, *Beyond Foundationalism: Shaping Theology in a Postmodern Context* (Louisville: Westminster John Knox, 2001). For the beginnings of evangelical engagement with postcolonial concerns, see Aída Besançon Spencer and William David Spencer, *The Global God: Multicultural Evangelical Views of God* (Grand Rapids: Baker, 1998). Evangelicals are still debating traditionalist complementarianism versus progressive

languages at Pentecost would herald the redemption of human cultures and religions; this means, again, not uncritical acceptance of all languages, cultures and religions, but their purification by Word and Spirit so that contemporary evangelical theology participates in the ushering in of all the nations of the earth and their gifts to the eschatological reign of God. Fourth, the fact of the Spirit's outpouring "in the last days" (cf. Acts 2:17) would mean that evangelical theology will have a robustly eschatological orientation that both recognizes the provisionality of the broad spectrum of its historical formulations—amid the passing away of the world and its conventional systems—even as it anticipates the full disclosure of the revelation of God. Combined, the dialogical and eschatological dimensions of evangelical theology would also involve its ongoing transformation in the here and now—*semper Reformandum*—by its encounter and engagement with the pluralism of human languages, cultures and religions (even as Peter himself was also transformed by his encounter with Cornelius).[43] Last, for our purposes, evangelical theology empowered by the Spirit of Pentecost would be performative in ways that go beyond the usual dichotomies—for example, of description versus prescription, facts versus values, epistemic relativity versus theological normativity—and precisely because the Spirit transforms our beliefs by enabling our practices and ethics.[44] The result will be an evangelical theology revitalized for engagement with the world of the twenty-first century.

ASIAN AMERICAN PENT-EVANGELICAL THEOLOGY: INTERPRETING DIFFERENT DISCOURSES

Having lain some of the theological groundwork for a pent-evangelical theological imagination in dialogical response to, at least initially, Asian pentecostal

---

egalitarianism—e.g., John G. Stackhouse Jr., *Finally Feminist: A Pragmatic Christian Understanding of Gender* (Grand Rapids: Baker Academic, 2005); Pamela D. H. Cochran, *Evangelical Feminism: A History* (New York: New York University Press, 2005); and Nicola Hoggard Creegan and Christine D. Pohl, *Living on the Boundaries: Evangelical Women, Feminism and the Theological Academy* (Downers Grove, IL: InterVarsity Press, 2005). Pentecostal contributions to the egalitarian cause include emphasis on the Spirit who is poured out equally on men- and maidservants in Acts.

[43]See Tony Richie, *Toward a Pentecostal Theology of Religions: Encountering Cornelius Today* (Cleveland, TN: CPT Press, 2013).

[44]E.g., Daniel Castelo, *Revisioning Pentecostal Ethics: The Epicletic Community* (Cleveland, TN: CPT Press, 2012), and Daniela Augustine, *Pentecost, Hospitality, and Transfiguration: Toward a Spirit-Inspired Vision of Social Transformation* (Cleveland, TN: CPT Press, 2012).

perspectives I now want to begin transitioning to the Asian American pentecostal and pent-evangelical contexts. The major problem with such a shift is that, to date and to my knowledge, there have been no efforts to formulate such a theological vision. There are certainly Asian American Pentecostals but they have written pentecostal or evangelical theologies rather than reflected explicitly as Asian Americans. Hence the following presents preliminary forecasts as well as a series of "thought experiments" regarding the possibility of an Asian American pentecostal and evangelical theology. In doing so, I invite others interested in such an task to consider how the Asian American diaspora has functioned as a host to Asian migration to the United States, and to take up their theological work within such a horizon. Such a posture opens up to the *how* of doing Asian American pent-evangelical theology. This is essentially a question about theological method. More specifically, it is a question about how to do pent-evangelical theology in the Asian American context and against a global horizon.

Discourses across the Asian American pent-evangelical diaspora. Elsewhere, I have argued the hypothesis that theological method involves a dialectical trialogue—a three-way conversation—among interpretation of the biblical text, interpretation of what the Holy Spirit is doing in the world and interpretation of the various contexts in which theology is being undertaken. Of course, this is itself a contextual hypothesis, formulated in dialogue with the discussions on methodology and hermeneutics in the wider theological academy.[45] For the purposes of doing Asian American pent-evangelical theology, the focus necessarily needs to be on what we discern the Holy Spirit is doing in and through the churches in their many situations throughout the Asian American diaspora. Remember that even for pent-evangelical theology in general, there needs to be contextual analysis and situatedness. There is no such thing as nonlocal theology. As I have argued in chapter one, the local is the global and vice versa. The key is whether or not the locality of any theological enterprise is admitted up front, rather than a pretense being put forward, perhaps out of ignorance or carelessness, that these are universal claims *simpliciter*.

I now want to suggest the further hypothesis that the task of Asian American pent-evangelical theology is to reflect on the experiences of Asian

---

[45]See my argument throughout *Spirit-Word-Community*.

American Christians as they attempt to discern what the Holy Spirit is doing in and through the church in their various contexts in light of the authoritative biblical and received theological traditions. Along these lines, Asian American pent-evangelical theologians need to be conscientious about how their theological reflection and work emerges out of the experiences of Asian Americans, and therefore pays close attention to what is happening "on the ground." At this level, Asian American pent-evangelical theology attempts to make sense of all that is happening in their churches—lives are being transformed; bodies are being healed; the gifts of the Holy Spirit are being manifest; and people are reconciled to one another and, most importantly, to God—under the light of Scripture. Historically, pentecostal and evangelical theology in general have focused on this level of transformative Christian experience.

From here, then, Asian American pent-evangelical theology needs to address the existential, social and political realities within which Asian Americans live and move. I wonder, for example, about bringing together pent-evangelical experiences, theological perspectives and scriptural resources to bear on the following issues and questions (listed in no particular order) that persist across the Asian American diaspora:

- What about a pent-evangelical theology of *shalom* in the context of relations—oftentimes across family lines—between North and South Korea, especially in light of the North's alleged nuclear capacities?

- What about a holistic pent-evangelical soteriology in response to natural disasters like the Banda Aceh tsunami, perennially flooding Bangladesh or hurricanes like Katrina?

- What about pent-evangelical theologies of race, justice and liberation inspired perhaps by Dalit Christianity in India, by Asian migrant enclaves in the ghettoes of San Francisco, New York City or other metropolitan areas, and among other communities impoverished by corrupt governments or globalizing market forces that threaten the economic survival of vulnerable people groups?

- What about a pent-evangelical theology of exile in the Himalayan context of Tibet, in the political context of Taiwan or among the many refugee communities in North America displaced by the wars in Southeast Asia? Concomitantly, what about a pent-evangelical theology of migration and immigration that engages the history of immigration to North American and contemporary global migration trends?

- What about a pent-evangelical theology of the land for indigenous Malays, Hmong (of Laos), Chin (of Myanmar) or Sherpa (of Tibet and Nepal), and how might this inform Christian theologies of space, nationalism and even the Holy Land?

- What about a pent-evangelical theology of technology for upwardly mobile Asians (i.e., Chinese, Japanese, South Koreans and Singaporeans who are now working in the high-tech industry) and Asian Americans (in Silicon Valley, for instance), or a pent-evangelical theology of medical technology, of which Asian Americans are at the forefront of development and which are also increasingly accessible to relatively impoverished Asian Christians?

- What about a pent-evangelical theology of dialogue and hospitality in Roman Catholic Philippines, in Muslim-dominated regions like Pakistan and Indonesia, in places where there are Buddhist and Hindu insurgent (fundamentalist) groups like Sri Lanka and India, and in pluralistic countries like Malaysia, and how might such theologies of dialogue and hospitality be relevant to Asian American migrant communities as well as to their Asian American and other evangelical hosts?

- What about pent-evangelical theologies of suffering (*dukkha*) or compassion, or of meditation, all dominant themes in the various Buddhist traditions of Asia?

- What about a pent-evangelical theology of the ancestors in light of the filial piety central to the Confucian tradition and persisting amid the global East Asian diaspora?

- What about a pent-evangelical theology of cultural diversity that can grapple with the complexities of the experiences of the different—first, 1.5 and second—generations, and how might such a theological perspective revitalize evangelical theologies of the coming reign of God?

- What about a pent-evangelical theology of contextualization that is sensitive to the similarities and differences of enculturation East and West, in Asia and in the United States?

- What about a pent-evangelical theology of politics and nation building that addresses minority-group experiences in engaging the issues related to democracy, citizenship and political responsibility, both in Asia and across the Americas?

- What about a pent-evangelical theology of globalization that is sensitive to the economic, political and ideological trends that shape the processes that intertwine East and West, Asia and the United States, along with the rest of the world?

- What about pent-evangelical cosmologies that can engage, critique and provide alternatives for the animist and other worldviews suggested by the religious traditions of Asia on the one hand, as well as for the materialistic, consumeristic and individualistic way of life in North America on the other hand?

- Last but not least, perhaps most abstrusely (but no less important for that), what about pent-evangelical philosophical theologies that take seriously the Buddha, Laozu, Kongzi, Shankara, Zhu Xi, Wangyang Ming and other Eastern conversation partners—rather than only Plato, Aristotle, Plotinus, Kant, Hegel, etc.—for theological and even dogmatic reflection?

The preceding, by no means meant to be exhaustive, suggests that Asian pentecostal theology is not necessarily circumscribed geographically by the Asian continent. Rather, in a globalizing world, "Asia" is a fluid category, identified not only by geography but also by phenotype (biology), culture, language and relationships.[46] In this global context, Asian evangelical theology is an enterprise that all Asians may have a stake in, even those who do not reside on Asian soil. To be clear, this approach does not presume an essentialist notion of either Asia or Asian America; in fact, I see that both lists are equally applicable within and outside of the Asian continent. The tasks proposed in either list could be engaged by Asian-based and non-Asian-based theologians, even as the results developed from such projects would also be relevant both within and outside these specific contexts. This aspect of the foregoing discussion is especially important since there are extant conversa-

---

[46]Thus R. S. Sugirtharajah talks about "shifting identities" as a marker of "Asianness" and even "orientalism"; see Sugirtharajah, *Asian Biblical Hermeneutics and Postcolonialism: Contesting the Interpretations* (Maryknoll, NY: Orbis, 1998), chap. 5.

tions afoot on many if not all of the preceding topics in wider ecumenical and Catholic theological contexts.

Asian American pent-evangelical method in a pluralistic world. What will such a reenergized pent-evangelical theology look like from Asian and Asian American perspectives? We can begin by asking what is Asian in Asian or Asian American evangelical theology. I suggest we follow the lead provided by Simon Chan (above) in his proposal to engage with Asian religious and cultural ideas (in his case, in dialogue with Daoism). But why should Asian or Asian American pent-evangelical theology bother with such Asian resources? Having already seen how difficult it is to determine what Asian means, I suggest that *one* way to explore this question about the meaning of Asia is to return to the wellsprings of Asia as manifest in its cultural heritage and to draw from them in a critical manner.[47] This is not, of course, to exchange one wellspring (Western) for another (Eastern) but to place them in dialogue with each other for a more holistic and reciprocal outcome. While some might be concerned that such a move may presume a reductionist view of Asia (as defined by its cultures, philosophies and even religions), I think such a risk is unavoidable but finally unfounded. Chief among challenges is that whatever Asia means cannot be negotiated in our globalizing context apart from Asia itself, nor apart from the immigrants who will continue to depart from Asia's shores for the foreseeable future. To be sure, 1.5 and later generations of Asian Americans who are interested in doing *Asian* American theology (evangelical or otherwise) will need to wrestle with the meaning of Asian in this new context, but they will not be able to do so in isolation from their contemporaries who remain closely tied to Asia in various ways. Further, the pentecostal-pneumatological approach I am recommending assumes that the glory and honor of Asia will also be brought into the eschatological Jerusalem (Rev 21:26). Might not Asians and Asian Americans return to and reappropriate elements from Asian cultural, philosophical and even religious traditions in ways that not only contribute toward this redemptive vision but also serve as a springboard for the church to speak

---

[47]This is neither to deny nor to ignore other salient elements that constitute Asian identities, whether languages, practices or customs; any sustained attempt to develop an Asian or Asian American evangelical theology will need to come to grips with these matters.

meaningfully to the Asian and Asian American worlds? But, finally, I attempt to conduct a retrieval of Asian religious traditions since from an evangelical perspective the dialogue with the religions of the world is the most challenging, and because I am convinced that Christian theology in the twenty-first century cannot proceed by ignoring this challenge.[48]

But engagement with Asian religious traditions needs to be done in a way that is respectful toward them while also being faithful to the Christian tradition.[49] Chan's suggestion is to draw from Daoist modes of thought in ways that allow the gospel to be more deeply rooted in the Asian heart and mind. I would further add that there are theological resources in philosophical Daoism that can be helpful for pent-evangelical theology. Daoism's "neo-naturalistic" cosmology can serve the kind of reenchantment of nature so desperately needed for a more robust pent-evangelical theology of the environment and for a pent-evangelical ecological ethic.[50] At the same time, as Chan argues, the rich Daoist cosmology overlaid upon the indigenous beliefs and practices of the Asian masses over the last millennia should not be completely demythologized. Pent-evangelical theology, cosmology and even demonology can be reconstructed in dialogue with Daoist notions. On the other side, of course, rather than placating the spirits, pentecostal theology would

---

[48]If Tillich is right that religion constitutes the "depth dimension" of any culture—and I believe he is close to the truth on this matter—then to engage Asian culture as if we could separate it altogether from Asian religions would mean engaging what it means to be Asian only on the surface. Hence, to take the *Asian* in Asian Evangelical and Asian American evangelical theology seriously requires that we come to terms with the beliefs and practices of Daoism, Confucianism and Buddhism, among other traditions. I have argued elsewhere for the importance of doing Christian theology in the twenty-first century in dialogue with the world's religious traditions; see Yong, *Beyond the Impasse: Toward a Pneumatological Theology of Religions* (Grand Rapids: Baker Academic, 2003), and *Discerning the Spirit(s): A Pentecostal-Charismatic Contribution to Christian Theology of Religions*, Journal of Pentecostal Theology Supplemental Series 20 (Sheffield, UK: Sheffield Academic Press, 2000).

[49]This is no merely rhetorical question. It has to do with whether or not we can simply adopt religious ideas from other faiths into our theologizing without either distorting the other or compromising ourselves. The issues are discussed from the Christian perspective in James R. Fredericks, *Buddhists and Christians: Through Comparative Theology to Solidarity* (Maryknoll, NY: Orbis, 2004), esp. chap. 1, and from a Buddhist perspective by Kristin Beise Kiblinger, *Buddhist Inclusivism: Attitudes Towards Religious Others* (Burlington, VT: Ashgate, 2005), chaps. 1-2.

[50]E.g., Norman J. Girardot, James Miller and Liu Xiaogan, eds., *Daoism and Ecology: Ways Within a Cosmic Landscape* (Cambridge, MA: Harvard University Press, 2001); cf. A. J. Swoboda, *Tongues and Trees: Towards a Pentecostal Ecological Theology*, Journal of Pentecostal Theology Supplement Series (Blandford Forum, UK: Deo Publishing, 2014).

insist on exorcism,[51] and, perhaps as important, pent-evangelical theology would provide an alternative vision of eternal life in contrast to Daoism's historic quest for immortality. Still, in either case, evangelical theology can only be enriched if challenged to return to its own sources, especially the biblical canon, in dialogue with the broad spectrum of Daoist traditions.[52]

Similar approaches are recommended toward Confucianism and Buddhism. Neither of these labels is monolithic, yet each presents opportunities for pent-evangelical theology to reconsider itself in dialogue with the assumptions and practices of many Asians. To be sure, the sexism and authoritarianism of traditional Confucianism needs to be criticized (as they do in certain forms of traditional Evangelicalism), along with popular understandings of Buddhist atheism, (karmic) determinism and nihilism. At the same time, pent-evangelical theology has much to learn from the filial piety, relationality and humanism characteristic of the main streams of Confucianism, as well as from the "middle way," nonviolence and meditative practices of historic Buddhism.[53] In any case, for especially those of East Asian descent, the Daoist-Buddhist-Confucian elements of cultural existence are so deeply ingrained that to ignore them is to be unconsciously informed by them; better to think through these matters intentionally than to mistake such features as being biblically evangelical.[54]

---

[51]Even if, I must add, that the traditional Pentecostal approach to exorcisms and traditional evangelical demonologies needs to be radically rethought in our time; see Yong, "Going Where the Spirit Goes . . . : Engaging the Spirit(s) in J. C. Ma's Pneumatological Missiology," *Journal of Pentecostal Theology* 10, no. 2 (April 2002): 110-28; "Spirit Possession, the Living, and the Dead: A Review Essay and Response from a Pentecostal Perspective," in *Dharma Deepika: A South Asian Journal of Missiological Research* 8, no. 2 (2004): 77-88; and "The Demonic in Pentecostal-Charismatic Christianity and in the Religious Consciousness of Asia," in Allan Anderson and Edmond Tang, eds., *Asian and Pentecostal: The Charismatic Face of Christianity in Asia* (London: Regnum International, and Baguio City, Philippines: Asia Pacific Theological Seminary Press, 2005), pp. 93-127.

[52]For various proposals emergent from the Christian encounter with Daoism, see James Miller, "The Economy of Cosmic Power: A Vision for a Daoist Theology of Religion," in Amos Yong and Peter G. Heltzel, eds., *Theology in Global Context: Essays in Honor of Robert Cummings Neville* (New York: T & T Clark, 2004), pp. 189-99; and Charles Courtney, ed., *East Wind: Taoist and Cosmological Implications of Christian Theology* (Lanham, MD: University Press of America, 1997).

[53]My own work to date has focused on the Buddhist tradition: Yong, *Pneumatology and the Christian-Buddhist Dialogue: Does the Spirit Blow Through the Middle Way?* Studies in Systematic Theology 11 (Boston: Brill, 2012), and *The Cosmic Breath: Spirit and Nature in the Christianity-Buddhism-Science Trialogue*, Philosophical Studies in Science & Religion 4 (Boston: Brill, 2012).

[54]See, e.g., Marc S. Mullinax, "Does Confucius Yet Live? Answers from Korean American Churches," *Journal of Asian and Asian American Theology* 3 (1999): 28-39, and Kyoung-Jae Kim,

These proposals do not suggest an uncritical embrace of all Chinese cultural traditions leading to a syncretistic hodgepodge of ideas and practices.[55] Any superficial interaction between evangelical theology and other traditions must be rejected. Instead, all viable intercultural encounters should emerge out of thick rather than thin descriptions of other cultural beliefs and practices,[56] from sophisticated applications of history-of-religions categories to the religious histories of East and West, and from sustained consideration of the various commentarial and hermeneutical traditions that inform contemporary traditions and ways of life. Hence, it is with caution and sympathetic attention that any contemporary Asian or Asian American pent-evangelical theology must responsibly engage that which is distinctively Asian, prophetically judging what needs to be judged according to the gospel, even while being reconciled to and transformed by all things good in Asian traditions.

The key for any Asian or Asian American pent-evangelical theology is to be resolutely and vigorously evangelical in the sense of being submitted to the authority of the scriptural narratives, in the sense of wrestling seriously with the major theological traditions of especially the Protestant Reformation, and in the sense of being committed to the task of the Great Commission in the contemporary world. But if the foregoing is correct, there is no ahistorical *euangelion* disconnected from Asia or Asian America other than the good news as encountered and received by Asians and Asian Americans. The result, even if unexpectedly, is that pent-evangelical theology is deeply trinitarian, by which I mean taking incarnation and Pentecost seriously in terms of em-

---

"Christianity and Cultures: A Hermeneutic Proposal of Mission Theology as Regards Inter-Religious Fusion of Horizons in an East Asian Context," *Journal of Asian and Asian American Theology* 7 (2005–2006): 64-80.

[55]Following the doyen of Pentecostal scholarship, Walter J. Hollenweger, I affirm a "theologically responsible syncretism" in view of the fact that all theology arises out of the crossfertilization of beliefs and practices in concrete historical contexts as Christian engage diverse sociopolitical realities and projects, although I would want to insist in the strongest terms possible that any theological proposal be biblically established and Christ centered; see Hollenweger, *Pentecostalism: Origins and Developments Worldwide* (Peabody, MA: Hendrickson, 1997), chap. 11.

[56]Evangelicals must come to grips with the fact that "religion" cannot be understood merely in terms of doctrines but that doctrines are intertwined with practices and vice versa; see, e.g., George Lindbeck, *The Nature of Doctrine: Religion and Theology in a Postliberal Age* (Philadelphia: Westminster Press, 1984); David S. Cunningham, *These Three Are One: The Practice of Trinitarian Theology* (Malden, MA: Blackwell, 1997); and Reinhard Hütter, *Suffering Divine Things: Theology as Church Practice* (Grand Rapids: Eerdmans, 2000).

bracing historicity, embodiment, social realities and environmental root-edness. Further, pent-evangelical theology must emphasize not only orthodoxy but also orthopraxis and orthopathy, by which I mean embracing both rightly-oriented belief and confession and rightly-oriented action and affection, and resisting any bifurcation of head and heart, mind and soul, spirit and body.[57] Finally, pent-evangelical theology must underwrite the whole gospel for the whole person for the whole world, by which I mean not only proclaiming and living out a holistic soteriology—with personal, confessional, embodied, social, environmental, spiritual, historical and eschatological dimensions—but also rejecting any attempt to reduce the redemptive work of the trinitarian God to any one of these aspects. At its best, evangelical theology speaks with confidence in the gospel of Jesus Christ as preserved in the Scriptures, but also with sensitivity, compassion and urgency to its audiences in order to stir up the question "What must we do to be saved?" When this happens, the Spirit once again lifts up Jesus the Christ, to whom all wealth, wisdom and strength belong, and who will receive in the end the glory, honor and splendor of all nations.

I am convinced that the theological reflection of the entire *oikeumenē* is needed to formulate such a robust theology appropriate to the biblical *euangelion*. Insights from Asian and Asian American pent-evangelicals will contribute indispensable perspectives, not only for Asians and Asian Americans but also for all Americans, all Evangelicals, the church catholic, even the whole world. Further, Asian and Asian American pent-evangelical theologies will also better enable evangelical Christianity's engagement with the twenty-first century since these will have emerged from Evangelicalism's performative interactions with the wider church, the theological academy and the world. In and through this hermeneutical spiral—wherein evangelical thinking emerges from its practices and returns to reform itself, not only theologically but also ethically and politically—the mission of evangelical Christianity will be dynamically propelled into and transformed by engagement with the world of many cultures, many religions, many political economies and even many dis-

---

[57]So, for example, any interpretation of the doctrine of justification solely in forensic terms will be inadequate from a Chinese perspective; see the various articles in the *Chinese Theological Review* 18 (2004), which addresses this issue.

ciplines (thus engaging the sciences).[58] Nothing less than this must characterize the future of evangelical theology.

Toward a pent-evangelical theology of hospitality. Yet amid this thought
experiment questions persist. Are Asian American pent-evangelicals up to the
task? This seems presumptuous since even the initial steps toward an Asian
American pent-evangelical theology have yet to be made. Is it not too far-
fetched to think that Asian American pent-evangelical theologians are ready
to engage with these matters?

I suggest three brief responses to these questions. First, theology is not only
a descriptive enterprise for Christian beliefs, but is also a prescriptive exercise
for the sake of Christian practices. It has long been known that pentecostal
and even evangelical Christians are pragmatists in terms of testing their beliefs
by the fruits that are produced.[59] Since I am hard pressed to think that pent-
evangelicals worldwide and in Asia and elsewhere do *not* confront these experiential realities, I think that their theologians need to reflect on these realities in order to provide a theological grammar that can shape and orient
Christians in ways that better enable them to engage the complexities of an
increasing globalized twenty-first century. In short, if these are the kinds of
realities confronting pent-evangelicals, then their theologians neglect their
vocation if they do not address these issues.

Second, I am convinced that it is part of the vocation of pentecostal and evangelical theology worldwide to mediate conversations and to do so by interpreting
(what Lamin Sanneh—see chap. 1—calls) the many vernacular languages and
discourses of various traditions, peoples, disciplines and research projects to one
another. In this sense pent-evangelical theologians should be not only conduits
of the spiritual gift of the interpretation of tongues but should also embody that
mediating posture amid the many conversations theologians are engaged in. In
other words, I am inviting pent-evangelicals to step out of their comfort zones so
as to be active participants at the global theological roundtable. The key to this
involvement, however, is that they engage in that discussion from out of the

---

[58]On the challenges and opportunities posed to evangelical theology by the sciences, see my *The
Spirit of Creation*.

[59]On pentecostal pragmatism, see Grant Wacker, *Heaven Below: Early Pentecostals and American
Culture* (Cambridge, MA: Harvard University Press, 2001).

strength of their own identities as Pentecostals and as Evangelicals—even as hybrids—rather than only on the terms set out by the existing conversation. In order for dialogue to be genuinely reciprocal, all parties have to contribute both to establishing the terms of the conversation and to its ongoing evaluation.

Third, I am convinced that pent-evangelical engagement in these projects will benefit not just these communities but also the wider Christian church and the wider theological discussion. In fact, I see no reason why the benefits of a holistic soteriology or a theology of technology or a theology of politics will be limited to only Christians. Rather, these kinds of theological undertakings will shape Christian practices that in turn benefit those outside the church as well. In that sense, the Asian American theological vocation casts an increasingly wide, beneficial net: from Asian Pentecostals to Asian Christians to Asians in general, and then extended across the Asian diaspora, even and especially in the North American context.

The way forward involves articulation of an Asian American pent-evangelical theology of hospitality.[60] The advantages of such a framework include the following. To begin, inasmuch as theology is never merely abstract or speculative but always already grounded in the church's experiences of the Spirit, so also is an Asian American pent-evangelical theology of hospitality both a descriptive task and a performative activity. A theology of hospitality cannot be merely *about* hospitality but has to emerge from out of the practices of hospitality and the interactions between guests and hosts. It is precisely such a pent-evangelical theology of hospitality that is capable of sustaining the work of pentecostal and evangelical theology both in Asia and in the Asian diaspora. With the advent of globalization, Asian Evangelicalism is now not only an Asian phenomenon but a worldwide set of fluid and dynamic practices and relationships. A pent-evangelical theology of hospitality serves in this global context to orient, shape and empower Christian theological engagement across the plurality of geographic, political, social, class, ethnic, race and religious boundaries that characterize not only the experiences of Asians and Asian Americans but also the emerging face of the postmodern theological conversation.

---

[60]See also my *Hospitality and the Other: Pentecost, Christian Practices, and the Neighbor*, Faith Meets Faith series (Maryknoll, NY: Orbis, 2008).

More important, if dialogue, relationality and mutuality are important virtues to be cultivated for doing theology in a postmodern, postcolonial and post-Christendom world, then a pent-evangelical theology of hospitality is precisely what is needed to provide a *biblical and theological* rationale for such a posture rather than allow it to be driven merely by politically correct concerns. By this, I mean that a theology of hospitality is first and foremost scripturally informed and theologically rooted. To be sure, there are social, political and ideological pressures exerted on Christian theological practices today calling for dialogue rather than proclamation. My claim, however, is to understand the dialogical imperative as driven by biblical, theological and, more precisely, pneumatological considerations.[61] I suggest, following pentecostal theologian Jean-Jacques Suurmond, that the outpouring of the Spirit on all flesh opens up and invites us to new dialogical opportunities previously not possible.[62] The gift of the Spirit enables the miracle of hearing and understanding strange tongues, as well as the miracle of interpreting and communicating in other languages. In other words, the presence and activity of the Spirit enables the kind of encounter between strangers—mediated through table fellowship, guest-host interactions and mutuality-reciprocity relations—that fosters listening, understanding, conversation, dialogue, proclamation and, finally, conversion. These elements were, of course, central to the evangelistic activities of the early church as recorded in the book of Acts. A theology of hospitality grounds the pent-evangelical witness present in hosting certain theological conversations on the one hand, and also empowers the pent-evangelical listening that is required when being guests at other theological venues on the other.

Finally, I wish to speak candidly about why Asian American pent-evangelical theologians should take the lead in developing and articulating such a theology of hospitality appropriate to the tasks of Christian theology in the twenty-first century. Increasingly, Asia and its various diasporic constituencies are becoming major players on the world stage. The face of the church has

---

[61]See David Lochhead, *The Dialogical Imperative: A Christian Reflection on Interfaith Encounter* (Maryknoll, NY: Orbis, 1988).

[62]Jean-Jacques Suurmond, *Word and Spirit at Play: A Charismatic Theology*, trans. John Bowden (Grand Rapids: Eerdmans, 1994), pp. 198-203.

been shifting from the West to the southern and eastern hemispheres of the globe, and the lines of im/migration are transforming peoples and churches so that we are now guests and hosts, alternatively and sometimes simultaneously, in relationship to one another, to non-Christians and even to the world.[63] In this fluid and dynamic world context, how might Asians in general and Asian Americans in particular contribute toward the kind of Christian theology of hospitality that can reshape Christian practices in a violent, turbulent and post-9/11 world? How is hospitality expressed in particular Asian cultures, and how might these social codes and expectations contribute to a pent-evangelical theology of hospitality in our contemporary global context? How might Christian practices of hospitality be informed by Thai and Japanese pent-evangelical reflection in dialogue with Buddhist concepts of compassion? In what ways might the Confucian notion of the "Six Relationships" contribute to an Asian American pent-evangelical theology of hospitality? What might we be able to learn from Malaysian and Indonesian theologians about hospitality in an Islamic state?[64] Are these not potentially ways in which the many tongues might be able to give glory to God if suitable interpretations and translations might be empowered by the Holy Spirit?

In the wider scheme of things, what about the theological task itself? Are not Asian voices more essential than ever to the health and vitality of the theological conversation? If so, perhaps this is the time for Asian American pent-evangelical theologians to take their place at the discussion table, and this involves both hosting moments of the conversation as well as being guests at appropriate junctures. I think Asian American pent-evangelicals can now speak not only for and to Asian Americans on the one hand or to Pentecostals and Evangelicals on the other, but also for and to other Christians and even the world church. In short, as Asian American pent-evangelical theology continues to mature, its contributions will be relevant beyond Asia and beyond Asian America, indeed to the church ecumenical, and even to theological conversations at the boundaries where the church meets the world.

---

[63]See Chandler Im and Amos Yong, eds., *Global Diasporas and Mission*, Regnum Edinburgh Centenary Series (Oxford: Regnum Books International, 2014).

[64]As suggested by Chinese Malaysian Roman Catholic theologian Jonathan Yun-Ka Tan, "Towards a Theology of 'Muhibbah' [Hospitality] as the Basis for Cross-Cultural Liturgical Inculturation in the Malaysian Catholic Church" (master's thesis, Graduate Theological Union, 1997).

5

THE IM/MIGRANT SPIRIT

Toward an Evangelical Theology of Migration

We next burrow deeper into the Asian American experience by examining the realities connected to migration and immigration in a globalizing world. While recognizing that migration is not distinctive to the Asian American experience, nevertheless we observe that Evangelicals have lagged behind in taking up questions related to theology of migration. Pentecostals, on the other hand, are migrants par excellence but have yet to think specifically about a theology of migration. Interestingly, at the heart of the modern pentecostal experience remains the Lukan text, especially the promise regarding the outpouring of the Spirit from on high to empower the Christian witness "to the ends of the earth" (Acts 1:8). This text calls attention to the migratory way of life of the earliest followers of Jesus as messiah. Yet I am unaware of any theological reflections to date about what it means to think about migration from an explicitly pentecostal perspective.[1]

This chapter outlines just such a pent-evangelical theology of migration and immigration. We begin with a brief overview about the appropriateness of such a theological task for pentecostal Christianity, observing in particular

---

[1]Leading the way in theology of migration are Roman Catholic scholars—e.g., Peter C. Phan, "The Experience of Migration as Source of Intercultural Theology in the United States," in Phan, *Christianity with an Asian Face: Asian American Theology in the Making* (Maryknoll, NY: Orbis, 2003), chap. 1; Daniel G. Groody and Gioachino Campese, eds., *A Promised Land, a Perilous Journey: Theological Perspectives on Migration* (Notre Dame, IN: University of Notre Dame Press, 2008); and Donald Kerwin and Jill Marie Gerschutz, eds., *And You Welcomed Me: Migration and Catholic Social Teaching* (Lanham, MD: Rowman & Littlefield, 2009). But see also a growing number of ecumenical voices, as in Elaine Padilla and Peter C. Phan, eds., *Contemporary Issues of Migration and Theology* (New York: Palgrave Macmillan, 2013).

its global migrant trends as well as situating such within a slice of the extant pentecostal, Asian American and wider theological literatures. The middle section of this chapter attempts to tease out from the book of Acts a basic framework for thinking theologically about migration, particularly through observing how the apostolic community can be understood as a dynamic community of migration. We conclude with some overarching theological reflections on migration and immigration that fuse the first-century horizons of the apostolic migrant experiences with the contemporary perspectives of the global pent-evangelical movement, especially refracted through the Asian American experience. Our goal is to be suggestive about how pent-evangelical perspectives might help us think constructively about migration in ways that simultaneously interrogate and, where necessary, reconceive discursive practices that are "too heavenly minded but not sufficiently of earthly good," as the saying goes.[2]

The argument, drawing from Pentecostalism's missionary emphasis, its global spread and its uniquely translatable spirituality derived from the many tongues of the Day of Pentecost event and the narratives of the early apostolic community, proposes a pneumatological theology of migration from an Asian American perspective that is focused on the immigrant Spirit who empowers the people of God in their migratory ventures across and into cultural, economic and political domains. The result is a deconstruction of at least some aspects of classical pentecostal theologies of mission even as it simultaneously presents a constructive Asian American pent-evangelical proposal that hopes to contribute to the emerging discussions of theologies of migration. Insofar as the forces of globalization and the continuously shrinking global village have touched all of us in various respects, perhaps the following can enable not just pent-evangelicals but all Christians, and even all migrants, to adapt as aliens in foreign lands, and motivate all hosts, regardless of ethnicity, to welcome migrant strangers.

---

[2]This is in part a reference to the by and large apolitical character of much of the global renewal movement. Things, however, are changing, as I discuss in my "Salvation, Society, and the Spirit: Pentecostal Contextualization and Political Theology from Cleveland to Birmingham, from Springfield to Seoul," *Pax Pneuma: The Journal of Pentecostals & Charismatics for Peace & Justice* 5, no. 2 (2009): 22-34.

CONTEMPORARY MIGRATION: A FUSION OF HORIZONS

The following seeks to situate our theological reflections appropriately at the intersection where pentecostal Christianity meets Asian America. We ought to keep in mind that trends noted throughout this section of the chapter are generalizable in multiple directions. The first part of this section paints a portrait of the migratory character of Pentecostalism as a renewal movement. As we proceed, remember that references to "pentecostal" and its cognates here in this chapter (and even elsewhere in the book) are shorthand for understanding this as both as subset and representative of global evangelical Christianity in the present time. Three aspects of pentecostal migration are especially noteworthy for our purposes: its missionary heart, its global extent and its translatability.

Migration in Pentecostalism. First, Pentecostalism is, in many and perhaps even its most fundamental respects, a missionary religion.[3] Yes, at its core, Christianity itself is driven by a missionary impulse, so in that sense, there is nothing distinctive to this claim. Yet on the other hand, it is also practically undisputable that whereas the nineteenth century featured the missionary emergence of Christianity as a world religion, the twentieth century has seen the missionary "pentecostalization" of world Christianity. In that sense, the missionary mantle for contemporary Christianity has been donned, like it or not, by Pentecostalism. And it has been precisely its missionary spirit that has led Pentecostals along the path of transnational migration, going here and there, wherever it is that they believe God has called them to the work of mission and evangelism.

More specifically, there are two aspects—historical and contemporary—to understanding the missionary identity of Pentecostalism. Historically, we must denote the missionary impulses that launched the movement as a global phenomenon.[4] More than anything else, early Pentecostals were motivated

---

[3]See Allan Anderson, *Spreading Fires: The Missionary Nature of Early Pentecostalism* (Maryknoll, NY: Orbis, 2007); cf. Anderson, *To the Ends of the Earth: Pentecostalism and the Transformation of World Christianity* (Oxford: Oxford University Press, 2013), esp. chap. 3.

[4]As documented by James R. Goff Jr., *Fields White Unto Harvest: Charles Fox Parham and the Missionary Origins of Pentecostalism* (Fayetteville: University of Arkansas Press, 1987); Cecil M. Robeck Jr., *The Azusa Street Mission and Revival: The Birth of the Global Pentecostal Movement* (Nashville: Nelson Reference & Electronic, 2006); and David D. Bundy, *Visions of Apostolic Mission: Scandinavian Pentecostal Mission to 1935* (Uppsala, Sweden: Uppsala University Library, 2009).

as missionaries because they believed that they also, like the apostles, had received the power of the Spirit to take the gospel to the ends of the earth. Thus from Azusa Street, one of the earliest pentecostal centers, missionaries went to Asia, Africa and Latin America, believing that they had been called by God to preach the gospel in order to make way for the soon return of Christ. On the contemporary scene, this missionary impulse has fed ever more intense initiatives directed toward the evangelization of the world. Thus have Pentecostals ventured courageously into unevangelized areas, obeying the call of God to bear witness to the gospel to every creature under heaven (Col 1:23). Many observers of the Christian mission have therefore recognized Pentecostals to have been at the vanguard of global mission and evangelism projects, even if Pentecostals themselves have not, at least to date, produced the widest-circulating missiology textbooks.[5]

Second, and related to the first point, concerns the spread and extent of pentecostal migration. If its missionizing heart has driven Pentecostals ever outward from their comfort zones, the result has been literally the globalization of the renewal movement over the last century.[6] There are various aspects of this global and globalizing phenomenon. Sociologically, globalization experts have noted recurring patterns, for instance the migration of people from rural to urban areas, in many cases reflecting a response to labor and market demands and fluctuations, the movements across established transnational routes, and the usual shifts forced by wars (civil and otherwise), famines and other tragic developments. Economically, pentecostal entrepre-

---

[5]Which is not to say that there have not been pentecostal missiologies written. For some of the leading pentecostal missiologies in the last two-plus decades, see Paul Pomerville, *The Third Force in Missions: A Pentecostal Contribution to Contemporary Mission Theology* (Peabody, MA: Hendrickson, 1985); L. Grant McClung, *Azusa Street and Beyond: Pentecostal Missions and Church Growth in the Twentieth Century* (South Plainfield, NJ: Bridge Publications, 1986); Vinson Synan and Ralph Rath, *Launching the Decade of Evangelization* (South Bend, IN: North American Renewal Service Committee, 1990); Edward K. Pousson, *Spreading the Flame: Charismatic Churches and Missions Today* (Grand Rapids: Zondervan, 1992); Harold D. Hunter and Peter Hocken, eds., *All Together in One Place: Theological Papers from the Brighton Conference on World Evangelization* (Sheffield, UK: Sheffield Academic Press, 1993); Andrew Lord, *Spirit-Shaped Mission: A Holistic Charismatic Missiology* (Waynesboro, GA: Paternoster, 2005); and Gary B. McGee, *Miracles, Missions, and American Pentecostalism* (Maryknoll, NY: Orbis, 2010).

[6]As sociologist David Martin puts it in the title of his book, Pentecostals consider the world to be their parish; see Martin, *Pentecostalism: The World Their Parish* (Malden, MA: Wiley-Blackwell, 2002).

neurship has not been overlooked.[7] Pentecostal boldness in witness, evangelism and missions has transferred over into their economic lives: many are adventurous in launching business initiatives and creative in expanding opportunities variously to engage with developments locally and globally. Often they are also at the forefront in taking advantage of and extending new media and communications technologies, both with regard to mission and evangelism on the one hand, and with regard to economic mobilization and expansion on the other.[8] What this means is that alongside mission-related migration, Pentecostals fully inhabit our globalized world: socially, economically and telecommunicatively. These developments mean that even those who "stay at home" are touched by migration, experiencing globalization through their friends and families who emigrate for whatever reason.[9]

All of this pentecostal mobility, however, raises the question of its adaptability. This concerns the third aspect of pentecostal migration I wish to highlight: its translatability across cultures. As we saw earlier (in chapter one), scholars such as Lamin Sanneh have called attention to the translatability of the Christian faith as a whole and how the emergence of world Christianity is itself a reflection of the religion's capacity to be contextualized and acculturated across time and space.[10] So again, I am not saying that this is a feature only of Pentecostalism. My claim, however, is that Pentecostalism is in a certain sense uniquely indigenizable across vastly different languages, cultures and environments, in part because the center of pentecostal spirituality itself is deeply shaped by the many tongues of fire of the Day of Pentecost expe-

---

[7]I discuss the economic dimensions of global renewal in my *In the Days of Caesar: Pentecostalism and Political Theology—The Cadbury Lectures 2009*, Sacra Doctrina: Christian Theology for a Postmodern Age series (Grand Rapids: Eerdmans, 2010), §1.2 and §7.1.

[8]E.g., Simon Coleman, *The Globalization of Charismatic Christianity: Spreading the Gospel of Prosperity* (Cambridge: Cambridge University Press, 2000); Pradip N. Thomas, *Strong Religion, Zealous Media: Christian Fundamentalism and Communication in India* (Thousand Oaks, CA: Sage Publications, 2008); and Jonathan D. James, *McDonaldisation, Masala McGospel and Om Economics: Televangelism in Contemporary India* (Thousand Oaks, CA: Sage Publications, 2010). See also David Edwin Harrell Jr., *Pat Robertson: A Life and Legacy* (Grand Rapids: Eerdmans, 2010), esp. chaps. 6-7.

[9]See Michael Wilkinson, *The Spirit Said Go: Pentecostal Immigrants in Canada*, American University Studies Series VII Theology & Religion 247 (New York: Peter Lang, 2006).

[10]His classic text is Lamin O. Sanneh, *Translating the Message: The Missionary Impact on Culture* (Maryknoll, NY: Orbis, 1989); cf. also my article, "The Church and Mission Theology in a Post-Constantinian Era: Soundings from the Anglo-American Frontier," in Akintunde Akinade, ed., *A New Day: Essays on World Christianity in Honor of Lamin Sanneh* (New York: Peter Lang, 2010), pp. 49-61.

rience. Harvey Cox refers to this as the primal spirituality of Pentecostalism, one that touches and more easily connects with the primal speech and primal piety of the indigenous cultures that underlie much of the cultural-religious traditions of the world.[11] In short, as pentecostal scholars Murray Dempster, Byron Klaus and Douglas Petersen have suggested, Pentecostalism is itself uniquely suited as "a religion made to travel."[12]

Pentecostal travel, however, has been in multiple directions, not just a few. On this note, we ought to briefly highlight the phenomenon of what some call "reverse migration": the movement of particularly Asian and African pent-evangelical Christians to the Euro-American West, motivated variously but especially evangelistically and missiologically.[13] This phenomenon of missionaries coming from the Global South to the Euro-American West is no longer new, especially not since the repeal of the immigration law in 1965 opened up the flow of traffic to the United States and since the formation of the European Union allowed for easier travel within its borders. People are moving for various reasons, many of them economic—related to economic trends, free markets and other transnational and international variables—and then adapting themselves socially and culturally. What is interesting is that pentecostal immigrants seem quite adaptable on all these registers, including the religious one.[14] From the perspective of practitioners of pentecostal faith, especially those concerned with how the global renewal interfaces with the free market, some have observed trends of "Spirit-empowered entrepreneurship" even as others note the emergence of a business ethic that over-emphasizes risk-taking in ways that marginalize nonconformists to the behavioral-economic practices associated with the capitalist status quo.[15]

---

[11]Harvey G. Cox, *Fire from Heaven: The Rise of Pentecostal Spirituality and the Reshaping of Religion in the 21st Century* (Reading, MA: Addison-Wesley, 1995).

[12]Murray W. Dempster, Byron D. Klaus and Douglas Petersen, eds., *The Globalization of Pentecostalism: A Religion Made to Travel* (Irvine, CA: Regnum Books, 1999).

[13]For starters, see Ogbu Kalu's *African Pentecostalism: Global Discourses, Migrations, Exchanges and Connections*, which is volume 1 of Wilhelmina J. Kalu, Nimi Wariboko and Toyin Falola, eds., *The Collected Essays of Ogbu Uke Kalu*, 3 vols. (Trenton, NJ: Africa World Press, 2010).

[14]See Katherine Attanasi and Amos Yong, eds., *Pentecostalism and Prosperity: The Socioeconomics of the Global Charismatic Movement*, Christianities of the World 1 (New York: Palgrave Macmillan, 2012).

[15]Rijk van Dijk, "Social Catapulting and the Spirit of Entrepreneurialism: Migrants, Private Initiative, and the Pentecostal Ethic in Botswana," in Gertrud Hüwelmeier and Kristine Krause, eds., *Traveling Spirits: Migrants, Markets and Mobilities* (New York: Routledge, 2010), pp. 101-17.

From a religious point of view, pentecostal migration is motivated perhaps even more by desire not only to nurture the faith of immigrant communities in familiar linguistic and cultural forms[16] but also to reevangelize a Western world considered lost in the maze of secularism. Pentecostal missionaries from the Global South have even adopted a posture that might be called "reverse colonialism" inasmuch as they believe they are called to "take Europe back for Christ," similar to how the European missionaries first brought Christianity to the colonies.[17] Filled with a sense of urgency and full of faith in a miraculous God who can meet the needs of the world, Asian and African pentecostal believers are moving into the Western world and bringing the healing and saving power of the gospel with them.[18]

Migration in Asia and the Asian diaspora. Veering quickly into the Asian and Asian diaspora context, the forces of immigration and reverse migration are at work there as well. Historically, of course, there is much to consider in terms of Asian migration to the United States over the past two hundred years.[19] Chinese immigration goes back to the early to mid-nineteenth century when many arrived to work in the mining, labor and railroad industries. But by the 1870s, the economic depression in the country along with xenophobic biases led to the reactions against the Chinese, including the Chinese Exclusion Act of 1882, which was repeatedly extended until 1943. During the first quarter of the twentieth century, Japanese immigration was strictly controlled, again in large part due to concerns that these obviously different looking, sounding and behaving peoples were not easily integrated into the broader culture and society. A variety of anti-Chinese and anti-Japanese bills were passed, culminating with a 1922 Supreme Court decision

---

[16]E.g., Michael Wilkinson, "Transforming Pentecostalism: The Migration of Pentecostals to Canada," in Michael Wilkinson, ed., *Canadian Pentecostalism: Transition and Transformation* (Montreal: McGill-Queen's University Press, 2009), pp. 249-63.

[17]Claudia Währisch-Oblau, *The Missionary Self-Perception of Pentecostal/Charismatic Church Leaders from the Global South in Europe: Bringing Back the Gospel* (Boston: Brill, 2009).

[18]See André Droogers, Cornelis van der Laan and W. van Laar, eds., *Fruitful in This Land: Pluralism, Dialogue, and Healing in Migrant Pentecostalism* (Geneva: WCC Publications, 2006), and Mechteld Jansen and Hijme Stoffels, eds., *A Moving God: Immigrant Churches in the Netherlands*, International Practical Theology 8 (Münster: LIT Verlag, 2008).

[19]A succinct overview is provided by Frank Ching, "The Asian Experience in the United States," in Frank J. Coppa and Thomas J. Curran, *The Immigrant Experience in America* (Boston: Twayne, 1976), pp. 192-214.

establishing the special status of these and other persons of Asian descent as being ineligible for citizenship. Throughout this time, vicious stereotypical portrayals of Asians appeared in the media, including in films that continued to appear on television for the rest of the century. During the Second World War more than 100,000 Japanese were interned as "enemy aliens," with two-thirds of them American-born citizens. These experiences have been internalized in the Asian American immigrant memory and community and continue to mark their "perpetual foreigner" mentality and self-understanding.

Expanding back to the global and especially Pacific Rim contexts, theologians have documented the political, socioeconomic, religiocultural and existential dimensions of migration movements across the Asian world, especially from the Philippines to Japan and Taiwan (albeit certainly not limited to this trajectory), even as they have reflected on the ethical, theological and pastoral aspects of such movements. One volume provides theological perspectives as well as policy recommendations.[20] The former includes reconsideration of the phenomenon of migration ecclesiologically, eschatologically and even vis-à-vis trinitarian theology, while the latter involves sensible policy recommendations such as the proposal that religious orders take up the responsibility to broker migrant labor movements since they would not be motivated to stretch the law or exploit the system (governments, employers and migrant laborers alike) for their own financial gain. As already noted, Roman Catholics have been at the forefront of such thinking, in part due to the long history of Catholic social teaching.

Gemma Cruz is a Filipina Catholic theologian and one of the few who has developed a theology of migration.[21] Her contribution lies in the new ground broken by books in a new series intended to bridge the gap between systematic theology and what the past generation has called contextual theology. Cruz's volume is a superb contribution to this project in at least the following ways: by foregrounding the fact of migration as a global phenomenon demanding systematic theological considerations; by analyzing migration

---

[20]Fabio Baggio and Agnes M. Brazal, eds., *Faith on the Move: Toward a Theology of Migration in Asia* (Manila: Ateneo de Manila University Press, 2008).

[21]Gemma Tulud Cruz, *An Intercultural Theology of Migration: Pilgrims in the Wilderness*, Studies in Systematic Theology 5 (Leiden: Brill, 2010).

through the particular lens of the plight of Filipina domestic helpers in Hong Kong; by bringing feminist theological sensibilities, informed by the domestic helper experience, into dialogue with womanist, Asian and Asian American perspectives; and by developing the systematic theological implications of the Filipino theology of struggle tradition in light of the reality of global migration. The argument is well researched, and Cruz works patiently, carefully and deftly in a multidisciplinary arena, respectfully engaging a wide range of theological and other sources, and bringing them into critical but creative and fruitful conversation. Most impressive is how the result is sensitive to the pastoral issues related to the Filipina domestic helper experience—on the one hand, acknowledging the challenges of migration among this group of workers but on the other empowering a holistic ethic of liberation and salvation with much wider relevance—thus illuminating the practical consequences of systematic theological reflection in our arguably new glocal situation. The result pushes theologians not only to develop the theology of migration but also to reconsider the method and task of systematic theology in global context.

Although Asian Catholic theologians have been at the forefront of this discussion, the increasing numbers of migrants from East Asian and other regions less dominated by Catholic presence will soon be motivating other theological forms of assessment. Nevertheless the theology of migration remains a nascent field, especially for evangelical theology, and this needs to be corrected, since migrants now number at least 200 million worldwide and show no signs of abating in our increasingly shrinking global village. All this movement, expansion and translation beg for more formal theological consideration on the phenomenon of migration.

Pentecostal theologians have begun to reflect theologically on the missiological implications of their spirituality, but this has yet to translate into a theology of migration. My suggestion, in the next part of this chapter, is that the distinctive character of pentecostal spirituality and missionary sensibility can be mined for insights that can contribute to the emerging discussions on theologies of migration. As should be clear from the foregoing, however, I am thinking about migration in exceedingly broad terms, across the spectrum of perspectives from those moving from a region or nation (emigrants) to those settling into a new country (immigrants) as well as including vastly different experiences of voluntary labor movements (migrants) and forced movements due especially to political turmoil (refugees, exiles, asylum seekers, etc.). Yet I will return in the last part of this chapter to suggest why we can think theologically more specifically about an Asian American pneumatology of *immigration*, following the work of the Spirit who always seeks to arrive, rest in and transform human hearts, lives and communities.

LUKAN MIGRATION: A PENT-EVANGELICAL READING

As a springboard for our thinking about migration, I turn to the pentecostal canon-within-the-canon, the book of Acts.[22] The following unfolds in three acts, according to the division that the author outlines in Acts 1:8, the first part of which has become central to the modern pentecostal movement's self-understanding: "But you will receive power when the Holy Spirit has come upon you; and you will be my witnesses *in all Judea and Samaria, and to the ends of the earth*" (italics added). My intention is to unpack this three-part migration of the apostolic experience in light of contemporary globalization trends.[23]

Act 1: The early church in Jerusalem as a migrant community. I want to make three broad observations about the migratory nature of the earliest messianic community that is described in the initial chapters of the book of Acts. First, it is clear that the initial followers of Jesus as the messiah were mostly Jews and God-fearers from around the Mediterranean who had come "home" to celebrate the Feast of Pentecost (Acts 2:5-11). Luke states that the original "congregation" of three thousand was constituted by these migrants "from every nation under heaven" (cf. Acts 2:5, 41).[24] Within a short time, the

---

[22]My work in pentecostal theology has repeatedly been developed from out of the Acts narrative; I provide an extended rationale for this in my *In the Days of Caesar*, chap. 3.1-2. See also Zevola Giovanni, "'What Are You Talking About to Each Other, as You Walk Along?' (Lk 24:17): Migration in the Bible and Our Journey of Faith," in Fabio Baggio and Agnes M. Brazal, eds., *Faith on the Move: Toward a Theology of Migration in Asia* (Manila: Ateneo de Manila University Press, 2008), pp. 93-117, which also uses Luke–Acts as a springboard for sketching a biblical theology of migration.

[23]The following thus complements and extends (1) my articulation of a theology of hospitality from Luke–Acts that emphasizes being both guests and hosts vis-à-vis people of other faiths, and (2) various aspects of my pneumatological theology of the public square developed from out of the Acts narrative; see Yong, *Hospitality and the Other: Pentecost, Christian Practices, and the Neighbor* (Maryknoll, NY: Orbis, 2008), esp. pp. 100-108, and Yong, *Who Is the Holy Spirit? A Walk with the Apostles* (Brewster, MA: Paraclete, 2011), respectively.

[24]I assume the traditional and scholarly consensus about Luke being the author of Acts and thus

number of messianists had grown to over five thousand, not including women and children (Acts 4:4), although their numbers were being added to by those from the countryside around Jerusalem (Acts 5:16). It appears that as a result of what had happened many of those who had returned from the diaspora decided to stay in the area, leading to major organizational conundrums for housing and feeding so many families in the longer term.

Thus, second, the earliest Christian community was confronted with its most severe challenge—and opportunity—because of its migrant constitution. As Luke records it, "During those days, when the disciples were increasing in number, the Hellenists complained against the Hebrews because their widows were being neglected in the daily distribution of food" (Acts 6:1). On the surface, this "problem" can be understood as no more or less than an economic one: migration brings with it economic risks and hazards. However, we have already been told that somehow, there were sufficient resources that the growing community pooled together to meet the needs of all (Acts 2:45; 4:34). Something more is going on, reflecting perhaps the inequalities common to migration experiences from the beginning of time. In this case, the local Hebrew widows, at least some of whom were Aramaic speakers, appeared to have been able to control the distribution of food, resulting in the neglect of the "outsiders," the Greek-speaking or Hellenist widows. Note, though, that the problem was not so much that Hellenist widows were not getting food but that they were not participants in the distribution of food, resulting, perhaps, in the lack of food not only for Hellenist widows but also for Hellenist families as a whole.[25]

Yet why should we be surprised that factions had developed in the early messianic community? No doubt there were miscommunications, misunderstandings and even jealousies that characterized such a diverse community, drawn together by Jewish and messianic commitments to some extent, yet deeply diverse in terms of linguistic, customary and cultural differences that inevitably emerged over time. Just as predictably, when such disagreements

---

will refer to him in shorthand vis-à-vis the responsibility for this early Christian historical narrative; however, the thrust of my exegetical and theological reflections do not depend on any naive one-to-one correlation between "Luke" and the authorship of Acts.

[25]See Reta Halteman Finger, *Of Widows and Meals: Communal Meals in the Book of Acts* (Grand Rapids: Eerdmans, 2007), chap. 11, for details of this argument.

boiled over, those "in charge," the Aramaic-speaking messianists, acted exclusively and maybe even condescendingly vis-à-vis the migrants in their midst. After all, outsiders, or at least those whose ties to the local area had been stretched or even broken for a time in some instances, did not deserve the same level of treatment as insiders. That has been the undeniable experience of migrants since human beings have launched or been cast out (as the case may be) from their home regions in search of a better tomorrow.[26]

This leads to my third observation about the burgeoning messianic community: they worked hard to develop an egalitarian leadership by putting migrants in charge. The apostles appointed seven deacons, all apparently—if their names are any indication—leading members of the migrant Hellenist Jews, one of which, Nicholas, is said explicitly to have been from the diaspora, that is, from Antioch in what is today called Asia Minor (Acts 6:5). Herein I think we learn a further lesson about theological indigenization commensurate with the Day of Pentecost narrative. If the outpouring of the Spirit empowered the speaking of many tongues and languages to declare "God's deeds of power" (Acts 2:11), then part of the outworking of this dynamic gift of the Spirit should be the empowering of people from many cultures to incarnate the gospel on their own terms. The Pentecost event did not erase the diversity of tongues but redeemed it, in fact, loosing the plurality of human expressions while orchestrating such dissonance miraculously for the glory of God. Similarly, then, the experience of migration, which brings very different people together, should result not in a homogenization of the messianic community but in its diversification. And appreciation for such diversity and pluralism depends on our following the Spirit's lead in empowering leadership across the spectrum, even when that means putting migrants in charge![27]

---

[26]See Robert D. Goette and Mae Pyen Hong, "A Theological Reflection on the Cultural Tensions Between First-Century Hebraic and Hellenistic Jewish Christians and Between Twentieth-Century First- and Second-Generation Korean American Christians," in Ho-Young Kwon, Kwang Chung Kim and R. Stephen Warner, eds., *Korean Americans and Their Religions: Pilgrims and Missionaries from a Different Shore* (University Park: The Pennsylvania State University Press, 2001), pp. 115-23; cf. also Young Lee Hertig, "Cross-Cultural Mediation: From Exclusion to Inclusion—Acts 6:1-7; also 5:33-42," in Robert L. Gallagher and Paul Hertig, eds., *Mission in Acts: Ancient Narratives in Contemporary Context* (Maryknoll, NY: Orbis, 2004), pp. 59-72.

[27]This builds off my discussion of the early church's ministry in "Conclusion—From Demonization to Kin-domization: The Witness of the Spirit and the Renewal of Missions in a Pluralistic World," in Amos Yong and Clifton Clarke, eds., *Global Renewal, Religious Pluralism, and the Great Com-*

Of course, this is not to say that the apostolic leaders had made all the right decisions in empowering the Hellenist Jews to take responsibility for their widows. In point of fact, initially there remained a distinction between the authority of the apostles themselves, as pray-ers and preachers/proclaimers, and that of the deacons, "to wait on tables" (Acts 6:2-4). Yet once released as deacons, the empowerment of the Spirit, which ultimately sought to take the gospel beyond the confines of Jerusalem and Judea, began to move upon these Hellenist Jewish leaders to undertake tasks beyond that of their initial assignment. It was Stephen the deacon who began to see, and to proclaim under the Spirit's inspiration, that the scope of the presence and activity of God's Spirit was not limited to Jerusalem or to the temple. Here was a Hellenist Jew who began to discern that this eschatological outpouring of the Spirit had diasporic implications. The entire history of Israel pointed to the universal character of God's redemptive activity (Acts 7). Stephen berated the Sanhedrin and other Jerusalem- and temple-centered Jews about their parochial perspectives, and the result was his stoning for blasphemy against Moses and the temple (Acts 7:44-53).[28] Is it too much to say that it was Stephen's migrant point of view, from the margins, that allowed him to realize the extent of the salvation in Christ that the more centrally located apostolic leaders might have discerned but failed to act out?[29]

Act 2: Philip, the first migrant evangelist to Samaria. In the aftermath of tragedy that ended Stephen's life and ministry, the local Jewish intelligentsia launched a severe persecution "against the church in Jerusalem, and all except the apostles were scattered throughout the countryside of Judea and Samaria" (Acts 8:1). Interestingly, while the Judean- and Galilean-based apostolic leadership hunkered down in Jerusalem, it was the migrant Hellenist Jewish

---

mission: Toward a Renewal Theology of Mission and Interreligious Encounter, Asbury Theological Seminary Series in World Christian Revitalization Movements in Pentecostal/Charismatic Studies 4 (Lexington, KY: Emeth, 2011), pp. 157-74, esp. pp. 167-68.

[28]See, e.g., Marcel Simon, *St Stephen and the Hellenists in the Primitive Church* (London: Longmans, Green, 1958).

[29]I came upon Justo L. González, "Reading from My Bicultural Place: Acts 6:1-7," in Fernando F. Segovia and Mary Ann Tolbert, eds., *Reading from This Place,* vol. 1: *Social Location and Biblical Interpretation in the United States* (Minneapolis: Fortress, 1995), pp. 189-47, after I completed this section, but am happy to note that our observations are largely consistent, although I come at this from a different angle than González's Latin American point of view. I did, however, nuance my discussion in a few places in light of González's chapter.

deacons who gave no second thought to the doors that appeared closed—that is, in Jerusalem—and moved to take advantage of open doors: in the wider countryside and, God forbid, in the land of Samaria. Recall that during that time, it was clearly known that "Jews do not share things in common with Samaritans" (Jn 4:9). In fact, things had so degenerated between Jews and Samaritans that the former had already begun to engage in the rhetorical demonization of the latter; thus does John record the Jewish leadership's polemic against Jesus: "you are a Samaritan and have a demon" (Jn 8:48)! In light of this background, let me proffer four sets of comments about the migration of the gospel to the region of Samaria and beyond.[30]

First, Luke records: "those who were scattered went from place to place, proclaiming the word. Philip went down to the city of Samaria and proclaimed the Messiah to them" (Acts 8:4-5). Although Jesus was himself an itinerant evangelist, the apostles he personally discipled did not initially follow in his footsteps. But migrants like Philip had embraced a messianic message with a much more extensive reach that was not geographically bounded. Not even the despised Samaritans were beyond the pale of the gospel's offering.

Second, Hellenist migrants like Philip had learned how to survive in hostile and foreign situations. Upon arrival in Samaria, then, he was able to engage with the locals in ways that the apostles may not have been able to. Along the way, he attracted the attention of Simon the sorcerer, who "for a long time . . . had amazed them [the Samaritans] with his magic" and commanded their attention (Acts 8:10-11). With skills honed from a life of migration, Philip was able to both engage the people and interact calmly and extensively with Simon—who "stayed constantly with Philip" (Acts 8:13)—even to the point of baptizing him into the faith. To be sure, when the apostles finally arrived from Jerusalem, they were much more forthright with Simon, but this was only possible because the groundwork had been laid by Philip. Still, the combined effect was a twofold subversion: first of the local Samaritan dynamics, with the authority of Simon being displaced by that of Hellenist and Jewish followers of the messiah, and that of the apostles themselves, by a migrant deacon who

---

[30]For background discussion, see F. Scott Spencer, *Journeying Through Acts: A Literary-Cultural Reading* (Peabody, MA: Hendrickson, 2004), esp. pp. 94-103 on "Philip the Evangelist in Samaria and Judea: 8.4-40."

while perhaps running for his life had not known better than to act politically incorrectly by building bridges with the perennial enemies of Israel.

But third, while the apostolic leaders returned to Jerusalem even after the relatively successful mission to Samaria (Acts 8:25), Philip was not done, emboldened instead to venture into the region of Gaza (Acts 8:26). Along the way, he met another migrant, one who had become adept at crossing boundaries and borders: sexual boundaries, no doubt intimidating for a eunuch who worked for a queen in a male-dominated world; ethnic boundaries, as an Ethiopian on sojourn far from home, in Palestine; international and political borders, as "a court official of the Candace, queen of the Ethiopians" (Acts 8:27a); socioeconomic borders, as one in charge of the treasury of Candace and of the Ethiopian people (Acts 8:27b); religious borders, as (in all probability) a Gentile who "had come to Jerusalem to worship" (Acts 8:27c); and personal/relational borders, as one perhaps without family, certainly without descendants, who felt alone in the world.[31] Maybe it was precisely in reflecting on his own existential state that he resonated with the man he was reading about: "In his humiliation he was deprived of justice. *Who can speak of his descendants?* For his life was taken from the earth" (Acts 8:33 NIV, citing Is 53:8; italics added). Did the eunuch empathize with this migrant stranger, who even as he "was led like a sheep to the slaughter . . . did not open his mouth" (Acts 8:32 NIV, citing Is 53:7)?

Philip, "starting with this scripture . . . , proclaimed to him the good news about Jesus" (Acts 8:35). This migrant Hellenist told the migrant Ethiopian all about the migrant Jew named Jesus, who not only had no descendants but also "nowhere to lay his head" (Lk 9:58). Thus here was a boundary and border crosser the Ethiopian could identify with, one who was indeed rejected by his generation, as he felt himself to be. Yet as his migrant evangelist recounted, the one who had no descendants had, through the gift of the Holy Spirit to all who would receive him, formed a new people of God, called after his name, and into this new family even eunuchs, Ethiopians, the sociopolitical elite and the economically affluent were all welcome. We are not told what happened to the eunuch after his encounter with Philip except that he "went on his way re-

---

[31]Abraham Smith, "A Second Step in African Biblical Interpretation: A Generic Reading Analysis of Acts 8:26-40," in Segovia and Tolbert, *Reading from This Place*, pp. 213-28, esp. pp. 225-27.

joicing" (Acts 8:39). Tradition says that the church in Ethiopia can be traced, at least in part, to this migrant's experiences on the road from Jerusalem to Gaza. If so, then from its inception, the migrating power of the gospel was manifest in Ethiopia, embodied by a migrant, without physical descendants, but with the power of the Spirit of God whose capacity to generate spiritual prosperity even from a eunuch continues unimpeded.[32]

Last but not least, however, this narrative ends with a migration experience for which nothing Philip had previously encountered would have prepared him. Upon baptizing the eunuch, suddenly "the Spirit of the Lord snatched Philip away; the eunuch saw him no more, and went on his way rejoicing. But Philip found himself at Azotus, and as he was passing through the region, he proclaimed the good news to all the towns until he came to Caesarea" (Acts 8:39-40). What is amazing is that Philip the migrant simply continued up the coastline, toward Caesarea, perhaps anticipating that this was simply one more stop in following out the call to take the gospel back to the ends of the earth from which he had come. And it would be in Caesarea that the next momentous occasions for the migration of the gospel would unfold.

Act 3: Peter, Paul and the ends of the earth. There is too much to comment on here, so let me cut to the chase and make a few general observations. We begin with Peter, who we saw was willing to venture at least into Samaria, following Philip, but who appears to have reconsidered his decision to remain in Jerusalem after all. But later on he embarked on his own itinerary trek, at least in the surrounding regions of Lydda and Joppa and later up to Caesarea (Acts 9:32–10:24). From here on, the horizons and borders of his own ministry expanded. Over time, he must have revisited his relationship with the migrant Hellenistic community that had become part of the fabric of the early messianic movement, to the point of establishing connections with the diasporic communities represented by these migrants. Thus later he writes to "exiles of the Dispersion in Pontus, Galatia, Cappadocia, Asia, and Bithynia" (1 Pet 1:1).

---

[32]Yet it is precisely the open-endedness of the story of the eunuch that constitutes it as a migration story par excellence; to see further how the characterization of the eunuch and the narrative location of this pericope deepen its function as a liminal account of what I would call the betwixt-and-between reality of the ongoing migration of the gospel to the ends of the earth, see Scott Shauf, "Locating the Eunuch: Characterization and Narrative Context in Acts 8:26-40," *Catholic Biblical Quarterly* 71, no. 4 (2009): 762-75.

If in fact the author of this epistle is the same person—and there are no good reasons to doubt the letter's authenticity[33]—Peter had clearly come to claim for himself a migrant identity, urging his readers "as aliens and exiles to abstain from the desires of the flesh that wage war against the soul" (1 Pet 2:11). In short, migrancy is not just an accidental feature of the lives of those who have crossed humanly construed borders, but rather it characterizes the pluralistic nature of what it means to be the people of God at its core.[34]

Paul, of course, was a cosmopolitan figure who was raised in Tarsus but who felt at home throughout the *Pax Romana*. He exercised his travel rights as a Roman citizen but did so by taking advantage of his educational achievements and elite status, possibly as one of the leading members of the Synagogue of the Freedmen (Acts 6:9). Of course, Paul's legacy has been as the missionary par excellence during the first generation of the messianic Christian movement. He made multiple missionary excursions around the Mediterranean world (which are recorded in Acts), even visited Rome (albeit as a prisoner in chains)—considered to have been the heart of the empire and, from the standpoint of Jerusalem, representing the "ends of the earth"—and long had aspirations to evangelize in Spain (Rom 15:28). In short, after coming to embrace the Hellenist interpretations (by Stephen et al.) of the message and meaning of Christ, Paul himself came to see the universal implications of the gospel. Yes, it was borne from out of the heart of God's covenant with the Jews, but it had from the beginning been intended to bless all the nations of the earth, as had been promised originally to Abraham.

My claim, however, is that Paul the migrant was not merely an itinerant evangelist or a peripatetic apostle. Rather, because he recognized that the power of a migrating gospel was only as strong as its roots in any local region, Paul established churches and worked to ensure that they were competently led and nurtured. Such local congregations were not explicitly subversive of

---

[33]See, e.g., Rebecca Skaggs, *The Pentecostal Commentary on 1 and 2 Peter and Jude*, Pentecostal Commentary Series 17 (Sheffield, UK: Sheffield Academic Press, 2004), pp. 3-7.

[34]For Asian American reflections on 1 Peter, see Russell G. Moy, "Resident Aliens of the Diaspora: 1 Peter and Chinese Protestants in San Francisco," in Tat-Siong Benny Liew and Gale A. Yee, eds., *The Bible in Asian America*, Semeia 90-91 (Atlanta: Society of Biblical Literature, 2002), pp. 51-67, reprinted in Viji Nakka-Cammauf and Timothy Tseng, eds., *Asian American Christianity: A Reader* (Castro Valley, CA: The Institute for the Study of Asian American Christianity, 2009), pp. 267-78.

the peace of Rome—after all, it was precisely such peace that enabled evangelical migration!—yet neither were they completely without imperial effect.[35] These effects could be measured economically, as exemplified in the communal way of life in the earliest days in Jerusalem; politically, as in how the followers of the Messiah could respect and pray for their political leaders but pledge their allegiances only to Jesus as Lord, rather than to Caesar; and socially, as represented by Peter's admonition to live differently from the world, especially when it lives after the flesh.

Beyond this, there were also more direct imperial engagements. Following Jesus, Paul mounted no revolutionary assault against the imperial regime. However, he confronted the forces of empire personally when opportunities arose, challenging its various manifestations in different domains. Economically, for instance, Paul did not shy away from burning scrolls devoted to sorcery and from exposing the character of local deities to the extent that such activities came to negatively impact the political economy of Ephesian craftsmen (Acts 19:17-27). Politically, Paul regularly appealed to his rights as a citizen, did not hesitate to interact with local leaders (Sergius Paulus of Paphos, the Philippian magistrates, Publius on Malta) and engaged with politicians about matters related to "justice, self-control, and the coming judgement" (Acts 24:25). Throughout, he discoursed about the reign of God (Acts 14:22; 19:8; 20:25; 28:23), no doubt a subversive idea when understood against the backdrop of Caesar's claims to lordship.[36]

---

[35]Here I summarize what I have elsewhere argued at length—i.e., in *In the Days of Caesar* and *Who Is the Holy Spirit?*—about the public or political dimensions of the early messianic experience. See also, e.g., Warren Carter, *The Roman Empire and the New Testament: An Essential Guide* (Nashville: Abingdon, 2006), and Christopher Bryan, *Render to Caesar: Jesus, the Early Church, and the Roman Superpower* (Oxford: Oxford University Press, 2005). For briefer explications from very different perspectives, consult N. T. Wright, "Paul and Caesar: A New Reading of Romans," in Craig Bartholomew, Jonathan Chaplin, Robert Song and Al Walters, eds., *A Royal Priesthood? The Use of the Bible Ethically and Politically—A Dialogue with Oliver O'Donovan*, Scripture and Hermeneutics series 3 (Carlisle, UK: Paternoster, 2002), pp. 173-93, and Richard A. Horsley, "Renewal Movements and Resistance to Empire in Ancient Judea," in R. S. Sugirtharajah, ed., *The Postcolonial Bible Reader* (Malden, MA: Blackwell, 2006), pp. 69-77.

[36]See Robert G. Reid, "'Savior' and 'Lord' in the Lukan Birth Narrative: A Challenge to Caesar?" *Pax Pneuma: The Journal of Pentecostals and Charismatics for Peace and Justice* 5, no. 1 (2009): 46-61; cf. also Sang Meyng Lee, "Marginalization and Its Driving Force: Eschatological/Apocalyptic Vision," *Journal of Asian and Asian American Theology* 4 (2001): 29-46, who makes the parallel argument that it is the eschatological and apocalyptic orientation of the apostolic believers that inspired and empowered their marginal voices and actions vis-à-vis the "powers" of the imperial center.

In all of this, I submit that Paul was simply following in the footsteps of his migrant savior. Jesus himself consistently crossed boundaries and borders: interacting with social pariahs such as tax collectors and prostitutes; touching the religiously polluted such as lepers, those hemorrhaging blood, or the bodies of dead people; welcoming the poor and other unclean people, including Gentiles and Samaritans; and so on. No, Jesus never left Palestine—unless one believes the apocryphal story of his visit to India—but once emergent on the public scene, he was constantly on the move, "through cities and villages" (Lk 8:1), relying on the goodwill, provisions and resources of others. Thus also did he commission his followers as migrant evangelists: "Take nothing for your journey, no staff, nor bag, nor bread, nor money—not even an extra tunic. Whatever house you enter, stay there, and leave from there. Wherever they do not welcome you, as you are leaving that town shake the dust off your feet as a testimony against them" (Lk 9:3-5; cf. Lk 10:3-12). Is it any wonder then that the earliest followers of Jesus set out as migrants, even to the very ends of the earth?[37]

AN EVANGELICAL THEOLOGY OF MIGRATION:
ASIAN AMERICAN MODULATIONS

We have now seen that the early messianic movement was constituted essentially by its migration experiences and that such movement both enabled the incarnation of Christian faith in a diversity of forms on the one hand but also the subversion of local hegemonic structures on the other. This final part of the chapter now reengages the contemporary discussion of immigration in evangelical circles. To do so, we begin via a conversation with a recent call for an evangelical theology of immigration and go on from there to sketch a Lukan, pneumatological and pent-evangelical theology of the same. Along the

---

[37]Much more can be said about Luke and his theological agenda that needs to be left out due to space and time constraints. Yet the preceding assumes that Luke is not only historian of the early church but also theologian in his own right—as fully documented by François Bovon, *Luke the Theologian: Fifty-Five Years of Research (1950-2005)* (Waco, TX: Baylor University Press, 2005). My pent-evangelical reading presumes a robust Lukan theological imagination, although I am aware that a full appreciation of this understanding will require reading Luke as theologian within a canonical framework. The following discussion returns to more contemporary interfaces (which is part of the prolegomenal task of this volume) rather than continuing prosecution of a full-fledged Lukan and scriptural theology of migration (the task of another book).

way, however, we intersperse our reflections with questions and considerations derived especially from an Asian American perspective.

Evangelical theology and migration. Matthew Soerens and Jenny Hwang
have recently invited Evangelicals to reconsider their views regarding immigration.[38] In the following I focus on the overall framework of their proposal, although in the next chapter we will look more specifically and at length at their
ideas regarding undocumented (as opposed to "illegal") immigration.[39] Soerens
and Hwang have extensive experience with immigrants through their work with
World Relief. Hwang, in addition, is a second-generation Korean American who
continues to wrestle with what it means to be Asian American in a white world.[40]
Three aspects of Soerens and Hwang's discussion—the biblical, sociohistorical
and ecclesial (these are my categorizations)—deserve to be noted.

First and most important for our purposes is Soerens and Hwang's important chapter on the biblical aspects of migration.[41] They note that the
biblical narratives are replete with migration stories. In fact, the people of God
are perennially migrants, even after settling in the Promised Land. More
pointedly, in the New Testament, the new people of God remain aliens and
strangers to this world, albeit now they are also fellow citizens, quite apart
from their cultural, linguistic, tribal or national affiliations and derivations of
the one body of Christ and the one reign of God. The divine admonition to
ancient Israelites to care for the stranger and the migrant is carried over into
the apostolic community. Followers of Jesus as Messiah are urged to care for
their neighbors, even if such care involves crossing previously established cultural and even religious boundaries (such as exemplified by the Good Samaritan). Migration is therefore a central biblical motif. Evangelicals ought to
make more of this theologically and politically, it would appear, than they have.

Second, Soerens and Hwang highlight various sociohistorical perspectives
in order to set in relief some of the issues that Evangelicals are often concerned

---

[38]Matthew Soerens and Jenny Hwang, *Welcoming the Stranger: Justice, Compassion and Truth in the Immigration Debate* (Downers Grove, IL: InterVarsity Press, 2009).

[39]Soerens and Hwang recognize that such immigration is illegal, but they resist using such language since it potentially reduces the identity of such people to this one feature (see *Welcoming the Stranger*, pp. 22-23).

[40]See Hwang's autobiographical narrative in *Welcoming the Stranger*, pp. 18-22.

[41]Soerens and Hwang, *Welcoming the Stranger*, chap. 5.

about. From a historical vantage point, they note that the United States is itself a land of immigrants. They mention the 645,000 Africans involuntarily brought into slavery, although they do not also mention that other voluntary European immigrants displaced Native Americans from their property and livelihood.[42] Beyond these dark sides of American immigration history are the various waves of migrants, including Asian Americans variously in the nineteenth century and after 1965. Although many white Americans—Evangelicals and otherwise—are concerned that immigration from the Global South taxes scarce public and national resources, strains the local economy and even poses threats to homeland security (concerns exacerbated in the new millennium), some of the deepest anxieties are more existential. The gradual unraveling of the former white cultural majority and the growing numbers of those from outside the Euro-American West are worrying. Soerens and Hwang deftly document the economic benefits that immigration brings, including cheap labor, heightened competition (which ought to be welcome for Evangelicals who believe strongly in a free market economy) and complementary entrepreneurial initiatives. Perhaps most importantly on this front, the duo urges that Evangelicals among all types of Christians should be committed to embracing cultural diversity according to the biblical vision of the coming reign of God, and in that case, immigration from the Global South ought to be welcomed rather than feared.

Ecclesially, then, our authors urge the church to be more intentional about its ministry to immigrants. Social ministries ought to be further developed on the one hand, even as, practically speaking, the church should model a multicultural life of reconciliation for the world. Asian American congregations, like many other ethnic churches and communities, provide such a safe haven for those transitioning as migrants. On the other hand, the church also should be a prophetic voice with regard to the injustices many immigrants face. Those who confess Christ need to be advocates for the poor and vulnerable immigrant and therefore be proactive in identifying root causes of population displacement and other factors inimical to the quests of migrants regardless of source or destination.

---

[42]See Soerens and Hwang, *Welcoming the Stranger*, p. 50; on the latter history, see also Barbara Brown Zikmund and Amos Yong, eds., *Remembering Jamestown: Hard Questions About Christian Mission* (Eugene, OR: Pickwick, 2010).

Soerens and Hwang thus urge that a Christian posture that is biblically informed should see migrants and immigrants as people first, not just as categories, numbers or costs. Christian compassion ought to be the rule of thumb for guests receiving those coming from outside. It ought not to be forgotten that among those on the move are other Christ followers, themselves motivated by the virtues of courage and perseverance, perhaps even feeling the divine call to bring the gospel back to the West. Koreans and Korean Americans in particular are coming as Christians and thus living out their faith as immigrant ministers of the gospel of Christ.[43]

Toward a pent-evangelical theology of migration. In the final pages of this chapter, I want to sketch the rudiments of a migrant theology as informed by my Asian American perspective and my pentecostal rereading of the book of Acts. My goal is to build on Soerens and Hwang's theological insights toward an Asian American and pent-evangelical theology of migration. There are three dimensions to my summary reflections: missiological, political and theological.

Missionally, any pent-evangelical theology of migration must begin with the missional character of the Spirit-filled life. On this matter, mission involves migration, and migration is undertaken for missional purposes.[44] Yet as our overview of the early messianic experience shows, at some point, roots are planted, and in those cases, migrants need to find homes. Note that the apostolic decision to receive leadership from migrants reflects the discernment that in that case, at that place and time, these migrants who were far from home (although having returned home in other respects) needed their own leaders. Here was a case of enabling local leaders on foreign soil, so to speak. Along the way, at least at the dawn of the modern world, including the begin-

---

[43]My own familiarity with the Chinese American experience leads in this book to a relative neglect of Korean American Evangelicalism, which demands greater scholarly and theological attention. I briefly mention some of the important research on this topic in chapter 2. An important discussion of the recent expansive growth of Korean evangelical Christianity is Timothy S. Lee, *Born Again: Evangelicalism in Korea* (Honolulu: University of Hawaii Press, 2010), while perspectives on the emergence of the Korean missionary enterprise are provided by Sung-hun Kim and Wonsuk Ma, eds., *Korean Diaspora and Christian Mission*, Regnum Studies in Mission (Eugene, OR: Wipf & Stock/Regnum Books, 2011). Any comprehensive proposal for an Asian American contribution to evangelical theology in the present time will need to engage extensively with Korean American voices and perspectives.

[44]See Jehu J. Hanciles, "Migration and Mission: The Religious Significance of the North-South Divide," in Andrew Walls and Cathy Ross, eds., *Mission in the Twenty-First Century: Exploring the Five Marks of Global Mission* (Maryknoll, NY: Orbis, 2008), pp. 118-29.

nings of the modern missionary movement, we have forgotten such truths so that the missional task of Christianization has been co-opted by the colonial project of westernization instead. Hence we have had to relearn the hard way over the last century many lessons about the importance of recognizing and empowering indigenous leaders.[45] Yet such should not be understood only in terms of what happens "out there," abroad, in the Global South; it may also be relevant here, "at home," in the Euro-American West, particularly in light of the reverse missionary movement from the rest to the West. Pentecostals have usually been alert to the need for establishing indigenous churches that are—following the famous missionary model of Roland Allen—self-supporting, self-governing and self-propagating, at least in (missiological) theory if not in (evangelistic) practice.[46] Yet the current task for any theology of migration relative to the needs of the twenty-first century needs to be sensitive to the challenges experienced by migrant communities and their churches wherever they may be found.

From an Asian American missiological perspective, any pent-evangelical theology of migration ought to be mindful that the forces of globalization are not only causing upheavals in population movements but also open up new opportunities for mission and evangelization.[47] The Asian diaspora around the world, not to mention to North America, provides alternative pathways for carrying out the Great Commission, particularly with regard to people groups who are less accessible in their Asian homelands. More pertinent in the American context, many if not most Asian immigrants are open to learning about if not embracing the Christian religion since they are already primed to conform to the dominant American culture. There are missiological challenges involved here, but the opportunities are there nonetheless. The key is to be sensitive to Asian cultural dynamics so that ecclesial forms of life are

---

[45]Elsewhere, I sketch the broad contours of a postcolonial approach to the missionary task: Yong, "The Missiology of Jamestown: 1607-2007 and Beyond—Toward a Postcolonial Theology of Mission in North America," in Yong and Zikmund, *Remembering Jamestown*, pp. 157-67.

[46]See Yong, "Many Tongues, Many Practices: Pentecost and Theology of Mission at 2010," in Ogbu U. Kalu, Edmund Kee-Fook Chia and Peter Vethanayagamony, eds., *Mission After Christendom: Emergent Themes in Contemporary Mission* (Louisville, KY: Westminster John Knox, 2010), pp. 43-58, esp. pp. 47-48.

[47]See Chandler Im and Amos Yong, eds., *Global Diasporas and Mission*, Regnum Edinburgh Centenary Series (Oxford: Regnum Books International, 2013).

nurtured that do not merely mimic Westernized church traditions. Empowering Asian American leaders to think through the contextual issues navigated by Asian American communities of faith will be central to the future of Asian American Evangelicalism in particular and to evangelical faith as a whole.

Politically: Our review of the Acts narrative also, however, highlights what we might not often hear much about in pentecostal circles—the political dimension of missional migration. Pentecostals have been, in general, so focused on the evangelistic dimension of missions that they have neglected to reflect more intentionally about the political relevance of their practices. In this respect, my initial efforts to construct a pentecostal theology of migration in this chapter involve also an element of deconstruction of pentecostal assumptions about missional migration.[48] What needs to be interrogated is the widely assumed notion in pentecostal mission and evangelism that the gospel is meant for human souls rather than for human lives in all of their political complexity. By political, of course, I am referring to the public constitutedness of human life, which includes not only the political narrowly conceived in relationship to the state but also the economic, social, cultural and civic domains. Pentecostals are right to insist that neither Jesus nor Paul were directly concerned with such public structures in their migration. However, this does not mean that migrants have nothing to say about or contribute to the political formation of human lives. In fact, the subversive power of the gospel is precisely its capacity to interrogate the status quo of our political, social and economic practices, even to the point of undermining the very nature of these presumed realities insofar as they do not measure up to the peace, justice and righteousness of the coming reign of God.[49] The power of migration is that it injects fresh perspectives into local situations, perspectives that can generate new insights into underlying causes of what needs to be fixed and that can identify what needs to be done. The key is that there need to be structures in place that welcome migrants and enable their settling into a new home yet that

---

[48]See further my "Global Pentecostalism and the Political," in Shaun Casey and Michael Kessler, eds., *The Oxford Handbook of Political Theology* (Oxford: Oxford University Press, forthcoming).

[49]As I try to suggest, with Samuel Zalanga, in "What Empire? Which Multitude? Pentecostalism & Social Liberation in North America & Sub-Saharan Africa," in Bruce Ellis Benson and Peter Goodwin Heltzel, eds., *Evangelicals and Empire: Christian Alternatives to the Political Status Quo* (Grand Rapids: Brazos, 2008), pp. 237-51.

do not assimilate them to the point that they can no longer maintain a critical vantage point.[50] The result should be a transformation of the margins so that new centers emerge in a globalized and post-Christendom world.[51]

From an Asian American perspective, the politics of migration are complicated not only ideologically but practically. In a real sense, this entire volume gestures toward a path forward for pent-evangelical Christians that includes but does not merely assimilate Asian Americans into the dominant (white) culture. If being yellow between black-and-white involves complex and challenging issues, perhaps we can take cues from how Jewish proselytes and Gentile Christ followers in the early apostolic period navigated between traditional Jewish demands on the one hand and Greco-Roman obligations under the lordship of Caesar on the other. In this case, the dilemmas confronted when the interests of Greek- and Hebrew-speaking widows collided in the early church becomes a window through which to think through an Asian American pent-evangelical political economy. The task involves the building up of vibrant ecclesial communities that can meet the needs of migrants in their many domains but neither devolve into a ghetto or ethnic enclave nor eventually get absorbed into the larger culture in ways that diminish or lose the gifts that each culture brings to enrich and beautify the body of Christ in anticipation of the reign of God to come. And when truly divine, the tribes and peoples of the church will also challenge the status quo from their sites of Spirit-inspired difference.

This leads, finally, to the theological axis: My pentecostal perspective that begins with the experience of Spirit infilling and empowerment for mission realizes that our migration is modeled on that of the Holy Spirit's.[52] The

---

[50]Or, to facilitate what Andrew Sung Park calls "transmutation," which is not assimilation (wherein the emigrating identity is lost), amalgamation (wherein the emigrating and the new cultural identities are improperly syncretized) or mere coexistence (perpetuating ethnic enclaves and ghettoes), but where there is the possibility of the mutual enhancement, enrichment and deepening of all groups by one another. See Park, "A Theology of Transmutation," in Eleazer S. Fernandez and Fernando F. Segovia, eds., *A Dream Unfinished: Theological Reflections on America from the Margins* (Maryknoll, NY: Orbis, 2001), pp. 152-66.

[51]As argued by Jehu H. Hanciles, *Beyond Christendom: Globalization, African Migration, and the Transformation of the West* (Maryknoll, NY: Orbis, 2008).

[52]Mine might be called an eschatological theology of migration, precisely due to its pneumatological dynamic, in which case it extends what Andrew Walls calls the Adamic (involuntary) and Abrahamic (redemptive) models of biblical migration; see Walls, "Toward a Theology of Migration," in Frieder Ludwig and J. Kwabena Asamoah-Gyadu, eds., *African Christian Presence in the*

Spirit's migration, however, is also more precisely, from our perspective, an *im*migration, a movement of the Spirit that is incomplete until the Spirit takes up residence upon our heads, blows between our ears, enlivens our tongues and gushes forth from within our hearts. Thus does Luke write

> And suddenly from heaven there came a sound like the rush of a violent wind, and it filled the entire house where they were sitting. Divided tongues, as of fire, appeared among them, and a tongue rested on each of them. All of them were filled with the Holy Spirit and began to speak in other languages, as the Spirit gave them ability. (Acts 2:2-4)

The movements of the Spirit are thus outward, from the Father on high (Lk 24:49) through the Son at his right hand (Acts 2:33) and then inward, into us (cf. Rom 5:5), so as to redeem us as the people of God. No wonder we are a migrant people, caught up in the migrations of the Spirit. Yet simultaneously, we are also an immigrant people, following the immigrations of the Spirit. But if the Spirit immigrates into human hearts, so do we, as living epistles, immigrate into the proximity of the lives of strangers, and there seek to take root, not in the sense of making their world our home, but in the sense of enabling the gospel to flourish deep in the hearts and lives of our hosts. Thus the call of the Spirit is the empowerment to take up and leave our homes and our comfort zones, to be guests of others in strange places, so that the triune God can become the home for us all. Herein is accomplished our own transformation, touched through the Spirit by the differences represented in the hearts and lives of others. The Spirit immigrates betwixt, between and through our own diasporic crossing (repeatedly: back and forth—sometimes literally but at least figuratively) over the borders and margins that had previously divided "us" from "them."

From an Asian American perspective, then, such a theologically funded hospitality works in multiple directions. On the one hand, Asian Americans, Christian or not, are guests and hosts in a multicultural United States; here Asian American Christians find ourselves playing multiple roles, depending on the context, with such roles often shifting. On the other hand, pent-

---

West: New Immigrant Congregations and Transnational Networks in North America and Europe (Trenton, NJ: Africa World Press, 2011), pp. 407-17.

evangelical Christians, Asian American or not, have the obligation, in following out the trinitarian life of God, to host others—nonevangelical Christians or even non-Christians—and to be guests of these neighbors as well; Evangelicals who may be more comfortable being hosts rather than guests in these contexts need to be more intentional about emulating Jesus, both the ultimate divine host yet also the ultimate human guest in his incarnational journey. Amid these trajectories of hospitality Asian American Pentecostals and Evangelicals find themselves relating to other (nonevangelical and non-Christian) Asian Americans, other non–Asian Americans, and other non–Asian American Evangelicals—being hosts in some circumstances and guests in others. Any pent-evangelical theology that is not capable of supporting or inspiring faithful Christian witness in these divergent and in some instances dissonant contexts will need to be reconstructed, since these are realities of the globalizing world of the twenty-first century that are not going to disappear anytime soon.

When all of this finally happens, the eschatological transmigration will occur, one that will involve the coming down of the new Jerusalem from out of heaven, and that will involve the renewal of the heavens and the earth so that they and all their inhabitants can become the final dwelling place of the living God.[53] This is the Christian and pent-evangelical hope, for sure; equally sure is that its realization, at least according to human standards, remains distant.

---

[53]As beautifully argued, in the thesis that the cosmos is destined to become the dwelling place of the Spirit and the inhabitation of the triune God, by Frank D. Macchia, *Justified in the Spirit: Creation, Redemption, and the Triune God* (Grand Rapids: Eerdmans, 2010).

6

THE SPIRIT OF JUBILEE

An Asian American Immigrant Consideration

Fumitaka Matsuoka (whom we met briefly in chapter two) has long been at the forefront of encouraging the North American church and its theological establishment to think about racism vis-à-vis the multidimensional complexities of globalization.[1] He has thus identified the need to "revisit our relationships in light of complex histories" in order to retain the credibility of Christian faith and of our faith communities in a racist, pluralist and globalizing world.[2] Both the truth-telling of heretofore neglected or silenced voices and the reconciliation between those in the center with those on the margins are needed for the church to effectively engage the public square. Such a prophetic posture is central to the peace witness of the ecclesial tradition, the Church of the Brethren, which has long informed Matsuoka's teaching and thinking.[3]

This chapter delves deeper into issues raised by immigration opened up in chapter five. In particular, we probe into the economics of immigration

---

[1]Matsuoka's most poignant books on this front are *Out of Silence: Emerging Themes in Asian American Churches* (Cleveland: United Church Press, 1995) and *The Color of Faith: Building Community in a Multiracial Society* (Cleveland: United Church Press, 1998).

[2]Fumitaka Matsuoka, "The Changing Terrain of 'Globalization' in ATS Conversations," *Theological Education* 35, no. 2 (1999): 22. "ATS" in the title of the article refers to the Association of Theological Schools, the North American seminary accrediting body that Matsuoka has worked with for some time.

[3]E.g., as reflected in the following Matsuoka essays: *"Jesus Christ Our Lord* from a Missiological Perspective," in Richard A. Kauffman, ed., *A Disciple's Christology: Appraisals of Kraus's Jesus Christ Our Lord*, Occasional Papers 13 (Elkhart, IN: Institute of Mennonite Studies, 1989), pp. 28-37; "Race and Peoplehood," *Brethren Life and Thought* 44, no. 3 (1999): 33-46; and "Reflecting on Theological Education at Bethany Theological Seminary," *Brethren Life and Thought* 49, nos. 1-2 (2004): 108-16.

wherein we are also confronted more starkly with the phenomenon of undocumented immigration (which I, following Matthew Soerens and Jenny
Hwang, prefer over "illegal immigration"). Hence we heed Matsuoka's call by
retrieving the voices of undocumented Chinese immigrants to New York City
(NYC) for a contemporary theology of immigration viewed from an economic angle. Yet, I want to shift the terms of the discussion away from either
development or liberation[4] (or any of the other dualistically constructed
categories like capitalism or socialism) in order to take a fresh look at the
issues through the lens of the informal economy. My hunch is that an informal
economic perspective will be suggestive for thinking creatively, liberatively
and normatively (i.e., theologically) about the interface between religious life
and contemporary globalization.

Toward these ends, three primary tasks are undertaken, corresponding
with the three main sections of this chapter, that of (1) situating our reflections
concretely within the complex and largely silent recent history of Chinatown,
NYC, and identifying the global and transnational economic structures and
their religious links that constitute the backdrop of Chinatown; (2) critically
mapping the informality of the Chinatown economy onto that of the apostolic
experience of the earliest messianic believers, and following out cues from
there to contemporary theological debates about especially undocumented
immigration; and (3) considering innovative and improvisational forms of
ecclesial ministry and praxis for the church that is *in* but not constrained by
the informal sphere while providing some perspective on the present discussion of undocumented immigration in evangelical theology. Our goal
throughout is to reexamine the relationship between race/ethnicity, religion,
globalization, economics and immigration by focusing on the informal
economy and how it interfaces and perhaps illuminates questions related to
undocumented immigration.

I should note that this chapter ought not to be read as direct intervention in
the debates, theological and otherwise, over undocumented immigration.
Rather, this is a tangential, albeit no less important, theme related to the economics of globalization and immigration. In this chapter, our case study of

---

[4]Which is not to slight the import of either of these projects, explicated superbly in Thia Cooper,
Controversies in Political Theology (London: SCM Press, 2007).

Chinese American immigration is a springboard to reflection on the social justice, economic and political aspects of globalization. Biblical and pentecostal perspectives on a theology of economics and a theology of migration are developed in this context in dialogue with evangelical and other theological resources. Hence our considerations, brief as they are, on undocumented immigration, need to be understood amid this wider set of concerns. The concluding sketch of a pneumatological theology of economics and migration thereby addresses this nexus of important issues, and does so by reconnecting to one of the central themes of Matsuoka's lifework as it has been shaped by the Brethren and Mennonite traditions, that of the shalom—the peace, justice and righteousness—of the coming reign of God.

INFORMALITY AND IMMIGRATION: THE CHINESE AMERICAN EXPERIENCE

Recent research of Asian American transnationalism has documented the precarious socioeconomic plight of many Asian immigrants to North America. Such research raises theological questions about the church's ministry and mission in the context of trends in globalization. This chapter begins by exploring especially the economic dimensions of the Asian American immigration as uncovered by a recent ethnographic study of Chinatown in NYC[5] in order to invite consideration of a migration theological model able to engage both the opportunities and challenges confronting the church vis-à-vis the processes of economic globalization.

Kenneth Guest is an anthropologist at Baruch College's Weissman School of Arts and Sciences in New York. His *God in Chinatown* explores the relationship between religion and the globalization and immigration processes between the region of Fuzhou, on the southeast coast of the People's Republic of China, and the ethnic Chinatown enclave of NYC. The religious diversity among the Fuzhounese of NYC is refracted in Guest's study through a Buddhist temple, a Daoist temple, two Roman Catholic parishes and two Protestant congregations. The last receives more extensive coverage: the Church of Grace derives from the Chinese Christian tradition of John Sun's Home of

---

[5]Kenneth J. Guest, *God in Chinatown: Religion and Survival in New York's Evolving Immigrant Community* (New York: New York University Press, 2003).

Grace, and the New York House Church has connections with the Little Flock churches of Fuzhou. An important point the book argues is that religious matters are not subservient to a more "fundamental" socioeconomic domain but rather inform that domain from within and, in doing so, reflect realities both in Fuzhou and NYC.[6] Hence religious beliefs and practices bridging multiple nationalities and ethnicities mediate the construction of alternative identities, in part in response to the perennial human quest for meaning, but also to the broader discourses of the ethnic enclave in dominant American society. Throughout, Guest combines theoretical analysis, ethnographic observation and testimonial narrative to underscore how the Chinatown enclave provides a site for mobilization of social capital for immigrants in terms of connecting existing social networks, enabling the exchange of information and (financial) resources, and supporting the processes of legalization.

Undocumented immigration in Chinatown. My focus in this chapter is specifically on undocumented Fuzhounese immigrants and their transnational quest to "realize America in their hearts."[7] Nondocumented immigration from Fuzhou began in the mid-1980s and continues to the present. Most undocumented Fuzhounese begin their trek as youths,[8] and they find their way to the United States usually through organized international smuggling syndicates. The going rates in the late 1980s had tripled to over $60,000 by the early 2000s, with up to 20 percent due up front and the rest upon arrival.[9] Immigrants thus incur indebtedness to their families and relatives or, if the latter are unable to pay the bill, become indentured servants to the smugglers or their local brokers (at best) or are beaten, even maimed, as punishment (at worst).

Of course, Fuzhounese immigrants brave the journey to the United States in search of a better life (on which more momentarily). But upon arrival, they

---

[6]The centrality of religion for immigration is documented also with regard to the very different experiences of middle-class Taiwanese in Southern California by Carolyn Chen, *Getting Saved in America: Taiwanese Immigration and Religious Experience* (Princeton, NJ: Princeton University Press, 2008).

[7]This is the title of Fumitaka Matsuoka and Eleazar S. Fernandez, eds., *Realizing the America of Our Hearts: Theological Voices of Asian Americans* (St. Louis: Chalice, 2003), which illuminates the longings and aspirations of Asian migrants to the United States.

[8]Kenneth J. Guest, "Liminal Youth Among Fuzhou Chinese Undocumented Workers," in Tony Carnes and Fenggang Yang, eds., *Asian American Religions: The Making and Remaking of Borders and Boundaries* (New York: New York University Press, 2004), pp. 55-75.

[9]Guest, *God in Chinatown*, pp. 28, 67.

find a highly stratified ethnic enclave. Unless one has connections, one finds him- or herself defined by their region or city of origin, dialect, the socio-economic class status of one's family "back home" or one's educational achievements. This stratification persists even within churches found in the enclave. The result is that most immigrant youths find themselves in the working class, with limited English skills, owing large sums of money to their families or relatives in Fuzhou, or to the snakeheads (smugglers) or their brokers. As Guest thus notes, "Save for a limited number who successfully apply for political asylum, all remain undocumented, outside the mainstream, working in the informal economy."[10]

Many, if not most, struggle to survive working (and sleeping!) in restaurants, garment shops and other nonregistered businesses. They work six days a week—and not atypically pick up hours on their "day off" for other "employers"—for more than twelve hours a day and are paid sometimes as low as $2 per hour. The majority are without medical insurance, childcare or any other benefits.[11] The most hardworking and entrepreneurial pay off their debts faster than others—and even after that many continue to remit funds to their families—and some even eventually make their way up the socioeconomic ladder, gradually obtaining promotions to higher-paying positions. So on the one hand,

> Fuzhounese immigrants, particularly undocumented immigrants, are extremely creative actors working to manipulate a system stacked with disadvantages. . . . At the same time, this isolated ethnic enclave is a trap for many Fuzhounese who, marginalized by language, culture, and class from both the mainstream U.S. economy and the Chinatown elites, have no way to escape.[12]

So why then do so many continue to make the journey without documentation to the United States? No doubt, those who "make it" send reports and remit money "back home" regularly in ways that build up the hopes and dreams of those without other viable options.[13] The fact of the matter is that

---

[10]Ibid., p. 31.

[11]Ibid., p. 42.

[12]Ibid., p. 43.

[13]For further discussion of this transnational dimension, see Guest's other essays, "Transnational Religious Networks Among New York's Fuzhou Immigrants," in Helen Rose Ebaugh and Janet Saltzman Chafetz, eds., *Religion Across Borders: Transnational Immigrant Networks* (Walnut Creek, CA: AltaMira Press, 2002), pp. 149-63, and, focused on the Buddhist temples, "Religion and

when the Chinese work ethic is factored in, the opportunity to earn even $2 an hour is more than what many could make if they stayed and worked in Fuzhou.[14] This is especially the case since rural Fuzhounese have long confronted a depressed economy and then are at a disadvantage if they move to the city as legal employment is in many cases limited to city residents. Further, the expansion of the human smuggling network combined with the pull of the US labor market make emigration more attractive, even without legal papers. Last but not least have been the executive orders entered that have been favorable to immigrants. Fuzhounese are undeterred by their lack of documentation, since on at least two occasions in the last half-generation they have been the beneficiaries of changing immigration laws: the Immigration Reform and Control Act of 1986, under the presidency of Ronald Reagan, which granted amnesty to those who could demonstrate their arrival in the United States before 1982, and the presidential orders of George H. W. Bush in 1989 and 1990 that granted asylum to Chinese students in light of the Tiananmen Square massacre and China's population control policies. There is always the hope that another executive order will legalize their status and make it possible to attain the American dream.[15]

Within the wider transnational and global context, however, people emigrate without documentation for many other economic reasons that they may not be able to clearly articulate. What they feel most palpably is the high unemployment or underemployment realities of their home region; and what they hear about is the lure of employment and upward socioeconomic mobility options in the United States, while seeing the "proof" of such in the comparatively affluent families who are on the receiving end of remittances sent home from relatives or family members working overseas. Yet global market demands and labor supplies are structured by trade agreements between nations, and by demographic shifts, especially aging populations of receiving countries versus growing populations of developing countries.[16]

Transnational Migration in the New Chinatown," in Karen I. Leonard, Alex Stepick, Manuel A. Vasquez and Jennifer Holdaway, eds., *Immigrant Faiths: Transforming Religious Life in America* (Walnut Creek, CA: AltaMira Press, 2005), pp. 145-63.

[14]Guest, *God in Chinatown*, p. 41.

[15]Ibid., pp. 66-67.

[16]See Mary DeLorey, "International Migration: Social, Economic, and Humanitarian Consider-

Further, market-determined exchange rates that do not favor developing nations drive the unemployed or underemployed to look for work elsewhere, while structural adjustments imposed on developing nations usually involve a decline in their social welfare protections. Also, transnational corporations increasingly monopolize economic production, leaving free enterprise to float perilously in the informal economy. These economic factors in the background lead us to probe more deeply into the nature of economic informality, a reality within which Fuzhounese immigrants to NYC in a significant sense live, move and have their being.

The informal economy: A sketch. By definition, the informal economy exists outside the regulated and legislated (formalized) economy. An extremely heteronomous domain, a phenomenology of the informal economy, globally considered, would include at least the following kinds of economic agents and activities: street vendors, rickshaw/cart pullers, shared transportation, recyclers, petty traders/hawkers, small item producers, (very) small business owners (often at street corners rather than in their own rented or owned buildings), casual living arrangements, homeworkers (garment and shoe makers, embroiderers, assemblers, etc.), piece-rate workers, sub- and sub-sub-contractors, offsite data processors, farm and agricultural workers, unregistered/undeclared workers, cooperative partners and partnerships, and part-time, temporary and self-employed workers. As should be clear from this very brief enumeration, informal economic activity cuts across explicitly economic initiatives but in many cases also connects these with other social, communal and cultural relationships and interactions.[17]

While there is some overlap between informal economic transactions and premodern economies, the former is now acknowledged to be a more or less permanent feature of the present global market economy.[18] Of course, informal economic activity is especially noticeable in regions (and nations) working to enter the global economy and during periods of economic crisis

---

ations," in Donald Kerwin and Jill Marie Gerschutz, eds., *And You Welcomed Me: Migration and Catholic Social Teaching* (Lanham, MD: Rowman & Littlefield, 2009), pp. 31-53.

[17]A classic analysis of the informal economy is Hernando de Soto, *The Other Path: The Invisible Revolution in the Third World*, trans. June Abbott (New York: Harper and Row, 1989).

[18]See Alejandro Portes, Manuel Castells and Lauren A. Benton, eds., *The Informal Economy: Studies in Advanced and Less Developed Countries* (Baltimore, MD: The Johns Hopkins University Press, 1989).

and recession in developed nations. But as we have now seen with regard to the Chinatown enclave in NYC, informal economic activity exists in the very heart of the Western world as well. Hence it is clear that there is enough continuity between the formal and informal economies, rather than a strict demarcation between them, so that even in industrialized environments upwards of one-fourth of all economic activity occurs in the informal sector.[19] In fact, economists are suggesting that we move beyond any rigid conceptual dichotomy between the formal and informal economy.[20] Certainly the thrust of the most active theoreticians working in this arena is to find ways to formalize informal economic activities in order to unleash the potential of these assets as a means of engaging the otherwise poor with the global economy.[21] This would certainly be helpful for our Fuzhounese immigrants except for the fact that they would still have to deal with the challenges related to their lack of documentation.

How else then might the informal economy be understood? On the one hand, the existence of the informal sector "can be viewed as a constructed response on the part of civil society to unwanted state interference";[22] in the Fuzhounese case there are, in addition to these economic considerations, immigration factors that motivate their avoidance of the state. On the other hand, however, it is also fair to say that the explosion of informality has occurred in reaction to the mercantilism and state, national or even international bureaucracies that hinder effective formalization of economic activity at the grassroots. As instinctive responses of the masses to poverty, underdevelopment and the inefficiencies of the legal-political system, the informal economy exhibits a good deal of energy, spirit, entrepreneurship, ingenuity, productivity, persistence and just plain hard work. By its nature, then, the businesses of the

---

[19]See "Women and Men in the Informal Economy: A Statistical Picture," International Labour Organization (2002), www.ilo.org/dyn/infoecon/docs/441/F596332090/women%20and%20 men%20stat%20picture.pdf.

[20]See Basudeb Guha-Khasnobis, S. M. Ravi Kanbur and Elinor Ostrom, eds., *Linking the Formal and Informal Economy: Concepts and Policies* (New York: Oxford University Press, 2006).

[21]E.g., Ahmed M. Soliman, *A Possible Way Out? Formalizing Housing Informality in Egyptian Cities* (Lanham, MD: University Press of America, 2004).

[22]Alejandro Portes, "The Informal Economy and Its Paradoxes," in Neil J. Smelser and Richard Swedberg, eds., *The Handbook of Economic Sociology* (Princeton, NJ: Princeton University Press, and New York: Russell Sage Foundation, 1994), pp. 426-49; quote from p. 444.

informal economy are unregistered, its transactions not computed (nor computable) in gross national products, and its incomes untaxed (and oftentimes untaxable). Yet while the informal economy certainly includes semilegal and even unlawful activity (involving undocumented immigrants, for example), it is probably more accurate to understand this global phenomenon in terms of extralegality.[23] But herein lie also the challenges: extralegal operations in the informal arena result in unprotected employment (workers are without benefits of any sort), impinge on the capacity of informals to grow, develop and expand their trade (at least in the formal/legal sector), and leave them vulnerable to theft, violence and extortion, not to mention unjust business practices on an unequal playing field (unequal for the Fuzhounese not only because of their undocumented status but also because of their linguistic deficiencies).[24] In short, life in the informal economy is not ideal, and it is probably fair to say that informal economic agents do what they do in order to survive on the economic margins of society.

Chinese American evangelical informality. It is such a quest for survival that drives a significant part of the activity of the informal economy. Our discussion of transnational Fuzhounese migration from East Asia to NYC reflects this human search for hope, opportunity and meaning, and this inevitably leads many to intersect with the religious institutions of Chinatown. Guest's discussion of religion in Chinatown, then, illuminates the role that such churches, temples and religious agents (e.g., fortune tellers) play vis-à-vis the "illegality and informality" of their parishioners. Focusing more specifically on the Christian churches in Guest's study—which by and large are limited to two once-related evangelical-type congregations—we can see how these have facilitated the strenuous adjustment processes involved in migration that covers half of the world. Churches provide what Guest calls "safe

---

[23]See de Soto, *Other Path*, pp. 13-14. As de Soto suggests elsewhere, whereas many see the informal economy as being on the underside of the world economic system, "In fact it is legality that is marginal; extralegality has become the norm. The poor have already taken control of vast quantities of real estate and production"; see Hernando de Soto, *The Mystery of Capital: Why Capitalism Triumphs in the West and Fails Everywhere Else* (New York: Perseus, 2000), p. 30.

[24]For an early study of the blurred lines between lawful and unlawful interactions in the informal domain, see George Jenkins, "An Informal Political Economy," in Jeffrey Butler and A. A. Castagno, eds., *Boston University Papers on Africa: Transition in African Politics* (1967; repr., New York: Frederick A. Praeger, 1968), pp. 166-94.

harbors" with familiar customs, smells, sights, foods and language.[25] Information exchange occurs, social networks are opened, socioeconomic capital is mobilized, and financial, medical and care resources are made available to vulnerable immigrants. Financial assistance most often occurs interpersonally between members and adherents as people with needs are brought into the orbit of the church, although in some instances there are compassion funds established by congregations "used to assist members who are ill or unemployed or stricken by other misfortune."[26] In some instances, church leaders or members also support immigrants through the legalization process.

But precisely because such churches are constituted by people who live in a domain of informality, they walk a fine line in their ministry. As evangelical churches, in general they are already disinclined to engage with the sociopolitical, economic or structural issues that are pertinent to life in Chinatown. Thus sermons do not tackle the social challenges of smuggling, sweatshops, indentured servitude, prostitution or gambling, and if these matters are mentioned in church newsletters, they "typically serve as background for testimonies of miraculous healing and exhortations to pray for comfort and relief."[27] Things may be gradually changing in some of Chinatown's churches, but even then, there are still challenges: the stratification of the wider community also exists within churches so that legal immigrants are not always sympathetic to the plight of the undocumented. After all, those who have survived the process of undocumented immigration and "made it"—that is, attained legalization—wonder why the next generation should get assistance that was unavailable before.

In short, religion in Chinatown also operates on the borders of legality and formality. And this is the case not only for immigrant destinations but also for their places of origin. Segments of Christianity in Fuzhou, for example, are nonlegalized in the sense that they are unregistered with the government. In addition, there are also theological expressions that are unorthodox when measured according to the traditional teachings of the church. In a sense, then,

---

[25]Guest, *God in Chinatown*, chap. 7.
[26]Ibid., p. 198; on this same page, Guest also notes how one of the Buddhist temples in his study has a revolving loan fund that is available for repayment of smuggling debts in extreme situations.
[27]Ibid., p. 182.

Fuzhounese immigrants to NYC have simply moved from one domain and type of illegality to another.[28] And this is not an experience peculiar to the Fuzhounese diaspora.[29]

JUBILEE AND MIGRATION: A PENT-EVANGELICAL REFLECTION

We now shift gears toward more biblical and theological reflection. We begin by reverting back to the apostolic experience, in particular to understand contemporary informal economic realities against those navigated by the early Christian community. This is not to say that we can argue a one-to-one correlation between apostolic economic activities and present-day working of the informal economy, for that would be anachronistic. Yet it should also be clear that the biblical narrative invites an imaginative inhabitation by later generations even as it also ought to empower prophetic engagement with the structures of the world.

The reflections that follow are wagered on the idea that thinking with and through the informal economy might also shed new light on the interface between ecclesia and economics, especially about how the church functions at least in part through providing an alternative set of economic practices. If the values and goals of the formal economy are based on competition, balancing the supply and demand market, the achievement of surplus/profit and the principle of reinvestment of such for the further generation of wealth, the minimal goal of the informal economy appears to be that of achieving subsistence and comfortability. Without access to the formal sector, informals nec-

---

[28]As Eleazar Fernandez suggests in his reflection on the Filipino American immigrant experience, the westward migration for Filipinos can be likened in some respects to the ancient Israelite search for liberation in Egypt since it is only after arriving in the United States the realization occurs that survival is much more difficult than initially realized, to the point that immigrants find themselves entrapped, unexpectedly, in what they thought was in the "promised land." See Eleazar S. Fernandez, "Exodus-toward-Egypt: Filipino-Americans' Struggle to Realise the Promise Land in America," in Eleazer S. Fernandez and Fernando F. Segovia, eds., *A Dream Unfinished: Theological Reflections on America from the Margins* (Maryknoll, NY: Orbis, 2001), pp. 167-81.

[29]Thus, for example, in Latin America, pastoral agents of both Catholic and Protestant parishes, both those deeper in the region and those at the border, often provide assistance for emigrants who are without documentation. In other words, the intertwining of religion and undocumented immigration persists not just in North American destinations but at various nodes and along the various migrant paths across the Global South. See, e.g., Jacqueline Maria Hagan, "The Church vs. the State: Borders, Migrants, and Human Rights," in Pierrette Hondagneu-Sotelo, ed., *Religion and Social Justice for Immigrants* (New Brunswick, NJ: Rutgers University Press, 2007), pp. 93-101.

essarily work in (nonformalized) subsidiary organizations and often find solidarity with one another as they seek common cause.

Elsewhere I have argued, in dialogue with the latest findings of contemporary biblical scholarship, that the practices of the earliest followers of the Messiah can be seen as an ecclesial but also prototypical expression of informal economics.[30] Jesus' calling for a retrieval and implementation of the Jubilee ethics—that is, his teachings regarding poverty and wealth, gift giving, sharing and mutuality[31]—were designed to overcome the disjunctions between the rich and the poor and to effectively empower new economic relations rather than support the prevailing economic status quo. His followers embodied, at least for a time, an egalitarian community that met the needs of its members through informal forms of reciprocity. In the following, I want to briefly examine the economic aspects of the early messianic community in light of our discussion of religion and informality in Chinatown.

Apostolic economics. We are told very specifically in the book of Acts that "All who believed were together and had all things in common; they would sell their possessions and goods and distribute the proceeds to all, as any had need" (Acts 2:44-45). Later, after the community had increased to over five thousand men (not including women and children—Acts 4:4), it is noted:

> Now the whole group of those who believed were of one heart and soul, and no one claimed private ownership of any possessions, but everything they owned was held in common.... There was not a needy person among them, for as many as owned lands or houses sold them and brought the proceeds of what was sold. They laid it at the apostles' feet, and it was distributed to each as any had need. (Acts 4:32, 34-35)

Such a set of ecclesial economic practices was part and parcel of the outworking of the presence and activity of the Spirit of Jesus, who the author of Acts tells us was poured out upon the world. This pneumatological economy unleashed the economic practices of mutuality and reciprocity taught by Jesus. Let me make three sets of comments about this

---

[30]See Yong, *In the Days of Caesar: Pentecostalism and Political Theology—The Cadbury Lectures 2009*, Sacra Doctrina: Christian Theology for a Postmodern Age series (Grand Rapids: Eerdmans, 2010), chap. 7.3.

[31]See Sharon H. Ringe, *Jesus, Liberation, and the Biblical Jubilee: Images for Ethics and Christology* (Philadelphia: Fortress, 1985), and Michael Prior, *Jesus the Liberator: Nazareth Liberation Theology (Luke 4:16-30)*, The Biblical Seminar 26 (Sheffield, UK: Sheffield Academic Press, 1995).

economic life of the Spirit seen in the early messianic community.[32]

First, the lines between the formal and informal economies were blurred in the early Christian experience. Yes, there were those who owned, bought and sold property according to the formal economic conventions of that time. On the other hand, there was also charitable giving, and distribution based on need, not merit (or labor). Further, there was communal "ownership" at least in the sense that none exercised their rights to private ownership. Most importantly, what we see here is not any intentional plan to establish a communal economy; rather the apostolic leaders simply responded to the massive migration from the rural areas. Those who had heard about the gospel or about the signs and wonders accomplished by the apostles were gathering "from the towns around Jerusalem" (Acts 5:16) and these needed to be fed, housed and cared for.

This leads, second, to our observation that by and large the earliest Christian community consisted of migrants. However, these were not just local migrants from the surrounding Judean countryside but also Hellenistic Jews and God-fearers from the Jewish diaspora around the Mediterranean world. The original three thousand who responded to Peter's sermon on the Day of Pentecost were those who had returned to Jerusalem for the Pentecost feast from the ends of the earth (Acts 2:5-11). While mostly Jews or proselytes to Judaism, these migrants were all at least bilingual, thus signifying their having been formed, perhaps deeply, by the various Mediterranean cultures. In part for this reason, miscommunication and misunderstanding eventually threatened to undermine the messianic community: some members of the diaspora who had returned home and stayed were neglected by locals who had taken the lead in food distribution and care (Acts 6:1-2). In short, internal divisions along migration lines ensued, and while the apostles were initially able to address the issues, these makeshift practices turned out to be unsustainable in the long run, at least in part because persecution broke out against the messianic community.

Such persecution highlights the third aspect of early Christian origins: its political character. The healing of a lame man at the Beautiful Gate was the first event that instigated a confrontation between the apostles and the local

---

[32]See also Yong, *Who Is the Holy Spirit? A Walk with the Apostles* (Brewster, MA: Paraclete, 2011), part three.

political leadership.[33] The local council decided to curtail the apostolic activities of preaching and healing: "Let us warn them to speak no more to anyone in this name"—in response to which the council leaders called the apostles in and "ordered them not to speak or teach at all in the name of Jesus" (Acts 4:17-18). Hence messianic proselytism in the name of Jesus was prohibited. But recall that there was also an economic dimension to the initial encounter between the apostles and the lame man. He initially asked for alms, but Peter said: "I have no silver or gold, but what I have I give you; in the name of Jesus Christ of Nazareth, stand up and walk" (Acts 3:6). In a sense, this established the economic and political trajectory of the early messianic community: they would be constrained neither by the formal economy (they were, after all, already sharing all things) nor by the political legalities (thus their response to the council's circumscription: "Whether it is right in God's sight to listen to you rather than to God, you must judge; for we cannot keep from speaking about what we have seen and heard"—Acts 4:19-20).

This apostolic boldness presses the questions percolating in the background of the discussion so far regarding the extralegal nature not only of informal economic activity but also, and even especially, of undocumented immigration. The Acts narrative certainly prioritizes the bearing of witness to the gospel of Christ and to the coming reign of God, to the point of inciting persecution for such activities and even of death. The structure of the book itself—"But you will receive power when the Holy Spirit has come upon you; and you will be my witnesses [literally: μάρτυρες or "martyrs"] in Jerusalem, in all Judea and Samaria, and to the ends of the earth" (Acts 1:8)—indicates that such witnessing includes martyrdom. This suggests that, whether Christ followers are willing to challenge the powers that be or not, their witness ought to be ready to stand up against whatever prohibitions might exist for the sake of their higher calling.

Yet such an apostolic posture is by no means license for wanton disregard of the rule of law.[34] We know that Paul, for instance, exercised his rights as a

---

[33]See ibid., esp. chaps. 8-9, wherein I provide brief exegetical reflections on Acts 3–6 in light of Jesus' teachings as recorded in the Gospel of Luke.

[34]For discussion of possible political readings of Luke and Acts, see Paul W. Walaskay, "And So We Came to Rome": The Political Perspective of St. Luke (Cambridge: Cambridge University Press, 1983).

Roman citizen and lived according to the laws of the *Pax Romana*. As such, he was not reticent, at the proper time, to demand accountability of legal authorities, as indicated by his response to the unwarranted beatings and imprisonment he and Silas suffered at the hands of the Philippian officers (Acts 16:33-39). This would be impossible unless Paul were a law-abiding citizen and innocent of wrongdoing. Further, the later occasion of the riot at Ephesus also suggests that these early followers of Christ as Messiah acted prudently and not just recklessly. Paul, for instance, wanted to engage the rioting mob in person, but he was retrained from doing so by his comrades and others friendly to his mission (Acts 19:31). The admonition to the mob that their grievances "must be settled in the regular assembly" (Acts 19:39) highlights the assumption that this ought to be the *modus operandi* for Christian witness itself, whenever possible. Last but not least, the last fourth of the Acts account unfolds Paul's sojourn, under lock and key, to Rome, having appealed to Caesar. On multiple occasions, not only does Paul declare his innocence of any illegality or other moral wrongdoing, but he is also declared innocent on four occasions: by Claudius, Festus, Agrippa and even some of his accusers, the Pharisees (Acts 23:9, 29; 25:18; 26:31-32).[35] What is consistently communicated is that messianic followers are law-abiding citizens of the empire, and this also ought to characterize Christian life in any subsequent era.

Migration and documentation. Yet it is also important to acknowledge that the Bible is relatively silent with regard to the contemporary issue of undocumented immigration that has exercised many, including Evangelicals. The recent efforts of one evangelical theologian, M. Daniel Carroll R., are helpful in clarifying what the Bible does and does not say about such contemporary concerns.[36] Although engaging the issue of undocumented immigration head-on, the overall analysis focuses on the biblical themes of refugees, exiles, sojourners and strangers. Ancient Israelite migration related to famines and life in forced exilic situations frames the biblical considerations. It is precisely reception of hospitality at the hands of others and in particular from God's own unconditional embrace of Abraham and his descendants as his

---

[35]An expansion of the preceding discussion can be found in Yong, *Who Is the Holy Spirit?*, parts 7-8.
[36]M. Daniel Carroll R., *Christians at the Border: Immigration, the Church, and the Bible* (Grand Rapids: Baker Academic, 2008).

people that undergird the Torah's legislation to practice hospitality to strangers and sojourners in their own land.[37]

When turning to the New Testament, Carroll R.'s focus dwells almost exclusively on Jesus, especially on Jesus himself as refugee and sojourner. Yes, Jesus represents the hospitality of God to the world, but he is also guest of humankind in many ways.[38] So while "there is no explicit teaching on immigration in the Gospels,"[39] there is much in Jesus' life and teachings about Christian attitudes and practices in relationship to those who are outsiders. In fact, emulation in the footsteps of Jesus requires his followers also to be sojourners, as expressed elsewhere in the New Testament Epistles. Christians are thus not only going to be guests of others, recipients of their hospitality (perhaps even as immigrants), but also hosts to others, here sharing divine hospitality in the name of Jesus with aliens and strangers.

Within this framework, Carroll R. is not ignorant of the argument especially among Evangelicals that support for undocumented immigration, not to mention the phenomenon itself, raises questions about the Pauline injunction that Christians ought to "be subject to the governing authorities" (Rom 13:1). Evangelicals in particular are often torn internally between doing justice to others on the one hand and lawful abiding on the other—both divinely urged. Included in any substantively evangelical consideration of undocumented immigration ought to be the rejection of any strategy that calls for "civil disobedience on a large scale" as a response to biblical texts like these.[40] What Evangelicals should be advocating are changes to legislation that better reflect the overall scriptural depiction of God's heart for the stranger, foreigner and alien. When, for instance, "the government turns a blind eye to many employers because the country needs the cheap labor, but then closes the door to social services on these same workers,"[41] they are not only sending mixed messages but also undermining the principles of equity upon which any legal system ought to stand.

---

[37]Ibid., pp. 106-7.
[38]I explicate this christological and apostolic dimension of hospitality against the broader biblical narrative in my *Hospitality and the Other: Pentecost, Christian Practices, and the Neighbor*, Faith Meets Faith series (Maryknoll, NY: Orbis, 2008), chap. 4.
[39]Carroll R., *Christians at the Border*, p. 123.
[40]Ibid., p. 132.
[41]Ibid., p. 134.

Soerens and Hwang agree that not all laws protect, preserve and sustain the well-being of humans and society, which is precisely what the law was given for.[42] Hence the question of immigration laws must always ask about their justness and whether they are reflective of divine law. More generous immigration policies, in their estimation, are not inconsistent with stronger border security measures, even as laws to protect immigrants ought to parallel evangelical efforts to protect unborn babies. Alongside more generous immigration policies that are welcoming of those wanting or needing to migrate, a biblically and theologically informed approach to the undocumented immigrants in any country ought to steer a *via media* between either "total amnesty or harsh consequences such as deportation."[43] Biblical principles with regard to justice, restitution and restoration ought to be enacted that provide opportunities for many to acknowledge their unlawful presence and suffer appropriate consequences related to such (i.e., reasonable fines) but nevertheless enable a path forward toward documentation and legalization in keeping with the other posture of equity and fairness to all (including those who are waiting in line for approval to legally migrate). What is needed is a "procedural justice" that addresses local, international and transnational realities as well as the lives of many who are affected by such forces.[44]

All of this is not to say that a biblically informed approach to the issue of undocumented immigration is thereby resolved. What we can see is that the earliest Christians operated on the borders of economic formality and political legality. With regard to the former, it might be said that the early church developed its own theological or ecclesiological form of economics, one that bypassed the conventional economic structures of its time by empowering the weak in their midst in the name of Jesus and by mobilizing the generosity of the faithful. With regard to the latter, we can see that the first Christians lived within the laws of their land, albeit always subordinated such to their commitment to bearing witness to the gospel and the coming reign of God embodied and proclaimed by Jesus. In this sense, the economics and sojourning

---

[42]See Matthew Soerens and Jenny Hwang, *Welcoming the Stranger: Justice, Compassion and Truth in the Immigration Debate* (Downers Grove, IL: InterVarsity Press, 2009), pp. 107-14.

[43]Ibid., p. 112.

[44]Ibid., p. 113.

of the first Christians can be understood as anticipating contemporary economic life in the informal sector and yet also instantiating the justice of the
coming reign of God. Might analysis of the practices of the early church from
the perspective of the informal economy unveil how ecclesial solidarity as a
way of life provides an alternative set of economic values to those propounded
by the formal economy, and might the migrant character of apostolic life also
provide windows into a vision of what it means for Christians to be aliens and
strangers in the present world in anticipation of the world to come?

Jubilee, markets and migration. To begin to transition back to the present,
perhaps the practices of the earliest Christians can serve as a model for the
kinds of economic arrangements that emphasize mutuality and sharing as well
as local accountability and initiative that are applicable for contemporary globalization.[45] Rather than being dominated by the economy of exchange and
its supply-and-demand transactions, can the church be guided by a pneumatological economy of grace[46]—a set of economic relations and practices inspired by the Spirit of Jesus—that highlights charity (giving without anticipation of return), forgiveness (not only of sins but also of debts) and
solidaristic fellowship (cultivated through interpersonal relations, common
meals and daily interactions) instead? If this is possible, might the explicitly
theological economy of the earliest messianic believers empower our own
rethinking about political economy vis-à-vis the informality and illegitimacy
of Chinatown, NYC, and other like environments in the twenty-first century?
More importantly, might such considerations also have implications for
thinking about an evangelical response to the challenges confronted by the
phenomenon of undocumented immigration?

Before we shift gears toward these more normative theological issues,
however, we need to take a brief detour to address head-on the question regarding the "American dream." I have already indicated (see the prologue)
how one way to frame my own life journey as a 1.5-generation immigrant is as

---

[45]Here I have been helped by the concrete discussions of Lee Hong Jung, *"Minjung* and Pentecostal
Movements in Korea,"* in Allan Anderson and Walter J. Hollenweger, eds., *Pentecostals After a
Century: Global Perspectives on a Movement in Transition* (Sheffield, UK: Sheffield Academic Press,
1999), pp. 138-60, esp. pp. 158-59.

[46]Here expanding on what I have elsewhere presented as a pneumatological theology of grace—
Yong, *Spirit of Love: A Trinitarian Theology of Grace* (Waco, TX: Baylor University Press, 2012).

a success story vis-à-vis the pursuit of the American dream. If the American dream was first forged by the Puritans with their work ethic, Asian immigrants to the United States have also diligently followed this path in quest of their own success. East Asian immigrants, in particular, informed by their own Confucian ethic, have risked all, worked hard and striven to make a better life for themselves on American soil (not to mention elsewhere, as the diffusiveness of the global East Asian diaspora indicates). As the above discussion of Fuzhounese immigrants to NYC illustrates, Asian Americans have come to the United States in part because of the promise of "the dream."[47]

Unsurprisingly, then, at least first-generation Asian American immigrants will be relatively uninterested in some, if not much, of the economic discussion so far in this chapter. They understand the challenges of the informal economy all too well, but these are, they believe, only temporary realities that can be overcome through hard work and, if they are believers, through prayer. The success of some perpetuates the "model minority" stereotype even as the failures of others do not deter those who have little else to hope for. The goal for undocumented immigrants is to work their way from the informal to the formal domain, to put themselves in the position to capitalize on assets gained, however informally. Success in this venture is what allows them to join other (legally present) immigrants and other Americans in enjoying the American dream.

Hence those with such aspirations are not often able to comprehend the critique of consumerism and materialism applied to the global capitalist economic system. They see only the laissez-faire aspects, and many strain within the system to improve their lot, mostly without complaining. Those who have "arrived" are allowed to enjoy the symbols of their labor. Asian American evangelical sensibilities along this trajectory highlight the biblical virtues of frugality, thrift and diligence, among other virtues. I am sensitive to these contextual dynamics, even if I am also wary that it is precisely along this pathway that the lines between acceptable and excessive consumption, and between private ownership and materialism, become blurred. I also think that pursuit of the American dream inculcates the kind of individualistic self-interest necessary to

---

[47]See, e.g., Francis L. K. Hsu, *The Challenge of the American Dream: The Chinese in the United States* (Belmont, CA: Wadsworth, 1971); although focused on the Chinese American experience, much of Hsu's analysis is applicable to Asian Americans across the spectrum.

survive amid and excel over the competition at the heart of a supply-and-demand system of exchange. Along the way, Confucian and other Asian cultural values regarding the family and community are threatened, however subtly, and Asian Americans awaken one day to find that their attainment of the American dream has exacted an interpersonal and relational toll. A further cost includes naive equation between the American dream and the received evangelical theology, as if there were a correlation between the two, leading to the kinds of challenges elaborated in chapter three. In that case, to question the dominant pent-evangelical way of thinking is to suggest that one's life commitments (the American dream, along with its promises for success, if not prosperity) have been misguided at best. It becomes difficult to disentangle the two.

This chapter cannot address all the questions across this economic spectrum. Part of any viable theological response, I hazard to venture, will involve some version of my "many tongues, many economies" thesis—which suggests that there is no one economic model required by Scripture but that there are various theologically defensible approaches to economics relevant to different sociopolitical contents[48]—applied to the heterogeneous Asian American domain. The argument to be unfolded in the rest of this chapter, however, presumes that there is no shortcut between the undocumented immigration and informal economic nexus on the one side to the American dream on the other side, and that therefore hard work needs to be undertaken to reconsider a viable theological economics and an economic theology in this challenging space.

MONEY, MIGRANTS AND MINISTRY IN ASIAN AMERICAN EVANGELICAL PERSPECTIVE

In light of the foregoing, I now want to reengage the issues at the intersection of religion, globalization and economics raised by Guest's work in light of the apostolic experience. I focus on the economic domain in order to, by the end of the chapter, come back to the issue of undocumented immigration. The

---

[48]See my In the Days of Caesar, §7.3; cf. also Yong, "A Typology of Prosperity Theology: A Religious Economy of Global Renewal or a Renewal Economics?" in Amos Yong and Katherine Attanasi, Pentecostalism and Prosperity: The Socioeconomics of the Global Charismatic Movement, Christianities of the World 1 (New York: Palgrave Macmillan, 2012), pp. 15-33.

following therefore sketches some basic theological proposals regarding economics, migration and ministry that may be pertinent not only in Chinatown but also in the transnational zones of the global economy.[49] As we shall see, the insights gained from the Acts narrative for a Christian theology of economics may be more relevant for our contemporary experience than initially anticipated, including providing perspective on Christian interface with legality in relationship to evangelical ministry and mission, and to the justice and compassion of God.

Toward an economic theology. To begin, I have highlighted how the earliest messianic believers were both *in* the world yet not *of* it. Economically, we saw that they worked within conventional economic constraints but experimented with an alternative mode of mutual care and gratuitous provision. Similarly, historically and today, Christian religious orders and congregations, come-outers and restorationist house churches have also operated both formally and informally vis-à-vis the established economic systems of their times.[50] In these cases, the various forms of mutuality, reciprocity, sharing and solidarity in ecclesial communities can be understood as providing a range of informal economic services within congregational and communal life both as an expression of their religious identity and as part of their Christian missionary and evangelistic witness. Similarly, world Christianity as a mass urban movement involves dynamic national, international and transnational populations that form new communities and networks in place of the family and clan relations that have been left behind, and it is within these new enclaves (churches, congregations and communities) that people find both spiritual and material comfort, support and aid.

Amid the present forces of globalization, the largely impersonal features of

---

[49]From an American point of view, note that almost one out of every ten undocumented immigrants in the United States is from Asia—see Gemma Tulud Cruz, "Expanding the Boundaries, Turning Borders into Spaces," in Ogbu U. Kalu, Edmund Kee-Fook Chia and Peter Vethanayagamony, eds., *Mission After Christendom: Emergent Themes in Contemporary Mission* (Louisville, KY: Westminster John Knox, 2010), pp. 71-83, at p. 72—so our thinking about illegality and informality at Chinatown has wider implications for considering a theology of migration in global (not just vis-à-vis the East Asian) context.

[50]These can be teased out, for example, from some of the contemporary literature—e.g., Andrew Walker, *Restoring the Kingdom: The Radical Christianity of the House Church Movement* (London: Hodder and Stoughton, 1985), and Luke Wesley, *The Church in China: Persecuted, Pentecostal and Powerful* (Baguio City, Philippines: Asian Journal of Pentecostal Studies Books, 2004).

the global market are tempered by ecclesially shaped relations that draw from, enrich, and network with local enterprises, communal associations and co-operatives, and kinship, extended household and other domestic economic ventures. Whereas the global economy is driven by speculative finance, credit extensions and the flexibility of money as *the* medium of economic exchange, the church serves God rather than mammon and nurtures relationship while providing (especially voluntary) services that enable a more discerning engagement with the needs of those who are otherwise struggling to survive on the margins of the neoliberal market regime. Fuzhounese immigrants, for example, are excluded from the formal economy precisely because of their undocumented status. As such, a theology of economics that is relevant to their situation must critically engage with the informal economy. In the informal domain, it is not what the church has on the books that matters, but how it empowers agents to survive and make meaning in life that counts.

In one respect, I would go beyond what political economists define as the margins of the informal economy and include the sphere of reproduction and care.[51] The church that privileges the poor also prioritizes widows, orphans, children, the aged, the infirm, people with disabilities and those otherwise vulnerable, so that the care of these groups of people is registered as most important from the standpoint of the economy of grace. For immigrants who are already vulnerable because of their undocumented status, losing spouses, getting sick, becoming disabled or growing old multiplies the challenges that are confronted. In this framework, there is an even more urgent need for various forms of what we may call collective entrepreneurship to emerge that on the one hand sustain vulnerable members who are on the margins if not the underside of history, even while they on the other hand inspire creativity not only for survival's sake but also for the wider communal good. Churches and congregations in Chinatown and various heavily populated transnational zones already function in some of these ways. I am simply urging that we attend more intentionally to the biblical and theological issues so that we can be more truthful, practical and relevant to the situations at hand.

---

[51]See Eva Feder Kittay and Ellen K. Feder, *The Subject of Care: Feminist Perspectives on Dependency* (Lanham, MD: Rowman & Littlefield, 2002), and Eric Gregory, *Politics and the Order of Love: An Augustinian Ethic of Democratic Citizenship* (Chicago: University of Chicago Press, 2008), esp. chap. 3.

The preceding reflections, however, should neither dull us into a false sense of accomplishment in the dialogue between religion and economics nor blind us to the challenges confronting the realities of life in the informal economy. Hence a number of clarifications are in order. First, note that such a consideration of the church from the perspective of the informal economy does not remove the church either from the world or from the global market.[52] This is neither a call for the overthrow of the neoliberal economy nor an advocacy of one or another form of socialism or communism, but rather a reminder about how the church, when going about its business of communal edification, will inevitably recommend an economic way of life. I am concerned that such recommendations be those in the footsteps of Christ by the power of the Spirit rather than that they are co-opted by the economic powers that be.

Second, especially in light of the work of the church in immigrant enclaves, I am simply wishing to highlight how conscientious ecclesial participation in the informal economy can serve as a protest against the self-interested greed, consumerist materialism and rampant hedonism that are pervasive in the neoliberal market economy. Communal solidarity, private initiative directed toward the public good, and local and interpersonal relations, exchanges and accountability—all of these should be advocated by the church since together they combine to ameliorate the debilitating effects of humanity's fall in our economic lives. Yes, life in the ethnic enclave is indeed a struggle for survival; if the church cannot speak and embody the gospel in such economic domains, so much the worse for its witness. However, to the degree that the church can model the mutuality, reciprocity and hospitality of the earliest followers of Jesus, to that same degree it can be subversive of the invisible hand that stratifies both the formal and informal economic domains.

Finally, my assessment of the church as operating in effect within the informal sector is not intended to naively affirm all that transpires in that do-

---

[52]Sometimes, Mennonite intellectuals are more predisposed to withdrawing from the capitalist order and forming an alternative economics based on local community and advocating moral and environmental critiques of the current order from the Mennonite margins. I am sympathetic to the theological motivations behind such concerns but do not think that a withdrawal from the market is either feasible or the best way forward. See Jim Halteman, "Mennonites and Market Capitalism," in Calvin Redekop, Victor A. Krahn and Samuel J. Steiner, eds., *Anabaptist/Mennonite Faith and Economics* (Lanham, MD: University Press of America, 1994), pp. 321-31.

main.[53] Obviously, the church should not legitimate the distribution of contraband (i.e., drugs, music and other goods), condone tax evasion, bribery, kickbacks and other forms of unlawful activity, or look askance at the delivery of illicit activities (i.e., prostitution and slave trafficking). The church must also not think that a functional informal sector is a means of pacifying the poor or that such thereby alleviates the church's responsibility to speak prophetically to the world (that includes the state) regarding the enactment of economic justice. Last but not least, the church should not ignore the wider structural forces of globalization that drive undocumented migration and unjust and criminal economic activity.[54]

These caveats raise the question of what the church should do to address the many injustices that are perpetuated by the informal economy. The fact is that the informal economy is dominated by the poor, who are exploited by both criminals (through unlawful activities) and the more well-to-do (e.g., who put the poor to work in sweatshops), besides having to negotiate the challenges of otherwise unjust political, social and economic systems. Desiring neither to idealize poverty nor sentimentalize or patronize the poor, I suggest that a pneumatological economy of grace according to Jesus' Jubilee paradigm enacted in the early church will be sensitive to global

---

[53]This is the job of a more expansively considered theology of economics, such as those proposed by Douglas Meeks, *God the Economist: The Doctrine of God and Political Economy*, new ed. (Minneapolis: Fortress, 2000), and Kathryn Tanner, *Economy of Grace* (Minneapolis: Fortress, 2005). See also the concluding reflections below.

[54]One of these issues is precisely that pertaining to the economic inequities between the Global South and the Euro-American West. On this note, I recommend both Nimi Wariboko, *God and Money: A Theology of Money in a Globalizing World* (Lanham, MD: Rowman & Littlefield, 2008), and Philip Goodchild, *Theology of Money* (London: SCM Press, 2007), for the not-faint-of-heart who are interested in rethinking the theological dimensions of the global economic system. What Wariboko calls the *Earth Dollar* (as opposed to dominant national currencies such as the dollar, the euro or the yen) works to level out the playing field economically between richer and poorer countries, tempering the violent shifts in the foreign exchange rates that exacerbate the economic conditions of the most impoverished and vulnerable regions of the world, and enabling the development of and entry into the global market of such regions without hindering the economic growth possibilities of the more established and affluent nations. Goodchild's major constructive proposal is to develop banks of evaluative credit that can provide religious and moral guidance for the assessment and investment of money in the market economy. My contribution to this discussion is primarily theological, reminding us of the equal importance of ecclesial practices that embody the values of the Spirit, since apart from such concrete relations we will in due course lack models for effective mutuality and cease to be able to develop viable criteria for the evaluation of money itself.

factors that impinge on unjust economies but will also be focused on local projects and initiatives especially at the congregational and parish levels. In other words, Jesus' meeting the needs of the poor in various aspects invites the contemporary church to be alert to the multiple levels of poverty that afflict people today.

Individual healing is therefore incomplete without the provision of basic material necessities, friendships and spiritual care, access to social, educational, political, economic, medical and civil resources, and attention to an environmentally and ecologically sustainable way of life. Solidarity with the poor thus requires formation of subsidiary organizations that include those outside ecclesial communities in order to identify and redress the causes of poverty at each level, and in order that feedback from lower levels can also trigger revision, reform and reorganization at the higher levels. Sociostructural inequalities related to gender, race, class, and physical, intellectual and other sensory disabilities must be engaged both at the grassroots, where such can be sensitive to the particular challenges involved, and the political levels, where more general and abstract policies can be formulated in order to forge a more just society.[55] In the latter domain, the church must be a prophetic voice that calls attention to the biblical vision of shalom but also provides instantiations of such shalomic practices that point toward a better way.[56]

This last set of recommendations also reminds us that besides operating at or "within" this informal domain, the church nevertheless also remains active in the formal economy at many levels. The preceding proposals should not be taken to suggest that the church ceases formal operations as an economic agent. In fact, the church in its various local forms and even global shape itself can and should be understood as corporations of various types and should be subject to the different political, social and legal strictures within that formal domain. To some degree, much of the church's contributions to political reform, social justice and economic development projects should be properly formalized.

---

[55]Andrew Hartropp, *What Is Economic Justice? Biblical and Secular Perspectives Contrasted* (Milton Keynes, UK: Paternoster, 2007), chap. 2.

[56]See the final chapter, "God, Christ, Spirit: Christian Pluralism and Evangelical Mission in the 21st Century," of Amos Yong, *The Missiological Spirit: Christian Mission Theology for the Third Millennium Global Context* (Eugene, OR: Cascade, 2014).

Toward a theology of migration. In dealing with the Fuzhounese to China-town, the issue of undocumented immigration is one that requires further attention. Yet there are at least two domains of political activity that must be engaged on this matter: one regarding the structural factors that pertain to international free trade agreements that impact developing economies, and the other regarding the rights and responsibilities of sovereign nations to protect their borders. In some respects, these work in tension with each other. One side emphasizes human freedom in economic and political agency while the other prioritizes governmental sovereignty. How might the preceding Asian American pent-evangelical perspective respond in these matters?

On the political-economic side, our case study of Fuzhounese undocu-mented immigration opens up windows into international relations in general and Chinese-American relations more particularly that foreground the opportunity for ongoing transnational dialogue about important struc-tural matters related to globalization. One can err on either the legal and procedural side (focused on the rule of law) or the humanitarian side (fo-cused on compassionate welcome of undocumented immigrants).[57] The preceding discussions by both Carroll R. and Soerens and Hwang are helpful precisely in urging consideration of a middle way that ignores neither aspect. This means that Christians can and ought to be engaged in the discussion at multiple levels: that of the local NYC political economy, that of American and Chinese laws and systems (by American and Chinese Christians on their respective fronts, although obviously the latter con-tingent is miniscule at present compared to the former) and that of American-Chinese relations. In terms of public policies and laws, discussions ought of course to be predicated by principles of the common good as these are intertwined and yet distinctive from local to national to international levels. These will require a back-and-forth adjustment between local and global realities, each responding to the other so that both the demands of con-cretely particular realities and that of the more abstractly formulated rules

---

[57]These two types of approaches are nicely and succinctly articulated by Marten Van der Meulen, "Being Illegal Is Like Fishing Without a Permit: African Churches, Illegal Immigration, and the Public Sphere," in Mechteld Jansen and Hijme Stoffels, eds., *A Moving God: Immigrant Churches in the Neth-erlands*, International Practical Theology 8 (Münster: LIT Verlag, 2008), pp. 49-60, esp. pp. 52-53.

of law are met (precisely parallel to the theological task mediating the local and the global, as discussed in the first chapter).

From the explicitly pent-evangelical perspective of the coming reign of God, however, there are also missional issues at stake. This concerns not only the Fuzhounese as a diaspora group now open to missionization in NYC (or other American sites) but also the Fuzhounese Christians (in NYC and elsewhere) who are mediating missionaries between the immigrant population on the one side and their broader American hosts (whether, evangelical, white, Asian and/or otherwise) on the other. Guest and hosts in this domain are therefore fluid, both synchronically and diachronically. This means that Asian Americans can be guests in one respect (as Chinese American Evangelicals in NYC are vis-à-vis their American locatedness) but also hosts in another respect (as the same are vis-à-vis the undocumented immigrants in their communities and even in their churches). It could also be that undocumented Fuzhounese are surely guests—some might call them "intruders," to be truthful—in a strange land, although they may also, at some or other points, become hosts (whether because of a change in documentation status or simply by virtue of changing roles over time) to others. These varying and fluid situations and identities characterize life in our global village. None of this is meant to ignore the illegalities pertinent to undocumented immigration; it is meant to suggest that any response to this level of the phenomenon must be informed by theological and biblical perspective regarding what it means to engage in mission and evangelization in today's global context.

That these are complicated matters that deserve extensive ecclesial and theological consideration is clear.[58] My focus in this chapter on the more concrete local church's response to the presence of undocumented workers negotiating the informal economy does not mean that these other aspects that are intertwined with such situations are undeserving of sustained deliberation.

---

[58]A helpful ecclesial document for further consideration in this regard is *Strangers No Longer: Together on the Journey of Hope—A Pastoral Letter Concerning Migration from the Catholic Bishops of Mexico and the United States* (2003), available online at www.usccb.org/mrs/stranger.shtml. Roman Catholic scholars have been at the forefront of articulating a theology of migration—e.g., Solange Lefebvre and Luiz Carlos Susin, eds., *Migration in a Global World*, Concilium 2008/5 (London: SCM Press, 2008) and other sources cited in the previous chapter.

So while appropriating the lens of the informal economy is helpful for engaging what is happening in the transnational zone that is Chinatown, NYC, we should also recognize that the church functions variously, and rightly, in the formal economic and political sectors as well. The practice of christomorphically formed compassion is not opposed to adherence to the rule of law, when these are understood as heralding the coming reign of God.

A theology of Jubilee and shalom. It is precisely along this line that I have proposed in this chapter that the church's economic witness is not exhausted in its formal transactions. In fact, the distinctiveness of the church's economic witness occurs, I have suggested, in the diversity of its formal and informal economic activities. There is much to discuss, for instance, about the more formal Asian American contributions to the American and even global economies that we could delve into given time and space. From a theological perspective, these broader and alternative ecclesiological economies can be seen as retrieving and channeling the pneumatological economy of grace unleashed on the Day of Pentecost. The many kinds of ecclesial economic activity can thus be seen as expressions of a pneumatologically shaped version of local autonomy and participation that empowers an ecclesially inspired form of creativity and initiative, and fosters an ecclesially rich sense of appreciation for the diversity of the global Christian body politic.[59] The account of Fuzhounese American immigration detailed in this chapter, as well as the wider Chinese- and Asian-diasporic realities within which the Fuzhounese experience is embedded, invite reconsideration of older themes from these relatively new vantage points.

Beyond this more general vision of the informal church, however, I suggest a more explicitly Lukan interpretation animated by the thesis that the many tongues of the Spirit are anticipations of the many gifts that are expressed in the economic sphere. From out of this more pneumatological and charismatic framework arise a set of ecclesiological alternatives, nurtured within the informal sector, wherein all members are honored, especially the weak, so that all are available to come to the aid of those who are suffering, even as each potentially contributes her or his own peculiar gift for the edification of the

---

[59]This is the thesis of my monograph *In the Days of Caesar*, the economic aspects of which are explicated in chap. 7.

whole.[60] Empowered by the Spirit, these informal economic ways of life and activities may also function as prophetic parables that challenge the corruption, injustice, hedonism and environmental degradation characteristic of neoliberal capitalism that sometimes runs unrestrained within a free market economy. Here also Asian American voices as well as others derived from the global Asian diaspora provide unique and distinctive accents that can contribute to such a pent-evangelical prophetic vision. In short, the Spirit not only provides for and edifies the needy through the generous dispensation of the gifts (charisms) of the body of Christ but also enables a solidarity of life across racial, ethnic and class boundaries that resists the world's political economy of domination.[61]

The result will not be *the* shalom of the coming divine reign but will be intimations of the peace, justice and righteousness that will be established on that day of the Lord. For the ancient prophets, the Hebrew word *shalom* referred to the wholeness, completeness, security, friendship, well-being and even salvation of the people both individually and collectively.[62] Herein will the sick find their healing, perhaps not necessarily in bodily cures but certainly in and through their integration in reconciling, caring and welcoming communities. Herein also will the gospel find its penultimate fulfillment, perhaps not necessarily in affluence and material wealth but certainly in and through the Spirit-inspired sufficiency of mutual, sharing and generous communities of faith. In our global context of pluralism, immigration, transnationalism and the neoliberal market economy, such a pneumatologically inaugurated shalom, initiated in part on the Day of Pentecost and perhaps unfolding variously in the church today even

---

[60]I have developed this line of thinking also with regard to our present understanding and experience of disability; see Yong, *The Bible, Disability, and the Church: A New Vision of the People of God* (Grand Rapids: Eerdmans, 2011), esp. chap. 4; cf. also Yong, *Theology and Down Syndrome: Reimagining Disability in Late Modernity* (Waco, TX: Baylor University Press, 2007), chap. 8, on ecclesiology.

[61]My call to try to see a way between or beyond formality or informality parallels that of finding a way between or beyond "good migration" or "bad migration"; a perceptive and programmatic argument calling for a theology of the neighbor in this regard is by a Lutheran theologian studying Chinese migration in Eastern Europe: Dorottya Nagy, *Migration and Theology: The Case of Chinese Christian Communities in Hungary and Romania in the Globalisation-Context*, Mission Studies 50 (Zoetermeer, The Netherlands: Uitgeverij Boekencentrum, 2009).

[62]E.g., Malinda Berry, "Mission of God: Message of *Shalom*," in Dale Schrag and James Juhnke, ed., *Anabaptist Visions for the New Millennium* (Scottdale, PA.: Herald Press, 2000), pp. 167-73.

among congregations situated in the ethnic enclave of Chinatown, NYC, may be a harbinger of the peaceful and just community that human beings have long sought. Such a Spirit-inspired people of God, a true fellowship of the Spirit, will bind the diversity of the ecclesial body together around the name of Jesus and will graciously generate and dispense with authentic health, wealth and shalom beyond the world's political economy of exchange.

7

TOWARD A GLOBAL EVANGELICAL THEOLOGY

Asian American Intonations

This volume has ranged widely, in particular over Asian American terrain, in search for a globally viable evangelical theology. Whereas the first two chapters explored the Asian and broader Asian American dimensions of such an Asian American evangelical understanding, the third moved specifically to discuss the opportunities and challenges before Asian Americans within the dominant (white) North American context. Chapter four factored in explicitly pentecostal horizons to the discussion, while the last two chapters focused on engaging such pent-evangelical perspectives with the phenomenon of migration. Part and parcel of the proposed pent-evangelical theology of migration deployed (in the previous chapter) the lens of the informal economy to retrieve and reread the socioeconomic experience of Chinese immigration against that of the apostolic church in order to develop a contemporary model of ecclesial ministry and mission that can be improvised and appropriated for engaging the dynamics of the contemporary church in transnational context.

This final chapter returns us full circle to the task of global evangelical theology but now informed by our forays into a few Asian American pent-evangelical perspectives. What follows is a programmatic sketch for evangelical theology, one that works out of the Asian American matrix to engage the wider North American and then global evangelical theological conversations respectively. All three levels of theological work need to be undertaken simultaneously and dialogically in order for the promise of a global evangelical

theology to continue unfolding and find greater traction.[1] It seeks to take seriously the contexts, histories and particularities attendant to the theological
task—in this case sounded through the complexities that are the Asian
American diaspora—but intone from those soundings the good news that is
pertinent for the globalizing world of the twenty-first century.

NEXT STEPS FOR ASIAN AMERICAN EVANGELICAL THEOLOGY

As this volume has unveiled, there are multiple important dimensions of contemporary Asian American evangelical life that ought to be addressed in any
more comprehensive set of theological considerations. In this section, I address three frames of references: that attending to immigrant generations, that
related to second and later generations, and that regarding women. While the
following is nowhere close to exhaustively engaging the vital issues, it triangu-
lates around a set of tasks significant for the ongoing maturation of Asian
American evangelical reflection.

Immigrant generations. By all accounts, migration will continue across a
global scale. Our world is shrinking, and people are now able to cross oceans
without much difficulty. The Asian diaspora will continue to diffuse as what
were once important destination sites will become new sending locations.
Diasporic routes will flow in multiple directions facilitated by new travel networks. As such, Asians will come to the United States through divergent itin-
eraries, including via Latin America and increasingly through Africa. Those
who arrive will now be potentially multilingual, fluent not only in Asian languages but also Hispanic (Spanish or Portuguese) in many cases.

Asian American Evangelicals will need to be more intentional about
thinking theologically through the practical realities on the ground motivating
and sustaining such diasporic expansions. Asian American ethnic churches
already serve as community hubs that assist migrants in transition and relo-
cation, and these practical aspects of Asian American ethnic ecclesial ministry
should be neither underestimated nor reduced. Yet more could be done to
close the hermeneutical circle between what might be called "migration praxis"

---

[1]The dialogical form of theology advocated in this volume is methodologically explicated in my *The Dialogical Spirit: Christian Reason and Theological Method in the Third Millennium* (Eugene, OR: Cascade, 2014).

and biblical interpretation and theological reflection. This is not in order to generate new creeds or doctrinal confessions (although there is no reason why the ancient dogmas might not be informed by contemporary experiential realities and updated in vernacular idiom) but so that churches and congregations can realize how theological reflection is intertwined with rather than removed from life's exigencies. As we have seen in this book, there are economic, political and social forces generating migration, and riding on that are existential, cultural and linguistic hurdles pertaining to diasporic challenges. Why ought Asian American ethnic churches to approach these not just as practical matters but also as theological opportunities?

The Bible is increasingly being touted (in part because of the explosion of migration since the latter part of the twentieth century) as a book about human movement. How might Asian Americans come to see their own sojourning as anticipated in the scriptural frame, or how might they map their own lives onto the biblical narratives of exodus, exile and voyage? Can these windows into the Christian canon also open up new perspectives on the economic, political and intercultural aspects of human journeying? What might a more fully developed theology of migration look, sound and feel like when such reflection is sustained?

An Asian American evangelical theology of diaspora and migration can and ought to be appropriately dialogical. Historic cultural travel narratives embedded in East and South Asian traditions might be profitably attended to within a scriptural framework. The innumerable island nations that constitute the Southern sphere of the Pacific Rim—the Philippines, Indonesia, the Melanesian and Oceanic island-states, and so on—have ancient seafaring traditions that can be read alongside the biblical accounts. Further, Asian migrants that arrive on American soil via Latin American, African or other routes can also draw from traditions of travel and exploration from these continents. Last but not least, how might Asian American migration narratives compare and contrast with European and Native American traditions of this genre? Such a process of cross- and intercultural reading enables the vernacularization of the gospel within the fluid and dynamic context of Asian American migration. More importantly, it enables recognition of how all of history, including that across the Asian American spectrum, has anticipated the migration of the Son of God and will be fulfilled through participation in the life of the triune God in the coming age.

While work on such a theology of migration will be relevant for as long as there are migrants (which will continue into the foreseeable future), the sociology of migration brings with it second and later generations for whom the journey motif is less significant. Any Asian American theology of migration thus also needs an Asian American theology of citizenship, broadly considered. What I mean here by theology of citizenship is related less to legal or other theories of political belonging and identity (on which more in the next section) than to those relevant to processes of adaptation and acculturation navigated by citizens in the making. Here the opportunities and challenges related to both "perpetual foreigner" and "model minority" stereotypes might provide some parameters for constructive reflection.

Second and later generations. The challenge for the descendants of immigrants is avoidance of either ethnic ghettoization (internalizing the "perpetual foreigner" identity) or uncritical assimilation into the wider American milieu (here acquiescing to the "model minority" expectations on the terms established by the host culture). The latter is especially problematic when considering how the present national citizenship for Christians ought to be subordinated to that of the coming reign of God. In the big scheme of things, then, neither end of the spectrum is conducive to prophetic perspectives that can only by generated by sources "outside" the group. To remain within the ethnic enclave is to immunize the self and community from outside perspectives, while to embrace the host culture wholeheartedly is to attempt the impossibility of displacing one's past with an entirely new set of norms and standards. Neither stance is open to the prophetic dimension of the gospel.

This is not to say that Asian Americans ought not to westernize, assimilate or Americanize in some respects. The fortunes of second-generation and later immigrants depend in part on their adapting, at least somewhat, to the host culture. The question is what that means practically and existentially. These matters remain urgent for younger Asian Americans who are struggling to understand themselves—as Asian, as American or as Asian American.[2]

---

[2]I have been helped with the remainder of this paragraph by Grace Hsiao Hanford.

Evangelicals who are also Asian and American are triply confused. The United States they know is ahistorical, a place where they are urged to escape their history and to start anew. It is a melting pot that encourages them to be alike, where the reward for their blending in is popularity. As already indicated, they are expected to be "model minorities"—that is the politically correct post- and nonracial attitude, posture and rhetoric. Hence they are urged to see their United States optimistically as a place where Asian Americans are further along than they really are. They are thus rewarded for being superficial, even as the Evangelicalism they know discourages the study of culture, particularity and historicity. If pre-1980 Asian American immigrants came from poverty, war-torn lands and trauma that are only now being articulated, their children have no such identity markers etched into their souls. The conformity, denial and reticence elicited from them has left them not knowing who they are.

For our purposes in this book, these questions are important also for what they mean theologically. My claim is that there is no one normative model for the assimilation process. Instead, following our pent-evangelical paradigm developed earlier, there ought to be multiple options dynamically configured. At the congregational level, for instance, this means that we ought to celebrate the spectrum of possibilities between the ethnic community and the majority (white) church. Within this scope of possibilities might be, for example, bilingual configurations, or pan-Asian, and hybridized or multiethnic (both Asian- or white-led/normed) options.[3]

Bilingual ecclesial environments include first-generation ethnic immigrant congregations with significant and growing numbers of children who are being raised and educated in both the home language and English. These churches are strongest in retention of ethnic identities, cultures and languages, often providing the local forum for instruction in the parents' language for their children. They are mostly ethnically homogeneous, although in some cases others will join the church, especially the English-speaking side of the congregation. Often, however, once children leave home for college or for

---

[3]See Sharon Kim and Rebecca Y. Kim, "Second-Generation Korean American Christians' Communities: Congregational Hybridity," in Carolyn Chen and Russell Jeung, eds., *Sustaining Faith Traditions: Race, Ethnicity, and Religion Among the Latino and Asian American Second Generation* (New York: New York University Press, 2012), pp. 176-93, esp. pp. 177-79.

other reasons, they also transition from such ecclesial arrangements.

The sociological trend from bilingual to pan-Asian congregational formats is being documented. For second and later generations who continue in the church, one option is to transform an ethnically defined ecclesial community into a pan-Asian environment. Here, second-, third- and later-generation Asian Americans across the spectrum—Chinese, Korean, Japanese, Filipino, Southeast Asian, South Asian, and so on—come together as Asians and as Christians. Here the opportunities are maximized for thinking through what it means to be Asian, American and Christian.

Similarly, a parallel trajectory would be hybridized or multiethnic congregations. The difference here is that Asian Americans of whatever stripe would be only one set of ethnic groupings alongside others, whether Hispanic, African American and/or white. Depending on how the congregation is structured (Asian- or white-led) and what its vision and mission involves (Asian- or white-normed), there will be opportunities also here for Asian Americans to take up the hard questions of what it means to be Asian, American and Christian. It is likely that such conversations will unfold alongside and even with those of non-Asian background. The challenge here is how to nurture a common Christian identity that nevertheless not only recognizes but also celebrates the diversity of ethnic realities that constitute the congregation.

My claim is that pent-evangelical theologians in general and Asian American pent-evangelicals more particularly ought to be at the vanguard of thinking about such dynamic and multifaceted theologies of citizenship. The biblical "metanarrative" of migration-incarnation-Pentecost-coming reign of God provides a ready-made template for those navigating such realities to develop a multipronged theology of citizenship that can support and empower churches, congregations and communities across this spectrum of possibilities. Each has important gifts for its members—even at different life stages—and for the wider body of Christ. In this way, important Asian American practical theologies come together and mutually crossfertilize with Asian American ecclesiologies and even more systematically framed theologies for the edification of the church as the people of God and the fellowship of the Spirit.

Asian American women. I now turn briefly to a discussion of women in Asian American evangelical theology. This is conflicted terrain particularly in light of the traditionalist and patriarchal East Asian and Confucian culture (recall chapter three above) that undergirds much of the Asian American evangelical landscape. Given space and time constraints, I can only very briefly chart the issues and identify a possible way forward.

On the one side are more traditional conservative evangelical views about women and their roles in the home and the church. "Complementarians" are Evangelicals who affirm the full equality of male and female created in the image of God but also hold that the Scriptures distinguish between male headship and other, supporting or complementary, female roles. Ethnic Asian American congregations often work at least implicitly, if not explicitly, within such a theological framework.

On the other side are more egalitarian evangelical and also pentecostal traditions that see much of the complementarity texts within other scriptural frames of reference. Evangelicals see the liberative principle of Galatians 3:28—"there is no longer male and female; for all of you are one in Christ Jesus"—as redefining male-female relations across the board (which is not to deny that they remain complementary in important respects), while Pentecostals see that the Spirit's outpouring equally on sons and daughters (Acts 2:17-18) inaugurates a new dispensation in which God's call is no respecter of gender, much less persons (cf. Acts 10:34). Women have been instrumental in pentecostal history across the twentieth century as missionaries, evangelists, pastors, teachers and church leaders on all levels.

Herein may lie one of the cleavages within pent-evangelical Christianity. It does not appear anytime soon that pent-evangelicals who do not ordain women will be able to come to agreement about this issue with those who do. Asian Americans will find themselves on both sides of this chasm, and it will require a good deal of willingness to dialogue on the difficult theological and other issues in order for a way forward to emerge. What all can do, regardless of where they land, is commit themselves to being intentional about the edification of women in our congregations and about their empowerment in all aspects of their lives. Empowerment is not a "feminist" value; rather it is a biblical and pneumatological one. What the edification and empowerment of women ought to accomplish, however, is not merely their success but that of the witness of the church in a hurting world. Hence a biblically envisioned ideal of what it means to be women of God will include also the edification and empowerment of males, not for their own sake but as men of God.[4]

In short, we do not need to pit male against female or vice versa. Rather a pent-evangelical theological anthropology can be intentional about recognizing all of God's intentions for women in whatever roles they may play within their ecclesial communities. Asian American pent-evangelicals, moreover, can contribute their own perspectives both as informing their own local discussions on the matter and as contributing to the wider pent-evangelical conversation.

Next Steps for North American Evangelical Theology

The preceding segues nicely into this section, which asks about the implications of Asian American insights for the broader North American evangelical theological task. The scope here is immense and the challenges substantial. We can only explore, and that very briefly, three arenas directly derivative from the contours of this volume: that related to an evangelical theology of culture, an evangelical public theology and an evangelical socioeconomic theology. How might Asian American perspectives shape next steps in these efforts?

Theology of culture. Asian American pent-evangelical theologians ought to be motivated to take up important questions being asked in the theology of culture. The discussions of the prior generation, shaped by H. Richard Niebuhr's *Christ and Culture* (see chapter three above), still presumed "gospel" and "culture" as two disparate and divergent categories and realities. An incarnational and pentecostal approach to culture realizes that while distinct, the gospel always comes through culture and that culture can—indeed, must!—be redeemed for the purposes of the gospel. This means both that evangelical theologians ought to think intentionally from out of their cultural horizons—whether as Asian Americans or otherwise—even as, simultaneously, the gospel always prophetically confronts the fallen dimensions of our cultural existences.

---

[4]Soyoung Park, "The Intersection of Religion, Race, Gender, and Ethnicity in the Identity Formation of Korean American Evangelical Women," in Ho-Yuan Kwon, Kwang Chung Kim and R. Stephen Warner, eds., *Korean Americans and Their Religions: Pilgrims and Missionaries from a Different Shore* (University Park: The Pennsylvania State University Press, 2001), pp. 193-207; see also Lisa P. Stephenson, *Dismantling the Dualisms for American Pentecostal Women in Ministry*, Global Pentecostal & Charismatic Studies 9 (Boston: Brill, 2011).

The point is that there is no such thing as an unacculturated gospel; the gospel is good news only within culture, even as the gospel is never captive to culture.

Asian Americans Evangelicals can and should join in with black Americans, African-diaspora Americans, Latino/a Americans and Native Americans to think about the diversity of cultural dimensions that need consideration for any North American evangelical theology.[5] Just as important is that each of these voices identifies dialogue partners within the theological establishment who are sensitive to the need for such conversations not only among Evangelicals of color but also among whites.[6] In other words, an evangelical theology of culture is not just the task of ethnic minority groups. Rather, all Evangelicals ought to recognize that critical perspectives on theology of culture are derived from marginal experiences. This means that those in the center of the theological academy (historically whites) will have important critical questions for those on the (relative) margins and vice versa. As such, all voices are essential to a robust deliberation. Within this matrix, Asian Americans can contest (in a healthy sense) the issues from their real and stereotypical positions.

Any theology of culture, of course, is not an end it itself. Rather, a theology of culture can be considered to be a specific theological locus within a larger evangelical theological or doctrinal system, without which an essential discourse would be missing. Yet if essential indeed, then such an evangelical understanding of culture also has implications for the full theological enterprise. This means that, for instance, evangelical notions of culture can and ought to inform discussions in the other loci—for instance, ecclesiology and missiology surely, but also soteriology, creation, anthropology (and the fall) and eschatology, as well as the more formal topics of theology proper: christology, pneumatology, Trinity and the doctrine of God. In all of these areas, of course,

---

[5]See the chapters in part three of Jeffrey Greenman and Gene L. Green, eds., *Global Theology in Evangelical Perspective: Exploring the Contextual Nature of Theology and Mission* (Downers Grove, IL: InterVarsity Press, 2012), for preliminary considerations in these directions.

[6]E.g., Kay Higuera Smith, Jayachitra Lallitha and L. Daniel Hawk, eds., *Evangelical Postcolonial Conversations: Global Awakenings in Theology and Praxis* (Downers Grove, IL: IVP Academic, 2014). A pioneering theological effort to think critically through the question of a North American theology of culture is by recently deceased Jesuit theologian Donald L. Gelpi, *Inculturating North American Theology: An Experiment in Foundational Method* (Atlanta: Scholars Press, 1988); see also my overview of Gelpi's project, "In Search of Foundations: The *Oeuvre* of Donald L. Gelpi, S.J., and Its Significance for Pentecostal Theology and Philosophy," *Journal of Pentecostal Theology* 11, no. 1 (2002): 3 26.

the received theological tradition informs the discussion, albeit it is neither slavishly repeated nor immune from critical questioning. Similarly, Asian American or any other cultural vantage point (even that of the white American perspective) is interrogated in light of the biblical and historic Christian traditions on the one hand even as they may shed new light on the latter as well on the other hand. All of this is accomplished in dialogical fashion involving as many cultural perspectives as may be engaged in the conversation.

Public theology. Evangelicals are at the beginning stages of engaging in the task of public theology.[7] Albeit it has a lengthy and diverse pedigree, the emergence of public theology in our time reflects the recognition that Christian faith is relevant to the public sphere in its many domains. As such public theological discourse includes but is not reducible to political theology, theology of economics, theology of civil society, theology of citizenship (an aspect of which we touched on above) and other related ventures. Each of these is an aspect of the whole (public theology), although individual strands can be considered substantively and on their own terms.[8]

The question is not whether but *if* and *how* Asian American Evangelicals in particular and pent-evangelical theologians more generally will engage in these tasks. Evangelicals are usually less motivated to invest significant energies in such endeavors since their missional horizons subordinate such concerns to other theological domains. Yet there are evangelical and missional implications both attending to such discussions and to their neglect. One point of entry into the public theological discussion is precisely from the missional perspective: if the "rest" are now coming to evangelize the "West," then this opens up matters for public theological consideration.

Readers who have followed the argument in this book so far ought to be able to see numerous springboards into the field of public theology in general and its various tributaries as well. These have to do not only with Asian

---

[7]E.g., John Bolt, *A Free Church, a Holy Nation: Abraham Kuyper's American Public Theology* (Grand Rapids: Eerdmans, 2000).

[8]Thus, for instance, my book *In the Days of Caesar: Pentecostalism and Political Theology—The Cadbury Lectures 2009*, Sacra Doctrina: Christian Theology for a Postmodern Age series (Grand Rapids: Eerdmans, 2010) is more accurately a public theology (it includes the political, the cultural, the social and the economic) than it is a political theology, more strictly understood. I chose the latter, however, as my major methodological point of entry into the public theology discussion, and so subtitled my book as such.

American processes of adaptation and assimilation (touched on in the preceding section) but also about what and how they can contribute to the national and hemispheric discourses that have long been in the making and remain continuously in flux. How might Asian American experiences arriving to and navigating the American public landscape open up new perspectives for evangelical public theology? Could Asian philosophical and cultural discourses on the relationship between individuals and the broader community be brought to bear on the public theological conversation? How might translational relations, affiliations and even to some degree commitments contribute not only to evangelical thinking on these matters but also to the field of public theology as a whole?

As with theology of culture, an evangelical public theology will fill what is now emerging as a gap in evangelical dogmatic and systematic theology. But more importantly, evangelical public theological considerations will also have implications across the theological spectrum. Asian American experiences, perspectives and voices thus can enrich the evangelical theological imagination and mobilize, across multiple (Asian American) fronts, its engagement with the public square.

Theology and economics. Before leaving this section on Asian American contributions to the North American evangelical theological discussion, I want to pursue further one aspect of public theology, that which concerns the sociopolitical and economic domains. This is not only because of our more explicit deliberations on theology of economics above but also because whatever else Western culture is or might be, there is no minimizing how the forces of the global market are shaping our lives and even our Christian identities and self-understandings. Human beings are economic beings—thus *homo economicus*[9]—and so any theology, much less evangelical theology, that neglects this dimension fails to work through some of the most important theological matters of our time. Evangelicals themselves are beginning to

---

[9]On *homo economicus*, see Tomas Sedlacek, *Economics of Good and Evil: The Quest for Economic Meaning from Gilgamesh to Wall Street* (Oxford: Oxford University Press, 2011), esp. chap. 11; see also the discussion of how *homo economicus* can either succeed in being, or also fail to fully live as, Christian in Paul Heyne, *"Are Economists Basically Immoral?" and Other Essays on Economics, Ethics, and Religion*, ed. Geoffrey Brennan and A. M. C. Waterman (Indianapolis: Liberty Fund, 2008), chap. 4.

wade into the waters of economic theology.[10] How might Asian American Evangelicals contribute to such a discussion?

Aside from the considerations previously offered (chapter six), Asian Americans who live betwixt-and-between Asia and the United States can bring more existential and interrelational resources to bear on the transnational and globalizing dynamics of the present time. Any evangelical theology of economics surely will be informed by North American perspectives, essential indeed given the United States' role in the global market. At the same time, the emergence and rapid development of foreign markets means that American monopolies will be increasingly challenged. The arrival of economic powers across the Pacific Rim means that Asian voices also cannot be ignored.

Yet more importantly, Evangelicals are as engaged, if not more, as other Christians in development and relief initiatives. Given that widespread and massive poverty continues to afflict human beings across the world, evangelical theologies of economics will also be theologies of shalom and of justice. This is part of the missional and evangelical dimension of the Christian theology itself. Asian American Evangelicals ought to be motivated to heed the call to engage with theologies of economic justice that are relevant not only for the impoverished in Asia but also for the poor in the North American hemisphere.

Last but not least along these lines, any evangelical theology of economics will also take up the related tasks of ecological theology. Economic sustainability into the twenty-first century involves environmental sustainability. Asian American transnational and diasporic connections open up multiple dialogical avenues that provide perspective on global and environmental issues confronting humankind. Such will also be interdisciplinary endeavors, and Asian Americans who work disproportionately in the engineering, technological and scientific fields that can inform such considerations can bring their expertise to bear on these discussions.[11]

---

[10]E.g., John Lunn, "Economics," in Gerald R. McDermott, ed., *The Oxford Handbook of Evangelical Theology* (New York: Oxford University Press, 2010), pp. 402-17.

[11]My initial efforts in this direction have been sketched in a project in comparative theology, engaging in particular Buddhist traditions; see Yong, *The Cosmic Breath: Spirit and Nature in the Christianity-Buddhism-Science Trialogue,* Philosophical Studies in Science & Religion 4 (Boston: Brill, 2012), esp. part 3.

NEXT STEPS FOR GLOBAL EVANGELICAL THEOLOGY

By entering into the domain of economics and the environment, we have now shifted from the North American to the global horizon. In this final part of the chapter, I want to explore the possibility of Asian American contributions to the global evangelical theological task. This is surely a stretch since, as this volume has documented, Asian American Evangelicals are still at the starting gate in theological inquiry. However, I want to conclude this volume with as expansive of a theological vista as possible in order to provoke curiosity and perhaps even inspire imaginative possibilities. To do so, I suggest Asian Americans might lead the way in critically retrieving and engaging with Asian cultural and philosophical traditions as a way of doing theology in global context.

Constructive theology in a multifaith world. Thinking about the environment, for instance, invites critical consideration of Daoist philosophical resources. On the one hand, the rich notion of *wu-wei* refers to the kind of "effortless effort" to live in harmony with the environment long touted in the Daoist tradition. On the other hand, of course, *wu-wei* could become an "inactive activity" that hampers intentional interventions in the created order. So while Daoist sources can contribute to evangelical thinking about the environment (as intimated by Simon Chan in chapter one above) biblical notions also can challenge Daoist conceptions. How might Asian American thinkers facilitate such dialogue across cultural lines?

The East Asian theology of harmony, of course, links Daoist and Confucian traditions together. Environmental concord includes human accord: *wu-wei* applies just as well to human relations as to our interface with the natural world and the cosmos. Arguably, Confucian interrelationality also emerged in response to nascent forms of dualistic and even individualistic thinking in early China,[12] resulting in what might be called the "cosmotheandric" intertwining of heaven-earth-and-humanity in the Chinese tradition. Evangelical theologians can engage profitably with these Confucian and Chinese sources in rethinking theological anthropology in global context. Simultaneously, the church as the people of God, the body of Christ and the fellowship of the Spirit can also add critical content to the heaven or transcendence dimension

---

[12]As recently asserted by Edward Slingerland, "Body and Mind in Early China: An Integrated Humanities-Science Approach," *Journal of the American Academy of Religion* 81, no. 1 (2013): 6-55.

of the Chinese conception in order to fulfill at least some of its aspirations regarding human community and relationality. What might Asian Americans do to facilitate such dialogical interchange on these and other related topics?

Last but not least, Daoist and Confucian traditions are two of the three spokes of the wheel that constitute the *san jiao* or "three teachings" of Chinese and East Asian spirituality and religiosity, the third being the dharma teachings of Indian Buddhism. If Daoism attends to the cosmos and Confucianism to human relations, then Buddhist traditions focus on the nature of the self, or the true nature of the nonself, as the case may be. So if the former two teachings are appropriate dialogue partners for evangelical theologians in global context, the latter might also shape evangelical theologies of spirituality and of the self where East meets West. Buddhist notions could open up new pathways into scriptural teachings on dying to self and living in Christ.[13] Evangelical commitments could, in turn, suggest how the Buddhist deconstruction of the false self might be reconstructed in ways that are fulfilled finally in the true self that is Jesus Christ. Might Asian Americans mediate such a dialogue and conversation?

Interreligious dialogue and apologetics. The preceding only poses possible avenues of exploration, in some ways inquiring whether the efforts of the Boston Confucians in philosophy might be paralleled among Asian Americans in theology. Inasmuch as Asian Americans are generally not motivated to engage with Asian philosophical and especially religious sources for their theological work, the preceding suggestions may be beyond the pale of possibility for many at this point. That is surely understandable given the defensive-minded apologetic approach to other faiths that has dominated evangelical thinking. My proposals, however, are not shorn of the apologetic dimension. As should be clear, the critical edge of the gospel will sever all that is against the goodness, beauty and truth of the triune God. Yet this applies to the Western and even Christian tradition itself, as not everything that we find within these canons will stand up to the gospel message. The point is that theology in global context will be apologetic yet also dialogical. Evangelicals who know the former all too well are invited in this volume to consider aspects of the latter opened up in global context, in particular in relationship to Asian discourses and ways of life.

---

[13]See my *Pneumatology and the Christian-Buddhist Dialogue: Does the Spirit Blow Through the Middle Way?* Studies in Systematic Theology 11 (Boston: Brill, 2012), esp. part 1.

Yet the preceding focus on the interfaith encounter is neither the only nor perhaps even the most urgent matter for evangelical theology in global context. To be sure, the details of any global theological conversation will eventually, if not even sooner, run up against the question of religious pluralism. The sooner Evangelicals in general and Asian American Evangelicals in particular become more adept at engaging these conversations, the more productive and effective their witness and missional initiatives will be. Again, the point is neither the uncritical adoption of other religious ideas or practices nor the syncretism of Christian faith in Asian or Asian American contexts but the translatability of the gospel into the Asian and Asian American cultural and linguistic vernacular.

Some pent-evangelicals are called to interreligious apologetics of what is called the negative sort, which is a nonpejorative designation for defending the Christian faith against the claims or criticisms of those from other traditions. This is an important task, and interfaith interactions going forward will certainly need to be attentive to this aspect of the encounter between religions in the twenty-first century. My own work, however, has focused primarily on what might be called positive apologetics, which includes constructive theological explanations that are more expansive than those proferred by other faiths.[14] It seems to me that one way to "make your defense to anyone who demands from you an account of the hope that is in you" (1 Pet 3:15) is to provide an account of the world from one's own religious and theological tradition that includes, rather than ignores or excludes, whatever truths, goodness and beauty are witnessed to by other traditions. There is no shortcut toward this goal, only authentic dialogue with those in other faiths. In the process, one is transformed by their witness even as a more deeply and more profoundly expansive Christian apologetic emerges for the pluralistic world of our time.

I am convinced that these developments on all of these fronts are essential for the evangelical witness in Asian America going forward for second and later generations. While many second-generation East and even South Asians are increasingly secular, they are no less spiritually oriented. Because

---

[14]For more on these various forms of interreligious apologetics, see Paul J. Griffiths, *An Apology for Apologetics: A Study in the Logic of Interreligious Dialogue* (Maryknoll, NY: Orbis, 1991).

the East Asian religious traditions are neither hierarchically structured nor institutionally organized, they are less likely to generate a public religious identity on American soil. Nevertheless, many second-generation Asian Americans remain spiritually engaged, and these projects are informed by Confucian, Buddhist and Daoist sensibilities, albeit now hybridized in global context.[15] As such, effective interaction with such persons will need to be at least conversant about how these traditions are portable across cultures in the late modern world.

Hence I believe the theology-of-religions work of some Evangelicals and Pentecostals can help inform global pent-evangelical reflection on religious pluralism and the interfaith encounter.[16] In brief, what is needed for our time is an eschatologically oriented theological approach to the religions that is capable of recognizing and redeeming whatever truth, beauty and goodness may be present in them for the purposes of magnifying the Christ to which all truth, beauty and goodness ultimately point.[17] The incarnational and pentecostal economies of the triune God suggest that human nature and human culture, while fallen, are redeemable in all their historicity, contextuality and particularity. The gospel comes both to critique but also to give hope—the former pointing out how our systems and conventions are deathly and destructive and

---

[15]See the three chapters in part four of Carolyn Chen and Russell Jeung, eds., *Sustaining Faith Traditions: Race, Ethnicity, and Religion Among the Latino and Asian American Second Generation* (New York: New York University Press, 2012).

[16]The most insightful Evangelicals I have found include Gerald R. McDermott, *Can Evangelicals Learn from World Religions? Jesus, Revelation and Religious Traditions* (Downers Grove, IL: IVP Academic, 2000); Veli-Matti Kärkkäinen, *Trinity and Religious Pluralism: The Doctrine of the Trinity in Christian Theology of Religions* (Aldershot, UK: Ashgate, 2004); Bob Robinson, *Jesus and the Religions: Retrieving a Neglected Example for a Multicultural World* (Eugene, OR: Cascade Books, 2012), among many others. For further articulation of a pentecostal and evangelical theology of religions and of interfaith encounter, see my books *Discerning the Spirit(s): A Pentecostal-Charismatic Contribution to Christian Theology of Religions*, Journal of Pentecostal Theology Supplement Series 20 (Sheffield, UK: Sheffield Academic Press, 2000); *Beyond the Impasse: Toward a Pneumatological Theology of Religions* (Grand Rapids: Baker Academic, 2003); and *Hospitality and the Other: Pentecost, Christian Practices, and the Neighbor*, Faith Meets Faith series (Maryknoll, NY: Orbis, 2008).

[17]Some excellent examples are a collection of articles by Seah David Jeremiah and his colleagues in Singapore, published in the *Journal of Asian Evangelical Theology* 15, no. 1 (June 2007), for instance: with Chiang Kok Weng, "A Comparative Study of the Hebrew Concept of Ruach and the Chinese Concept of Qi" (pp. 15-45); with Jodi Choo May Eng, "Ascetic Theology for Asian Pentecostal-Charismatics" (pp. 68-97); with Tham Chee Kin and Sylvia Chua, "A Conceptualization of Chinese Christian Spirituality in the Counseling Context" (pp. 130-56); and Lee Kian Cheng and Chua Bian Hin, "*Bhikkhu* Spirituality and Thai Christianity" (pp. 98-129).

the latter pointing a way forward that transforms the potentiality of the present world—so that the many languages, cultures, peoples and traditions might finally declare the wondrous works of God illuminated in the light of Christ through the work of the Holy Spirit. It is such a pent-evangelical approach to theology of religions and of the interfaith encounter that will be adequate to the global context of present time on the one hand but also sufficiently particular for engaging with many different local realities on the other hand.

Global engagements. All Christian theologians, evangelicals included, would do well to recall that the advance of the gospel from Jerusalem through Judea to the ends of the earth has always borrowed, adapted and transformed from pagan traditions. This can be seen even in the pages of the New Testament, where the apostolic leaders used pagan terms and concepts for their own purposes.[18] It is certainly prevalent during the "Europeanization" of Christianity during the medieval period, not to mention also the "Americanization" of the faith in the New World later. As already discussed in the first chapter, Christianity's translatability has led to its contextualization, indigenization and vernacularization, each of which involves various aspects of embracing pagan ideas and even practices—in Asia, Africa and Latin America—albeit for Christian purposes.

What is important to emphasize, then, is how Asian American Evangelicals might facilitate global theological conversations across multiple lines. As this volume has shown (chapter one), Asian Evangelicals are already beginning to forge their own pathways by heeding the contextual demands and opportunities on the Asian front. Asian American Evangelicals can link those discussions with North American evangelical efforts. Yet Asian American Evangelicals can also potentially mediate discussion with nonevangelical Asian American theologians on the one side and nonevangelical Asian theologians on the other side. And in terms of the global frontier, Asian American Evangelicals might connect Asian evangelical theology with African and Latin American evangelical theologies, not to mention the range of European evangelical theologies that are also gestating on the horizon. What is being suggested, in other words, is that Asian Americans ought not to be so defer-

---

[18]E.g., Andrew F. Walls, "The Ephesian Moment," in Walls, *The Cross-Cultural Process in Christian History* (Maryknoll, NY: Orbis, 2002), pp. 72-81.

ential to others that they minimize the importance of their own witness for the evangelical theological enterprise. The full scope of Asian American perspectives ought to be sounded out, not just so that more noise can be generated but so that it might be heard in the wider theological academy even as it was voiced on the Day of Pentecost: "in our own languages we hear them speaking about God's deeds of power" (Acts 2:11).

When this happens, a pent-evangelical perspective can then believe and hope for the orchestration of the Holy Spirit to bring about good news for Asian America, for the United States and for the world in the twenty-first century. This will be because Asian American voices will reflect the blended set of sensibilities that is informed by life betwixt and between. From this interstitial and liminal region will come forth the living word of God in the power of the Holy Spirit, able to address new realities precisely through their juxtopositioning. The Asian American witness can resound just because it emerges out of the hybridity that is increasingly a part of the global experience. Perhaps for that reason it can bear new forms of witness to the ultimate hybrid, the God-man Jesus Christ, and his Spirit who has been poured out on all flesh.

EPILOGUE

Evangelical Theology in the Twenty-First Century: Hybrid Soundings from the Asian American Pent-evangelical Diaspora

Growing up evangelical and pentecostal, I had been taught that our cultural identities did not matter since we had converted to Christ and were now part of "Christian culture." This was a standard evangelical and pentecostal understanding of what conversion entailed through the middle third of the twentieth century. Yet I have come to see that the central acts of God's saving history actually invite us to think otherwise. That Jesus the Logos of God took on flesh means not only that he became biologically human but also that he took up within himself first-century Palestinian languages, cultures and even religions (of the Second Temple Jewish form), surely transforming them in the process. Then the Day of Pentecost outpouring of the Spirit upon all flesh means something similar: not just that men and women, young and old, slave and free from the Jewish diaspora around the Mediterranean world received the Spirit as individuals, but that their languages, cultures and, I have argued in various places, even religious traditions were being somehow redeemed in order to declare and speak "about God's deeds of power" (Acts 2:11). In short, Christian initiation and conversion involves not just a turning away from the world and a turning to God but also constitutes God's ways of purifying, transforming and redeeming the world in all of its complexity.

I have come to these theological convictions in part through reflecting on my own journey. Reflecting and expanding on my autobiographical ruminations in the prologue of this book, I was born to pentecostal pastors who were also first-generation Chinese converts from a nominal form of Buddhism in postcolonial Malaysia. This aspect of my early life itself needs unpacking at least at three levels. First, Malaysia in the late 1960s and early 1970s—these were my growing-up years, before our family emigrated to the United States, about which more momentarily—was a Muslim state attempting to finds its bearings after achieving independence from the British in 1957. Even then, and until now, the slight majority population of indigenous Malays (the *bumiputra* or "children of the soil"), all legally understood as Muslims, were socio-economically and politically privileged. Yet the fact that the 20 to 25 percent Chinese population has always contributed a much larger percentage to the nation's GNP has meant that there have always been racial and ethnic tensions between Malays and Chinese. As Christians in Malaysia were mostly non-Malays (Chinese, but also South Indian Tamils, who make up about one-tenth of the population), they have always been a marginalized minority (around 10 percent), not only religiously but also politically and socially. Yet there are further complications, as when intermarriages occur, including my aunt who married a Malay *datuk* (a chief and elite member of the Malay social hierarchy) and had three children with him. Her own religious identity, needless to say, has continuously been betwixt and between, neither Christian nor Muslim, at least not in any orthodox sense with regard to either tradition.

At a second level, my parents believed that their being made new in Christ (cf. 2 Cor 5:17) meant that they had left behind their Buddhist beliefs and practices once for all. However, growing up I learned about filial piety, a traditional Confucian value; about the importance of natural and herbal forms of health maintenance and health care, derived from the long history of indigenous and Daoist-based Chinese medicine; and about doing all things in moderation. The last, while arguably a gloss on certain biblical proverbs, was also a clear Buddhist virtue, a central element of Buddhist teachings advocating a middle path between extremes. Of course, these aspects of my upbringing were always presented as common sense; I did not know of their cultural and religious backgrounds until I undertook graduate studies in comparative religion later in life. In any case, we celebrated a partially Christianized version of Chinese New Year (partially, since not all of our relatives at that time were converts). Yet were we successful in leaving our (Buddhist) past behind, or were we right to desire to reject that past completely as the missionaries had taught us to?

At a third level, my parents were converts not to more established forms of Catholic or Protestant Christianity (the latter dominated by its Anglican and Methodist expressions in Malaysia) but to Pentecostalism. In the third quarter of the twentieth century, Pentecostalism was still viewed almost as a sectarian form of Christianity, the latter already a marginal religion in the Muslim political context and amid the Buddhist religious environment that most Malaysian Chinese inhabited. My parents have told me of being persecuted at a young age for their Christian faith, even by their own family members. Eventually, their parents (my grandparents) also converted to Christianity. The point is, however, that conversion in such situations no doubt also contributed to the theological view that insisted on defining Christian faith over and against other religions. At the same time, given the small numbers of Christians in the Malaysian context, less and less was made of sectarian, denominational or ecclesial differences over time, with most Christians thinking it more worthwhile to collaborate with others to achieve common goals, especially in the political venue. In that sense, in the Malaysian context, Pentecostals have remained distinctive, but not absolutely so from other Christians.[1]

My family immigrated to Northern California when I was ten to pastor among other Chinese-speaking immigrants who were pouring into North America in the wake of the immigration reform laws passed in 1965. I was thus part of the Chinese diaspora twice removed—first in Malaysia and now in the United States. Having spent the rest of my growing up years in the United States and having completed all of my graduate and postgraduate studies here, my education is thoroughly Western. Along the way, I married a fifth-generation Mexican American woman, and together we have had three children who continuously have to decide whether they should check "Latino," "Asian" or other boxes related to their ethnicity. Although I am now

---

[1]For an overview, see Tan Jin Huat, "Pentecostal and Charismatic Origins in Malaysia and Singapore," in Allan Anderson and Edmond Tang, eds., *Asian and Pentecostal: The Charismatic Face of Christianity in Asia* (London: Regnum International, and Baguio City, Philippines: Asia Pacific Theological Seminary Press, 2005), pp. 281-306.

a naturalized Asian American citizen of the United States and am a lifelong adherent to and for the last twenty-five years a credentialed minister with the Assemblies of God, I remain very sensitive to the dynamics of globalization, especially as these have affected my own transnational, intercultural and even interreligious set of experiences.

As a theologian shaped by this history, then, I find myself continuously navigating betwixt-and-between various identities, realities and relationships. What has emerged can be considered a hybridized identity. By this, however, I mean not just a jumble of confused elements drawn from hither and thither, although sometimes it might feel that (for me) or even seem that (from the perspective of others). Rather, I mean that who I am is the result of a range of histories and particularities that are now interwoven into the fabric of who I am. I can still distinguish the Asian and the American features, although they hold together more in creative tension than they do as if their seams were obliterated. Jesus Christ, himself the "reflection of God's glory and the exact imprint of God's very being" (Heb 1:3), nevertheless took up in his person human nature as well, albeit without either confusing such with or separating such from the divine nature, as the early church taught. By the grace of God, then, according to the image of the incarnate Son into which I am being transformed through the purifying and sanctifying power of the Holy Spirit, these various elements of my identity are being eschatologically redeemed, not eliminated.

Hence my Asian American hybrid identity cannot be understood apart from the other more specifically theological domains that also constitute my life (hi)story. Hybridity does not just cut across our lives variously in the globalizing world of the twenty-first century but is fundamentally theological. In order to see this, let me elucidate ten axes of creative and hybridic tensions that I find intertwined in my own life, each representing distinctive realities that yet precisely in their togetherness inform my testimony and witness to the saving work of God. I explicate these in no particular order.[2]

First, I find myself always between East and West, between Asian and American cultural traditions. In some respects, I am comfortable in either

---

[2]I apologize in advance for the brevity of these presentations, although I have cited mostly my other work wherein I engage with many of these issues more substantively. I urge readers who are interested in my own constructive thinking on these matters to consult these prior publications.

world, but in other respects, I find myself belonging in neither. This is in part because of my ethnic and racial identity, complicated certainly by the dominant black-white framework through which such issues are adjudicated in North America (to which I return in a moment). It is also in part because I now believe that various cultural aspects of my identity are constitutive of the primordial goodness of creation and, in that sense, also anticipate the redemptive work of God. This is not to say that all cultural realities are to be naively adopted into Christian faith. It is to say that there is much more to be considered about the cultural dimensions of Christian life than we have heretofore been open to. Beyond these factors, I ought to note that while I am grateful for the opportunities afforded to me and my immediate family in the United States, I know that part of my identity will always belong in Asia, with my extended family members and their children who remain there. As a person of Chinese descent, I will be on the margins of American life in some or other respect at least for the rest of my lifetime, even as my family members (and myself, if I were to ever return to Malaysia for more than a short-term visit) will remain at the margins of Malaysian life for the foreseeable future. In short, neither can be an ultimate resting place. And I cannot even return to China: any relatives going back a few generations would not know me, not to mention that my American Chinese would be largely incomprehensible to native speakers. Some people might find this situatedness between East and West debilitating; perhaps being *both* Asian *and* American—rather than *either* one or some unrecognizable or synthetic *tertium quid*—it can be a resource for theological reflection relevant to the contemporary global context instead.[3]

Second, I live as yellow between white and black, but this is now also complicated by shades of browns, not to mention other spectra. As already indicated, my yellowness renders me both a perpetual foreigner and a model minority; yet the latter is also a threatening signifier for the darker hues of browns through blacks. More complexly, my interracial marriage (to a Mexican American woman) cuts against the unspoken prohibition, in the West, of

---

[3]See, e.g., my two books, *Pneumatology and the Christian-Buddhist Dialogue: Does the Spirit Blow Through the Middle Way?* Studies in Systematic Theology 11 (Boston: Brill, 2012), and *The Cosmic Breath: Spirit and Nature in the Christianity-Buddhism-Science Trialogue,* Philosophical Studies in Science & Religion 4 (Boston: Brill, 2012).

yellow men marrying nonyellow women even as our children are racial hybrids—"Chexicans," as my son has publicly embraced—who may still be best characterized by what they are not: neither white nor black; neither yellow nor brown, "purely" speaking. Still, there are more and more of "them" even if in overall numbers, "they"—Chexicans, that is—are relatively few. Similarly, there are more and more black-white, black-yellow, black-brown, brown-white, brown-yellow, yellow-white and other "combinations," and these will only increase going forward. None of this means that the history of race and ethnicity, in fact and as socially constructed, will be any less important. Their significance, however, will need to be freshly construed by each generation.[4] Perhaps being yellow allows for mediating between other "colors" in ways that preserves their distinctive witnesses while yet also forging a new whole that anticipates the fullness of the coming reign of God. This book presents one effort to think theologically through the implications of Asian American racial and ethnic hybridity within the broader discussion.

Third, I live uneasily between a colonial and postcolonial world. We are about a generation or two removed from independence of most colonized nations. At one level, as a Christian, there is much to be grateful for about how missionaries brought the gospel to the Majority World, including, in my case, pentecostal missionaries who went to Malaysia. And while there were certainly missionaries who were supported and benefited from the colonial enterprise, many were also not politically motivated or directly implicated. On the postindependence side of things, it is also essential to note that the various countries of the world that have emerged from under colonial rule need to take responsibility for themselves and not blame the history of colonization for their woes. Many nations have made successful adjustments since independence, so others can as well. Still, the legacy of colonialism remains to this day, and its mechanisms, deeply embedded in countries and regions of the world across the Global South, continue to reverberate in our shrinking global village. In the United States, the long history of slavery and

---

[4]My work in this area is limited to some articles and one edited book—e.g., Yong, "Justice Deprived, Justice Demanded: Afropentecostalisms and the Task of World Pentecostal Theology Today," *Journal of Pentecostal Theology* 15, no. 1 (2006): 127-47, and Yong and Estrelda Alexander, eds., *Afro-Pentecostalism: Black Pentecostal and Charismatic Christianity in History and Culture*, Religion, Race, and Ethnicity Series (New York: New York University Press, 2011).

Native American racism remain palpable in certain parts of this country and continue to haunt our existence in a subterranean manner despite the gains made during the civil rights revolution in the 1960s. In this context and as a member of the Chinese diaspora (twice removed, as I indicated above), I wrestle with the fact that the dominant theological tradition has been implicated in the colonial enterprise. New postcolonial voices and perspectives are emerging, some resisting and rejecting the historic tradition, others (among whom I count myself) seeking to revise, retrieve or reappropriate the Christian faith for a postcolonial—not to mention postmodern, post-Western, and post-Enlightenment—world.[5] What does it mean to think Christianly and to reconceive Christian theology in light of the historical, social and political realities after colonialism, not only for Malaysia but for the United States as well? Can we preserve the gains of the Enlightenment while being open also to what late modernity has to offer through subaltern perspectives? How in the end can a hybridic identity that is trinitarianly shaped—christomorphic and pneumatically empowered—redeem the colonial legacy on the one hand yet inspire postcolonial efforts on the other?[6]

Fourth, I live with some ambivalence on this course of upward socio-economic mobility that I and my family have been traversing. As immigrants to the United States, we came "sponsored" (that is the technical term that includes the promise of financial support for as long as needed) by a missionary and a network of churches, and I looked forward every Christmas to receiving hand-me-downs from charitable Christians who would bless us missionary families who could not otherwise afford to purchase new clothes. My wife was born on the Mexican American migrant trail (her Texan parents were picking

---

[5]See my concluding reflections to a volume on the Christian mission to Native America: Yong, "The Missiology of Jamestown: 1607-2007 and Beyond—Toward a Postcolonial Theology of Mission in North America," in Amos Yong and Barbara Brown Zikmund, eds., *Remembering Jamestown: Hard Questions About Christian Mission* (Eugene, OR: Pickwick, 2010), pp. 157-67; cf. Amos Yong and Christian T. Collins Winn, "The Apocalypse of Colonialism, Colonialism as Apocalyptic Mission; or, Notes Toward a Postcolonial Eschatology," in Kay Higuera Smith, Jayachitra Lalitha and L. Daniel Hawk, eds., *Evangelical Postcolonial Conversations: Global Awakenings in Theology and Praxis* (Downers Grove, IL: IVP Academic, 2014).

[6]Two books of mine address different aspects of this issue: theologically in *In the Days of Caesar: Pentecostalism and Political Theology—The Cadbury Lectures 2009*, Sacra Doctrina: Christian Theology for a Postmodern Age series (Grand Rapids: Eerdmans, 2010), and scripturally in *Who Is the Holy Spirit? A Walk with the Apostles* (Brewster, MA: Paraclete, 2011).

cucumbers in Wisconsin when she arrived) and remembers working in the
fields every summer even through her college years. Now our combined
income places us solidly in the upper-middle-class bracket, and we are awash
in our consumerist and materialist cultural way of life. While our fortune in
life makes it easier to talk about the providence of God, it also removes us
somewhat from the solidarity with the poor that the Scriptures enjoin. In fact,
sometimes I think that the individualistic, evangelical gospel of justification
by grace through faith legitimates my way of life: it justifies my home ownership while being presumptive about others who lack such as simply not
working hard enough. After all, my own Asian American upbringing instilled
in me that if I worked hard enough, got straight A's and completed medical
school (I did a PhD instead!) that I could live the American dream. So when
I read about Jesus having nowhere to lay his head and Paul being a missionary
tentmaker who was content in whatever situation he found himself, I ask
myself if my contentment derives from Christ or from my relatively finan-
cially secure situation. John Wesley's maxim regarding generosity—that is,
"Having, First, gained all you can, and, Secondly saved all you can, Then 'give
all you can'"[7]—is haunting since I am sure we can give more, especially to
those less well-off. I justify our condition saying that compared to others, we
are only relatively comfortable, but it is undeniable that a much larger percentage of the world lives with much, much less than we do. In short, we
sometimes are guilty about our prosperity, yet also often are thankful that
our debt load is minimal and that we have enough to pay our bills at the end
of the month. What is the fine line here between having enough and having
too much, between living in a plentiful United States (or any other "promised
land") and elsewhere in regions struck by famine, war and other conditions
inimical to economic stability, development and growth? Perhaps it is possible to live faithfully and creatively either in simplicity or in plenty—or between them—as appropriate in accordance with various life stages, voca-
tional calls and circumstantial periods.[8]

---

[7]See Wesley's sermon (1760), "The Use of Money," in Albert Cook Outler and Richard P. Heitzen-
rater, eds., *John Wesley's Sermons: An Anthology* (Nashville: Abingdon, 1991), p. 355.
[8]See my chapter in Yong and Katherine Attanasi, eds., *Pentecostalism and Prosperity: The Socioeconomics of the Global Charismatic Movement*, Christianities of the World 1 (New York: Palgrave
Macmillan, 2012).

Fifth, I struggle strenuously with how my Christian faith commitments are in some ways fundamentally opposed to yet also in other ways not exclusive of other faiths. This is my reality—I cannot deny that what I am as a person of Chinese descent is already a hybridic combination of the philosophical, cultural and religious traditions of East and Southeast Asia. In the West, we might think these various strands are detachable from one another and therefore that it might be acceptable to embrace the cultures but not the religions of the East. But in reality, these are overlapping domains. Part of the challenge is that at least some traditions of Christianity consider any association with other religious traditions in negative terms as "syncretism." I desire neither an uncritical syncretism nor a bland, lowest-common-denominator theology that is inclusive of other faiths. Simultaneously, I also do not think that some versions of theological exclusivism can account for the complicated interreligious lives and identities that are being formed through the gospel. While being for Christ will entail being against some aspects of other faiths, perhaps this leads not to complete repudiation but anticipates their eschatological fulfillment.[9] If Paul's identity in Christ, for instance, did not eradicate his Jewishness even as it prompted substantial interrogation of what it meant to be a faithful Christ follower, might this not also be the case for those in other faiths? Meanwhile, then, perhaps the tensions amid these domains can serve as a resource for creatively rethinking Christian commitments in a global multireligious context as outlined at the end of the previous chapter.[10]

The preceding Pauline example leads, sixthly, to discussion of identity in Christ that is between ancient Israel and contemporary Judaism. Is Christianity Jewish or not? Yes and no are probably both correct answers. The issues are particularly urgent in light of the long history of Christian anti-Semitism culminating in the Holocaust. Post-Shoah Christian self-understandings cannot afford to ignore how Christian views of the Jews have had tragic political and historical consequences. Complicating contemporary Christian and Jewish relationships are the emergence of messianic Jews and back-to-

---

[9]As expertly argued by Ivan Satyavrata, *God Has Not Left Himself Without Witness* (Oxford: Regnum International, 2011).

[10]I have long wrestled with these matters, most recently in my *Hospitality and the Other: Pentecost, Christian Practices, and the Neighbor*, Faith Meets Faith series (Maryknoll, NY: Orbis, 2008).

Jerusalem movements. The former are certainly well received in evangelical Christian circles but severely contested among Jews, while the latter are prominent in East Asian contexts and growing in global influence. On the one hand, many Christians insist on the ongoing evangelization of Jews; on the other hand, our theological self-understanding is not as deeply informed by the Hebrew Bible as it ought to be. In fact, there is a spectrum of response across the Christian community about how to understand the relevance of that portion of the biblical canon in relationship to the New Testament. Has the ancient covenant with Israel been subsumed into the church, or does it persist in some respects parallel to that of the new covenant in Christ? Therein lies part of the challenge about how Christians should relate to Jews in the contemporary world. No doubt, intermarriages between Jews and Christians have complicated this question of identity for both Christians and Jews. Rather than having to be either for or against Judaism today, the Christian way forward may be more adequately charted as one that embraces the Jewish roots of Christian faith in a post-Holocaust world. If so, then Christian faith is neither Jewish nor anti-Jewish but involves instead a hybridic posture between these options, one with the potential to transform the world in anticipation of the coming reign of God.[11]

Seventh, as a Pentecostal I ride the tension that persists between more evangelical and more ecumenical forms of Christianity today. To be sure, such tensions are more relaxed today than at any time in the last century. Nevertheless, there are still debates between "conservatives" and "liberals," between "orthodoxy" and "progressivism," between confessional and mainline Protestantism (and Catholicism and Orthodoxy as well). In the United States, and especially in the Asian American evangelical arena, the lines between "right" and "left" are more hard and fast than in other parts of the English-speaking world, even if the emergence of postconservative forms of Evangelicalism is erasing some of the rigidity. Certainly, as I have indicated above, in some parts of the Majority World, there is much more cooperation when confronted by the need to mobilize smaller numbers for common causes. This is not to say that Pentecostals and Evangelicals need to give up on all their

---

[11]I struggle with this question in the final (eighth) chapter of my *In the Days of Caesar*; see also the literature cited there.

theological convictions. Neither is it to say that both sides are beyond critique in their respective commitments. It is to say that there may be better ways of holding to at least some of these convictions that more appropriately engage contemporary challenges. My point is that a hybridic response requires neither a negation of the good and true on either side nor some unwieldy and inauthentic both-and amalgamation but rather a redemptive way beyond either-or that seeks to be faithful to Scripture according to the image of Christ by the power of the Spirit.[12]

This leads, eighth, to a discussion of how pentecostal identity has existed in creative tension from its emergence at the beginning of the twentieth century with the self-understanding of the broader Christian tradition. On the one hand, the pentecostal belief in the baptism of the Holy Spirit that empowers Christian witness, as evidenced by speaking in tongues, suggests that those without such experiences are second-tier Christians (at best), if not members of nonvital churches from which they should depart (at worst). This view fosters a kind of pentecostal elitism that, not surprisingly, rubs other Christians the wrong way. On the other hand, the fact that Pentecostals often attract nominal Christians from other churches has led also to concerns and accusations about pentecostal proselytism and "sheep stealing." These tensions are exacerbated in Asian and other ecumenical contexts internationally when pentecostal missionaries and evangelists approach other putatively Christian groups with an aggressive message of conversion. Against this backdrop, how can I maintain my pentecostal commitments without perpetuating the triumphalism characteristic of pentecostal attitudes from earlier eras? In addition, there is also the phenomenon of Oneness Pentecostalism—trinitarian Pentecostals do not like to acknowledge this aspect of the modern renewal movement, but it is present nonetheless, especially in the ways that even trinitarian Pentecostals count the demographics of global renewal. Is it possible to consider pentecostal Christianity as presenting certain gifts to the churches, even from the Oneness perspective,[13] while yet inviting Pentecostals to be open to re-

---

[12]I would argue that the issues are in part hermeneutical and in part methodological; see my *Spirit-Word-Community: Theological Hermeneutics in Trinitarian Perspective*, New Critical Thinking in Religion, Theology and Biblical Studies Series (Burlington, VT: Ashgate, 2002).

[13]As done so brilliantly by David A. Reed, *"In Jesus' Name": The History and Beliefs of Oneness Pentecostals*, Journal of Pentecostal Theology Supplement Series 31 (Blandford Forum, UK: Deo, 2008).

ceiving the gifts of other churches at the same time? Can such a mutual gift exchange preserve the distinctiveness and uniqueness of the pentecostal message—even across the trinitarian and Oneness divide—while not demeaning those of other Christian traditions? Is this what it might mean to receive the many gifts of the Holy Spirit that are given through the many and different members of the church?[14] Again, the hybridic response is that pentecostal Christianity remains distinctive yet is not set off completely from the broader Christian tradition; instead, there are opportunities for distinctive witness to resound, resulting in mutual edification and even transformation.

Ninth, I am a committed egalitarian when it comes to gender relations yet one who is continuously navigating the via media between evangelical complementarianism on the one side and evangelical feminism on the other. As already discussed, from a pent-evangelical perspective, the biblical case for the Spirit's empowering women across the full range of ministries is clearly arguable. However, many Asian American evangelical churches and congregations are hesitant about reading certain epistolary passages in light of the Day of Pentecost narrative in Acts, an attitude consistent with wider swaths of the evangelical world that affirm that male and female are equal in the sight of God yet assigned complementary (distinct) ministerial and other roles. On the other side, it is also undeniable that the renewalist fire that has swept across the world, even in the Asian context, has been lighted by women, both going back to nineteenth-century evangelical missionaries and certainly featuring consistently across the twentieth-century pentecostal and charismatic renewal movements. How to affirm this basic pentecostal principle while honoring culturally particular perspectives and alternative readings of the Scriptures in global context? How to empower women within biblical frames of reference while distancing from the more radically construed feminist political ideologies? How might the work and ministry of women be lifted up in ways that are edifying for others—for men, for the church and for the world—and yet not imposed (imperialistically) on those who do not currently see such matters similarly (and may never come around to this egalitarian po-

---

[14]I confront the Oneness challenge plus explicate an expansive pentecostal theology in my *The Spirit Poured Out on All Flesh: Pentecostalism and the Possibility of Global Theology* (Grand Rapids: Baker Academic, 2005), esp. chap. 5.

sition)? In some circles, church unity is threatened precisely on this point. A hybridic response, however, would neither minimize nor exacerbate the differences but rather seek for mutual understanding within the broader quest for common witness in Christ. As in every one of these cases, perhaps what is needed is nothing less than a fresh and global outpouring of the Holy Spirit.[15]

Perhaps the nine tensions that have been described so far participate in this last one I will describe: that of living between now and eternity. The New Testament does, in various places, identify followers of Jesus Christ as "aliens and exiles" (1 Pet 2:11) who are seeking another, heavenly, city and country (Heb 11:17). Thus we are sojourners, continuously living a diasporic existence, thrust into a world that is in some ways not our home. At the same time, the goal is not merely to escape from the world, as we anticipate a transformation of the present world and its remaking as a new one fit for the presence of God and the new city of God. Thus the book of Revelation clearly indicates that "the kings of the earth will bring their glory into it [the new Jerusalem that descends to the earth]," and that "people will bring into it the glory and the honor of the nations" (Rev 21:24, 26). In that sense, then, we live between the now and the not-yet, between this world and the coming reign of God, between the Asian America of the present era and the whole world that will be redeemed by the triune God. There are certainly discontinuities between the present age and the one to come; but there are also continuities in how the redemption of this world will contribute to the glory of the one that is coming. This is hybridic Christian life: fully in but not of the coming world, while yet now anticipating, in Christ, the coming reign of God.[16]

I am motivated also by the scenario in Revelation that there will be around the throne of the Lamb "saints from every tribe and language and people and nation" (Rev 5:9; cf. Rev 7:9; 14:6). This tells me that God's final redemptive work will include not just souls in the abstract but real flesh-and-blood peoples in all of their linguistic, cultural, sociopolitical and historical particularity. This

---

[15]See Amos Yong and Estrelda Alexander, eds., *Philip's Daughters: Women in Pentecostal-Charismatic Leadership*, Princeton Theological Monographs Series 104 (Eugene, OR: Pickwick, 2009).

[16]I develop such an eschatological theology in my book (with Jonathan A. Anderson) *Renewing Christian Theology: Systematics for a Global Christianity* (Waco, TX: Baylor University Press, 2014); cf. Yong, *The Spirit of Creation: Modern Science and Divine Action in the Pentecostal-Charismatic Imagination*, Pentecostal Manifestos 4 (Grand Rapids: Eerdmans, 2011), chaps. 3-4.

is also consistent with the description of God's salvific work manifest through the Day of Pentecost narrative that lies at the center of my own pentecostal faith. The outpouring of the Spirit was also not on souls in the abstract but on men *and* women, older *and* younger, free *and* slave, from various regions of the known world, and embodying different histories, sufferings, experiences and hopes. These pilgrims to Jerusalem, while all Jews at varying depths of commitment, were encountered by the living God. Their lives in all their complexity were there and then recruited to declare the wondrous works of God.[17]

My claim would be that our status as aliens and strangers invites us to think about diaspora and hybridity not as marginal or incidental aspects of Christian faith but indeed as central to it. Hybridized identities hold together particularities in productive tension; as such, historical identities are also never pure, as if untinged by otherness. This does not mean that all languages, all cultures, all ethnic or racial aspects of human identity and all religious traditions are equal. The gospel comes to judge as well as to purify. But my account here suggests also that the gospel comes to redeem, which means literally to "buy back." This means that in God's scheme of things, various aspects of our histories and life stories will find new meaning in light of our encounter with the God of the divine-human Jesus Christ, whose light has shone into every heart (Jn 1:9) and whose Spirit has been poured out upon all flesh (Acts 2:17) and potentially also into each human soul (Rom 5:5). This also means that we no longer have to be ashamed of our hybridized identities, neither as individuals nor as congregations, churches and even as the church catholic. Instead, it is the nature of the church as the people of God, the body of Christ and the fellowship of the Spirit to be constituted by manyness, difference and plurality, albeit not in ways that perpetuate hostilities or antagonisms. To embrace our hybridized identities—whether yellow or "red," or even black or white—is to not have to assimilate to the dominant culture in ways that erase our differences but to be able to maintain solidarity in differentiated ways, with others nearer and further, and to be able to navigate these multiple spectrums, colors and discourses in order to participate in and facilitate the pentecostal fel-

---

[17]As developed in my book *Spirit of Love: A Trinitarian Theology of Grace* (Waco, TX: Baylor University Press, 2012).

lowship of the one Spirit with its many voices.[18] Hence for me as an Asian American and pent-evangelical yet ecumenical theologian, this is a redemptive word that I hope resounds also for others—all of us in some way or other—caught betwixt-and-between multiple worlds.

I present these soundings from the Asian American diaspora to my evangelical and Christian sisters and brothers in part because I think any centering of the church on any of these axes (rather than on Christ) portends its ossification. When the above tensions are resolved, voices from the margins, from the diasporas wherein the winds of the Spirit blows, will need to infuse new life into institutionalized forms of faith. The diaspora now no longer remains the frontier where Christianity is expanding, and the hybridic is now no longer, in Christ and the Spirit, the marginalized alien or mulattic other. Instead, diaspora captures the very heart of God's saving work, no matter when, where or among whom, and hybridity reflects the promise of trinitarian redemption of the many into the eschatological harmony. No tribes are too "primitive"; no languages are too "barbaric"; no peoples are too uncultured; and no nations are too pagan. All are hybrids in some or other respect, and anyone, anywhere, anytime, may represent the surprising work of the Spirit in anticipation of the coming reign of God. Perhaps the preceding pages will help us to recognize the gospel notes within what otherwise might be no more than a cacophony of Asian American and pent-evangelical voices in the contemporary global situation.

---

[18]See also Yong, *Who Is the Holy Spirit? A Walk with the Apostles* (Brewster, MA: Paraclete, 2011).

SUBJECT INDEX

AUTHOR INDEX

SCRIPTURE INDEX